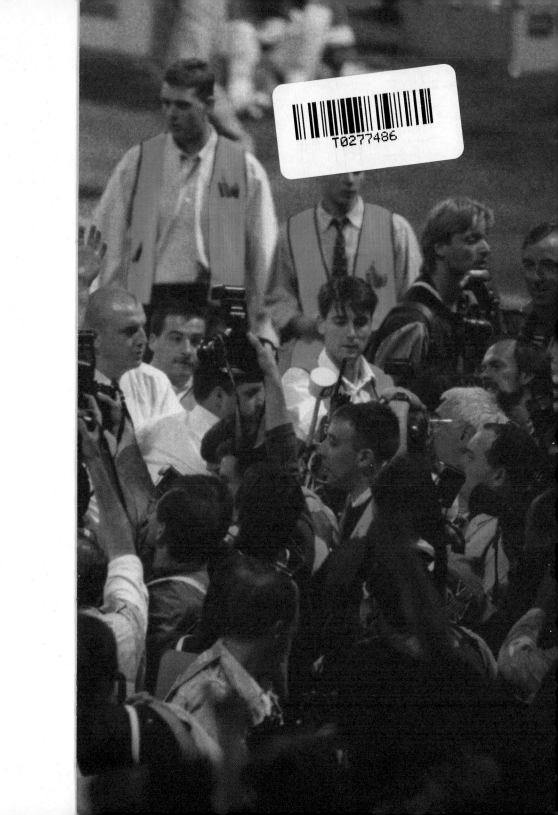

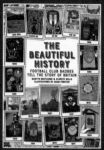

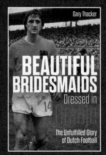

Aly Mir

TEN BIG EARS

An Alternative Account of FC Barcelona in Europe

First published by Pitch Publishing, 2022

Pitch Publishing
A2 Yeoman Gate
Yeoman Way
Worthing
Sussex
BN13 3QZ
www.pitchpublishing.co.uk

info@pitchpublishing.co.uk

ISBN 978 1 80150 132 3

Typesetting and origination by Pitch Publishing
Printed and bound in India by Replika Press Pvt. Ltd.

Contents

Acknowledgements

FIRSTLY, I would like to thank Jane at Pitch for publishing this book.

I would also like to acknowledge the Barcelona supporters who contributed with their comments and agreed to be quoted in the book: Angelo, Anna, Cesar, Chris, Florin, Geoff, Joan, Jorge, Kuba, Mubarik, Naheed, Raimon and Xi. Assistance was also provided by Eduard, Jason and Peter. Thanks should also go to a couple of my former work colleagues, Tom and Alan, for their memories of two contrasting Barcelona European semi-finals. My fellow Leeds United supporter Will was also very helpful with his comments on the manuscript.

I am also grateful for having been invited to make a spoken contribution to the Dutch film *Bestemming Wembley* made by Wasserman and Captains Studio and broadcast on Ziggo Sport about Ronald Koeman's winning goal at the 1992 European Cup Final. Thanks to Stefan at Wasserman for providing permission for me to describe that day's filming in such detail.

I ought to finally thank my wife Josie for showing me how to turn on a computer. Perhaps one day she'll explain how to turn it off.

Introduction

MAY 2022 marks 30 years since FC Barcelona's first European Cup win, arguably the greatest moment in the club's 123-year history. In 2017, I was invited to return to the venue of that famous event, Wembley Stadium, to participate in a television documentary commemorating the 25th anniversary of the 1992 final. The idea for writing *Ten Big Ears* came from that afternoon's filming, starting off as a study of Barcelona's five European Cup/ Champions League triumphs, before evolving into a first-hand account of not just those finals but the club's wider participation in UEFA competition, including the Super Cup and Cup Winners' Cup.

While touching on the club's early history, the story begins in earnest with my first attendance at a Barcelona game in 1983, before looking at 24 matches in European competition. The last of the games to get the full eyewitness treatment is the 2019 Champions League semi-final, but the book also considers the massive financial, political and footballing crises that hit FC Barcelona in 2020 and 2021. While the difficulties were partly caused by years of overspending and the impact of the coronavirus pandemic, this book will argue that the crises also resulted from the club overstretching itself in the quest for European glory, making a study of the team's performances in UEFA competitions all the more important.

Central to *Ten Big Ears* is an eyewitness approach, providing an account from direct observation of football matches I have attended. When I worked as a leader of guided walking tours in central London it was sometimes said that I had a photographic memory. Sadly, that is far from true, and consequently some details of the matches have been checked by consulting written reports or film footage during the writing of this book. However, the emphasis is on personal recollection, to try and give a flavour of what it was like to be in the stadiums during these sometimes epic encounters.

Different to existing football club histories, what follows is an alternative and occasionally satirical account, drawing on a wide variety of themes, ranging from Greek philosophy to reality television dance shows, presenting a deliberately quirky take on the Barça story. The book is written by a fan of another football club, and does not represent the views of FC Barcelona or any of its supporters' clubs or associated organisations.

1

Xi and the Art of Motorcycle Maintenance

Saturday, 28 November 2015, Hotel Avenida Palace, Barcelona

LOCATED NEAR two of Barcelona's most famous streets, Paseo de Gracia and Las Ramblas, the Hotel Avenida Palace was the perfect venue for a celebratory dinner. One of the 130 guests, Zhenzhong Xi (known as Xi), had travelled all the way from the People's Republic of China by motorcycle. The most direct route overland from China to Barcelona is about 12,000km, but Xi had chosen an even longer journey, which the gauge on his motorbike measured at 39,070km, so that he could meet certain people on the way. Even though the food at the dinner was excellent, Xi hadn't ridden his motorbike the equivalent of the equatorial circumference of Earth just for something to eat. What was it that had encouraged him to travel such a vast distance, and who were the people that warranted such detours?

With swept-back black hair, spectacles and a goatee beard, Xi looked like a modern-day Chinese philosopher, except for one item of clothing that revealed the purpose of his epic journey – a blue and dark red football shirt. Xi had crossed all of Asia and Europe to see his destination's local football team, FC Barcelona, and some of the people he arranged to meet on his journey were supporters of that club.

Xi was born in 1985, 30 years before the dinner, in Changsha, Hunan province of the People's Republic of China. In 1999 at the age of 14 he became a supporter of FC Barcelona, an interest stimulated by the club's Dutch star Patrick Kluivert who had arrived the previous year. When asked if there was a particular performance from Kluivert which prompted his interest, Xi replied, 'I can't remember. I know it from a newspaper, because we couldn't watch La Liga [Spanish football league] matches on TV before 2003.' In 2015 he finally decided to go to watch Barcelona play at its Camp Nou stadium for real, as opposed to on television, and to travel all the way by motorcycle. Equally surprising was the fact that Xi embarked on such a long journey only ten days after his wedding. Xi departed on 14 May 2015 and during a journey that lasted six months he passed through 21 countries, meeting members of Barcelona *penyes* (supporters' clubs) in many of them.

At Camp Nou, Xi was officially received by Josep Barnils, director of FC Barcelona's Social Commission, and Antoni Freire representing the international organisation of Barcelona supporters' clubs, before watching a match against Real Sociedad. In the evening Xi attended the dinner, which was organised by Penya Blaugrana London (meaning 'Blue and Red Supporters' Club London', or more accurately blue and dark red). The meal was merely one of a whole number of events that weekend, including the match against Real Sociedad in the main stadium, a futsal five-a-side game at the Palau Blaugrana and a Barça B fixture (the club's second team) in the Mini Estadi. The weekend trip was organised by Penya president Eduard Manas and the rest of the PBL board to celebrate the 30th anniversary of the London branch's formation. The main event, however, was the dinner where PBL members from the UK were joined by representatives of Barcelona *penyes* from across the world, including Argentina, Cuba, France, Greece, Morocco, Poland and the United States of America.

Speaking to the diners in excellent English, helped by the fact that his wife was a teacher of the language, Xi explained that this was his first trip to Europe and that while he used a bicycle in China it would take too long travelling to Europe with that, so he came by motorbike. I asked Xi what his new wife thought about him leaving only ten days after their wedding and he told me that she was 'a little bit angry', but added that he would be coming back in early December and hoped 'it would all be okay when I got home'. I wished him luck with that. Xi told me that he intended to donate his motorbike to FC Barcelona and fly back to China. He also gave the club a large flag signed by members of the different *penyes* he had met on the journey. When asked if he had encountered any major problems or unpleasant incidents during his epic motorbike ride, Xi replied, 'Nothing, everything made my life happier and stronger.'

The vast function room that hosted the dinner in the Hotel Avenida Palace contained a number of round tables, each with places for ten people to sit and eat, with a raised stage at one end. On this stage was a silver object, 62cm tall, weighing 7.5kg. Looking in need of a good polish after all the hands that had touched it, this was the UEFA Champions League trophy, formerly known in English as the European Champion Clubs' Cup or European Cup for short. A few months before the dinner, Barcelona had won its fifth European Cup, and for one of the guests the trophy was especially meaningful, because, as we shall hear later, he played for the club in its second appearance in the final of this competition, European football's leading club tournament, 30 years earlier.

The first European Champion Clubs' Cup trophy was commissioned by French sports newspaper, *L'Équipe*. In 2001 I visited Real Madrid's Estadio Santiago Bernabéu and explored the club's museum, which displayed six of these trophies, all looking like tall silver vases with two small handles. In 1967 UEFA, European football's governing body, decided that Real Madrid should keep the original European Champion Clubs' Cup in honour of its sixth victory in the tournament, recorded the previous season. UEFA provided a budget of 10,000 Swiss Francs for a new trophy to be produced and commissioned a

Swiss jeweller to manufacture it. Some of the national football associations within UEFA contributed different suggestions and preferences, meaning that the eventual design was a compromise and hybrid[1]. One of the main ideas was to make the new trophy more eye-catching, particularly by making its handles much larger, which caused the trophy to become known as 'the cup with the big ears'. This book tells the story of how I achieved a personal ambition of seeing Barcelona win its first five European Cups by being present at all the finals, in other words ten big ears altogether.

Some *penya* members had to fly back to London the day after the dinner, but a few remained and on the Sunday evening I accompanied a hardcore of five of them, Tony, Caroline, Peter, Katarzyna and Seb, to the George Payne Irish Bar in Plaça d'Urquinaona, just slightly east of the hotel. There they ordered one of the aptly named 'Barcelona Blackout Trays', consisting of sangria, a carafe of vodka and Red Bull, Sex on the Beach cocktails, with shots of Jäger, tequila and sambuca, all for the bargain price of €20. They enjoyed it, so ordered a few more! It was a lot of booze, but that day, 29 November, justified a celebration because it was the anniversary of the formation, not of a supporters' club, but of the whole Football Club Barcelona. On 29 November 1899 the club had been founded at a meeting in the Solé Gymnasium in Barcelona organised by Hans Kamper, a 20-year-old Swiss citizen who had recently moved to the city. He

---

1   Official programme, UEFA Champions League Final 2017.

become known by the Catalan version of his name, Joan Gamper, and the football club he started would later grow into one of the biggest in the world.

The club's famous nickname first appeared in a publication called *Auca* in 1921 as 'Barsa', before a magazine called *Xut!* changed this to 'Barça' the following year[2]. In this book 'FC Barcelona', 'Barcelona', 'Barça' and 'FCB' will all be used at different times to refer to the club. Although Barça has won a great many domestic honours, the focus of this book is the club's involvement in European competitions. These were slow to develop into continental-wide tournaments. Steps on the way included the Mitropa Cup, which just involved clubs from parts of central Europe, and the Copa Latina (Latin Cup), a tournament only open to clubs from Spain, Italy, Portugal and France. Barça won the inaugural Copa Latina in 1949, then repeated the success three years later. However, the first proper European Cup, open to winners of domestic leagues across the continent, wasn't set up until the 1955/56 season, soon after the formation of UEFA. Unfortunately for Barça, its rival Real Madrid won the first five of these. The fifth of Real Madrid's triumphs was in the 1959/60 tournament, when the club from the capital qualified as holders and met Barcelona in the semi-finals. This was Barça's first season in Europe's elite club competition, having qualified as reigning Spanish champions, but the team was eliminated after Real Madrid won both legs of the tie.

---

2   fcbarcelona.com.

The following season, 1960/61, Barça gained some revenge by becoming the first side to knock Real Madrid out of the European Cup, on the way to reaching the final against the Portuguese team Benfica in the Swiss city of Berne. Barça, featuring star player László Kubala, hit the woodwork several times, and despite managing to score twice still lost because Benfica did so three times. This European Cup Final defeat in May 1961 was to be one of the most disappointing days in the history of FC Barcelona.

Although Barça had not won the European Cup, the club's first two entries into the tournament led to a semi-final and a final. Surely it would not be long before the club went one better and took home the trophy? In fact, Barça couldn't even enter the European Cup again for another 13 years because of a lack of domestic success, caused partly by financial difficulties relating to the cost of building Camp Nou in 1957 and delays in the sale of its old stadium. These money problems forced the club to sell some of its best players, and unfortunately the replacement signings didn't always work out. Barcelona didn't qualify for the European Cup until it won La Liga in 1974, and had to settle in the meantime for victories in a lesser competition, the Inter-Cities Fairs Cup (forerunner of the UEFA Cup/Europa League), claiming victories in 1958, 1960 and 1966. When Barça did re-enter the European Cup, in the 1974/75 season, it met the English champions in the semi-final. This was how I entered the story.

In April 1975, aged 13, I went to Mallorca for my first holiday abroad. Then, as now, the Mediterranean island was part of Spain. At that time General Franco, the right-wing dictator who had come to power during the Civil War in the 1930s, was still alive and despite failing health would remain head of state until he died in November that year. I remember seeing an elderly woman begging outside a church in Palma, the island's capital. Since the 1980s beggars have been common in the UK, but they were unknown to me in the 1970s, so it was quite a shocking sight. Clad in black, with a weathered face and hooked nose, she looked like a witch from a children's fairy tale. It was one of my two main memories from that holiday. The other recollection was a sign in the port advertising ferry crossings from Palma to mainland Spain. What was so special about the sign? The destination of the boat was Barcelona, and on 23 April during my holiday, Barcelona would play Leeds United in the second leg of the European Cup semi-final.

Like most boys growing up in the 1960s and '70s I was football mad. My team was, and still is, Leeds United. In the mid-1970s live televised coverage of football games was a rarity in England. Usually only major games such as important internationals, FA Cup finals and European Cup finals were broadcast. Finals, not the semi-finals, so before flying to Mallorca I had to be content with watching highlights of the first leg on television. Played on 9 April 1975 at Elland Road, Leeds beat Barça 2-1. Although thrilled that my team had won, I was also fascinated by my first sight of FC Barcelona. The two Johans in the Barça side that night, Cruyff and Neeskens, were already household names in

Britain because of their exploits for Holland in the World Cup finals the previous summer, but that night I also had my first glimpse of the likes of Carles Rexach and Juan Manuel Asensi, who scored Barça's potentially vital away goal. I was also drawn to the Barça kit of blue and red stripes, contrasting with the all-white of Leeds.

It was a case of so near yet so far, because my mother told me I wasn't old enough to make that ferry crossing from Palma to Barcelona to go and see the second leg of the semi-final at Camp Nou. Instead, I had to console myself by buying a pennant from a souvenir street stall in Palma commemorating Barça's triumph in La Liga the previous year. The pennant, in blue and dark red stripes with gold edging, featured the names and faces of Cruyff and his title-winning team-mates. The second leg ended in a 1-1 draw, meaning Barça was eliminated and Leeds progressed to the final in Paris. That match ended with Leeds being beaten by Bayern Munich, after some highly dubious refereeing decisions. More disappointment was to follow when the Barça pennant was lost during a house move several years later.

Many thought that it wouldn't be long before Barcelona would get another chance to win the European Cup, especially having Cruyff, then the world's best player, in the side. In fact, Cruyff left the club in 1978 without further league titles and it would be 11 years until Barça again won La Liga and got a fourth crack at Europe's top club competition. Luckily, I didn't have to wait that long before seeing the team live for the first time.

2

Tarzan, Wolf and the Animals

ON WEDNESDAY, 26 January 1983 I was spending a lazy afternoon drinking beer in the student union bar at Warwick University. Aged 21 and studying in the final year of a history and politics degree, I found myself in a discussion with someone who turned out to be an Aston Villa fan. After introducing myself as a Leeds United supporter and telling him about my recent trip to Elland Road to see an FA Cup third-round tie against Preston North End, he trumped that by saying he was about to head to Villa Park to see his team play Barcelona, which I had to admit was slightly more impressive than Preston. The match was the European Super Cup, and he added that I was welcome to tag along as it wasn't necessary to get a ticket in advance because you could simply turn up and pay on the gate.

Now known as the UEFA Super Cup, the competition is an annual event between the winners of the two main European club tournaments, the Champions League and the Europa League, in a one-off showpiece match. Back in the 1980s it was played over two legs, home and away, between the winner of the previous season's European Cup (in this instance Aston Villa) and the holder of the European Cup Winners' Cup, a tournament for teams that had triumphed in domestic cup competitions. Barça won the Cup Winners' Cup for the first time in 1979 by beating Fortuna Düsseldorf 4-3 in the final, then repeated the success in 1982 with a 2-1 victory over Standard Liège, so qualified for the Super Cup.

Usually the Super Cup was played in the same year that the two competitors won their European trophies, but no convenient date could be found in 1982 so the fixture was delayed to the start of the following year. The first of the two legs, on 19 January 1983 at Camp Nou, resulted in a victory 1-0 for Barça, with the second leg a week later at Aston Villa. The previous summer Barça had signed Diego Maradona, then the world's greatest player. Unfortunately, Maradona wasn't available for the Super Cup after being diagnosed with hepatitis the previous month, but it would still be a chance to see Barcelona play 'in the flesh' for the first time and to take a look at some of the team's other players. One of these was Bernd Schuster who had been a star performer for the West German national side in the 1980 European Championship, which I remembered seeing on television. So I finished my drink and accompanied the student on the short train journey to Birmingham.

My first view of Villa Park was the rear entrance to the Holte End, a grand facade of red brick with elegant gables, decorated with claret and blue details and the name of the football club inscribed in gold lettering. After climbing a steep flight of steps I joined a queue outside the turnstiles, then paid about £2.50 to enter the stadium. Reserved for the home side's most passionate fans, the Holte End is now full of seats but back in 1983 it was still a huge stretch of terracing. Even though it was a UEFA final there was no pre-match entertainment in those days, apart from reading the match programme which, unlike today's glossy publications, was a flimsy 24-page stapled effort costing just 40p. The inside back page offered young fans the opportunity to buy half-price tickets to see a Dick Whittington pantomime at the Birmingham Hippodrome starring the actor Paul Henry, better known to people of mature years as Benny in the television soap opera *Crossroads*. The match programme also contained an advert which read, 'Vacancy. Aston Villa require an experienced person to operate their video camera for selected home matches. Anyone interested in this position on a voluntary basis please contact the Club Secretary, Steven Stride, for further information.'[3] In other words, the reigning European champions wanted someone to work unpaid to film matches, and they needed to supply their own video camera; the club wouldn't even provide the equipment!

As the Holte End was terracing, there were no reserved places and you could stand where you wanted. I selected a spot to one side of the goal, about a third of the way from the front. Ahead of me at the bottom of the

---

3 Official programme, Aston Villa vs Barcelona, 26 January 1983.

Holte End were sturdy metal fences. Designed to keep hooligans off the pitch, fences like these contributed to the Hillsborough disaster six years later which led to the deaths of 97 Liverpool fans. The fencing at Villa Park may have been brutal, but not nearly as brutal as what the crowd of 31,750 was about to see on the pitch.

These days FC Barcelona is synonymous with beautiful passing, movement and football emphasising skill rather than physical strength, so it may surprise younger fans to read that Barça, in the 1983 Super Cup at Villa Park, was the dirtiest team I have ever seen. Barça had already acquired a bad reputation in England after persistent fouling in the previous year's Cup Winners' Cup semi-final against Tottenham Hotspur, leaving White Hart Lane to chants of 'animals' from the outraged home supporters.

In charge of Barça at Villa Park was the West German, Udo Lattek, who held the distinction of being the first coach to win all three of Europe's main club competitions, the European Cup with Bayern Munich in 1974, UEFA Cup with Borussia Mönchengladbach in 1979 and Cup Winners' Cup the previous season with Barça. In those days clubs didn't always take the Super Cup very seriously (in 1981 it wasn't even held) but Lattek was reported as being keen to win it, partly to complete the set of personally winning all four European club competitions and also because taking a trophy back to Camp Nou might ease some of the pressure that was building on him as his team struggled domestically, standing only fourth in La Liga before the game.

Lattek's team lined up in a 4-4-2 formation, consisting of Javier Urrutikoetxea (known as Urruti) in goal; captain José Sánchez, Migueli, José Ramón Alesanco and Julio Alberto in defence; Víctor Muñoz, Schuster, Ortega Urbano and Miguel Alonso (known as Miguel) in midfield; then up front were Francisco José Carrasco and Alonso Marcos (known as Marcos). In the first leg at Camp Nou, Barca's goal had been scored by Marcos and the team played in a 4-3-3. The change at Villa Park was the introduction of a fourth midfielder, Urbano, instead of a third forward, showing Lattek's intention to defend the lead.

Villa's domestic form was even worse than Barcelona's, having already lost 11 league games that season and languishing in mid-table in ninth place. Coached by Tony Barton, the reigning European champions lined up in a 4-3-3 made up of goalkeeper Nigel Spink; Gary Williams, Allan Evans, Ken McNaught and Colin Gibson at the back; a midfield of Andy Blair, Des Bremner and Gordon Cowans; with a front three of Gary Shaw, Peter Withe and Tony Morley. Barça, playing in a change kit of yellow shirts with blue shorts and socks, kicked off playing towards my end, while the Villa players wore their traditional home kit of claret and light blue shirts, white shorts and light blue socks.

For some games I shall focus on particular players to tell the story of the match, and the first of these is Miguel Bernardo Bianquetti, known as Migueli, and a Barça legend. Born in 1951 in Ceuta, a Spanish city on the north coast of Africa bordering Morocco,

Migueli joined Barcelona from Cádiz in 1973, aged 21, earning a reputation as a brave and tough defender following matches such as the 1979 Cup Winners' Cup Final where he played the whole game despite having a broken collarbone. Migueli was nicknamed 'Tarzan' by a Barcelona team-mate in the 1970s, after the character in Edgar Rice Burroughs's novel *Tarzan of the Apes*. The novel introduced the fictional Viscount Greystoke, who was raised in the African jungle by apes. Although both Migueli and Tarzan had connections with Africa, it was the fictional character's famous bravery, strength, athleticism and long hair that earned the footballer his nickname. During the 1970s Migueli sometimes grew his hair quite long, but by the time of the game in Birmingham he was 31 years old and had shorter hair, although he kept his moustache which gave him a passing resemblance to Freddie Mercury, singer of rock group Queen. In the original novel Tarzan is cultured and educated, but in some later screen adaptations is depicted as primitive, almost savage. At Villa Park 'Tarzan' inclined towards the latter, although to be fair he wasn't the only one.

Despite wearing his usual number three shirt at Villa Park, Migueli was actually a central defender, not a left-back, with a reputation as one of the toughest tacklers in Spain. Migueli mainly shielded the left of the central defensive area, with Alesanco looking after the right. Both players shared the task of marking Withe and Shaw, although Migueli tended to deal with any high balls that came into the box. After nine minutes Migueli played a one-two with Schuster before bursting forward, but poor ball control caused him to lose possession. Thereafter, Migueli focused on rugged defending, either heading the ball away or hoofing it into touch.

One thing that passed unnoticed by me in the stadium at the time, although it could be heard on the film, was the presence of a small group of travelling fans chanting 'Barça! Barça!' at the start of the match and on the few occasions when their team launched an attack. Lattek must have hoped that such attacks would involve Carrasco, a Spanish international nicknamed 'El Lobo' ('The Wolf'). Then aged 23, Carrasco was a skilful winger, known for his ability to dribble with the ball. Unfortunately, Carrasco was injured in a robust tackle from Villa right-back Gary Williams near the goal line in front of me at the Holte End after only a quarter of an hour. The home fans unsympathetically chanted 'Wanker! Wanker!' at Carrasco while he received treatment, before returning to the action with his left ankle supported by white strapping. 'The Wolf' tried to run off the injury before being substituted and replaced by another forward, Quini, after 29 minutes.

The first big chance in the match came a few minutes later. A Shaw cross from the Villa right landed perfectly for Withe, who for once managed to evade the attentions of Migueli and Alesanco, only to blast his shot high over the bar. The game had started as a scrappy contest, then slowly but surely petty fouls designed to break up play were followed by nastier ones as the game degenerated. I remember quite a few off-the-ball incidents not shown on television, one being right in front of the Holte End when Schuster showed the under-soles of his boots to an opponent, threatening him with the studs. The first foul which sparked a reaction was just before the break when Quini was challenged by McNaught near the halfway line, but it wasn't clear whether it was a foul or play-acting by the Barça striker.

Half-time arrived with the game still scoreless. Ten minutes after the restart, Barça defender Julio Alberto, who had already been booked for a foul, received a second yellow card for deliberate handball after reaching up to stop a lobbed pass even though it wasn't a dangerous situation, so giving the referee no alternative. Immediately following the sending-off Lattek made another substitution, sacrificing a striker and bringing on a defender, Manuel Manola, to try and secure the aggregate lead. The departing player, Enrique Castro (widely known as Quini), had signed for Barça in 1980 from his local club, Sporting Gijón. Quini came on after 29 minutes at Villa Park only to be replaced in the second half, therefore becoming the first player I had seen come on as a substitute and then be taken off later in the same game. This was because second substitutions were allowed in UEFA competitions, but would not be introduced to England until 1987. Quini was sacrificed by Lattek following Julio Alberto's sending-off to reinforce the defence. Sadly for Quini, his substitution at Villa Park wasn't the first time he had been taken away against his will.

A couple of years before the Super Cup game, on 1 March 1981, Quini had just scored two goals in a game at Camp Nou when he disappeared while travelling to meet his wife at the airport. Alesanco was then contacted by a criminal gang demanding a ransom for his colleague's release. Investigations confirmed that Quini had been abducted by armed kidnappers. Barça was due to play the league leaders Atlético Madrid and it appears that the kidnapping was intended to undermine the club's title challenge, as well as earn the gang some money. After part of the ransom was paid the gang withdrew the money from a bank account, and it was that which led to the police finding Quini incarcerated in a garage in Zaragoza in eastern Spain, over 300km from the site of his abduction. He was released after 25 days in captivity[4].

Not surprisingly, the kidnapping badly affected Barça's results, with the players anxious for their team-mate as well as missing his goalscoring. Barça was defeated in the big game to Atlético and lost four of the next five matches. Despite his ordeal, Quini was soon back playing, and even though he missed a month of the season he still ended up as Barça's top scorer, helping win the 1981 Copa del Rey, which qualified his team for the 1982 European Cup Winners' Cup (where he scored the decisive goal in the final) and subsequently the Super Cup in Birmingham. Quini's three kidnappers were sentenced to ten years' imprisonment, although Quini strangely declined to claim the compensation his kidnappers were ordered to pay, instead saying that he forgave them.

---

4   Jason Pettigrove, 'Barça Rewind: Quini's kidnapping', fcbarcelona.com.

Less forgiving was this Super Cup contest. Soon after Quini's substitution Schuster came close for Barça, hitting a free kick which took a deflection off the Villa wall before rebounding off Spink's left post. The West German had performed well in the first leg, directing play from midfield with his long passes and contributing to the goal, but showed little of his ability in the second leg, carelessly conceding possession on several occasions. With 20 minutes remaining Barton withdrew Morley and replaced him with Mark Walters. Marcos then launched what looked like a karate kick at Blair, but although the referee awarded a free kick, the Barça player escaped further punishment.

With ten minutes remaining, Schuster launched a two-footed lunge at Gibson, who went down injured. The Villa fans then started to slow handclap in protest at the visitors' behaviour. Schuster's foul proved costly for Barça, as the resulting free kick led to Villa scoring 11 minutes from time. Up until then, Migueli had dealt effectively with Villa's centre-forward, Peter Withe, but that was about to change. Following the free kick, the ball arrived in the zone usually protected by Migueli, but seconds before Withe had elbowed Migueli in the face, enabling Shaw to score from close range in a crowded area. The Barça players surrounded the Belgian referee, Alex Ponnet, pointing to the blood spattered all over Migueli's yellow shirt (think Freddie Mercury combined with Terry Butcher). Like me, the referee didn't spot the foul at the time, so the goal stood.

After receiving treatment, Migueli lived up to his hardman image by playing on until the end of the game, holding a pad to his face which kept on bleeding. For the rest of the contest Migueli stayed even closer to Withe than before, and looked determined to take revenge, going through the back of the Villa man twice before the end of normal time. After the second of these fouls Migueli was spoken to by the referee, but no card was produced.

With no further score, and the tie level 1-1 on aggregate, it went to 30 minutes of extra time. Soon after the restart, Barça launched a counter-attack towards our end and Alesanco gained possession on the edge of his own penalty area before playing a superb ball with the outside of his right foot to the sprinting Marcos on the halfway line. Alesanco's pass was arguably the only moment of real quality in the entire 120 minutes, but unfortunately for Barça Marcos wasted the opportunity. Soon after, Migueli used his left elbow on Withe when they both went up for a high ball in the middle of the field. This time Migueli, still holding the bloodied pad to his face, was finally booked.

A brief spell of actual football followed, culminating with Williams playing a long ball for Walters to chase, before he was brought down in the box by Sánchez. It was a clear penalty and the referee pointed to the spot, only to be surrounded by protesting Barça players. Urruti seemed momentarily to be the peacemaker, ushering his team-mates away, but his real intention was quickly revealed when he pushed the referee himself! The foul happened nine minutes into the first period of extra time. After a lengthy delay Cowans went up to take the penalty. What followed was extraordinary.

Cowans hit his spot kick towards a corner of the goal. Urruti dived low to his left to make a save, but only succeeded in pushing the ball back towards the penalty taker, who smashed the ball into the centre of the goal from close range. Cowans's momentum took him to the goal line. The keeper immediately jumped up and deliberately kicked Cowans in his right leg, scything him down and into the goal. Mayhem broke out and from my vantage point at the other end of the stadium (and television pictures later) it looked like Urruti was shown a red card by the referee. However, the keeper remained on the pitch for the remaining 21 minutes of extra time. *World Soccer*'s report endorsed this view, writing that Urruti having 'kicked Cowans into the net as well, was seen to be shown the red card but stayed on'[5]. It is possible that Urruti stayed on the pitch because Ponnet had flourished a red card in error and told him he didn't need to leave; however, given the severity of the offence what is more probable is that the referee simply lost control.

Following a tackle by Evans, Marcos stayed down holding his head, suggesting he'd been stamped on. Chants of 'Cheat! Cheat!' rang out from around me in the Holte End. Shaw was then hacked down twice in a minute, both times by Manolo. It was the second time that a Barça foul was to prove costly, because from the resulting free kick after 104 minutes Cowans crossed to McNaught who scored with a diving header from close

5 *World Soccer*, March 1983, p6.

range. Before the restart Barça was reduced to nine men when Marcos was sent off for spitting at Walters (more about that incident later).

The second period of extra time began with yet more fouling, in the form of a fierce bodycheck from Alesanco on Evans, followed by Migueli going through the back of Withe yet again. It could easily have been a second yellow and a sending off for 'Tarzan', who was then booed by the home fans each time he received the ball. Villa then tried to waste time (and humiliate Barça) by stringing together a lengthy series of passes, including keepy-uppies by Evans, to a soundtrack of 'olé, olé' from the fans surrounding me. However, this backfired when possession was lost and Barça broke forward, leading to Evans fouling Miguel. For this, Evans received a second yellow and was sent off.

Villa's 'olé, 'olé' sequence included defenders twice kicking the ball back to Spink for their goalkeeper to pick up, even though there were no Barça players nearby and there was plenty of time to play the ball forwards. Nine years later in 1992 a change in the rules meant that goalkeepers could no longer handle the ball when it was kicked towards them by defenders, but in 1983 the back-pass was still a major part of the game. In the Super Cup Aston Villa made 12 back-passes to Spink, while Barca's Urruti received 16 balls from his defenders, making a total of 28 back-passes. Analysis of the back-passes in this match shows the extent to which they were used as a deliberate tactic to waste time and slow down play. Taking into account extra time, the game lasted 120 minutes, yet half of Villa's back-passes came in the final 15 minutes when the home side was ahead and wanted to see out the game. Similarly, most of Barça's back-passes occurred before going behind in the tie. When the aggregate score meant Barça needed a goal the visitors suddenly felt less compelled to knock the ball back to Urruti. I estimate that each back-pass took about ten seconds for the keeper to pick up the ball, consider where to direct it and then finally kick it. This meant a total of approximately 280 seconds, or nearly five minutes, was lost by this activity.

After the final whistle the Barça players walked off towards the tunnel in the far corner. The next day, *The Times* headlined its report 'Spaniards shamed in defeat: The bloody battle of Villa Park' and the newspaper pulled no punches in its coverage of the game, detailing Barcelona's persistent fouling and violent play[6].

In the nearly 40 years that have followed, various changes to the rules concerning tackling and criteria for yellow and red cards have been introduced, with referees ordered to take action against simulation (diving), tackles from behind and out of control or reckless challenges. In the 1983 Super Cup Barça had three players red-carded (although one is confusing because the offender refused to leave the pitch) and six yellow-carded, while Villa received one red and three yellow cards. Watching the match again on film, and applying today's rules to it, I believe that Barça could also have seen second yellows for

---

6   *The Times*, 27 January 1983.

Urbano, Alesanco, Manola and Migueli, plus a straight red to Schuster for his two-footed lunge on Gibson. This would mean Barça having eight players sent off. Even Villa, who had Evans harshly sent off, should still have lost another player because Withe would be ordered off these days for elbowing Migueli.

After the match, UEFA's disciplinary committee met to consider banning Barcelona from European competition, but in the end decided to just fine the club and suspend four of its players: Manolo for one game, Julio Alberto for two, while Urruti received a four-match suspension, not for the assault on Cowans or pushing the referee, but for pulling down his shorts and baring his backside at the match officials. I didn't notice this incident at the time, probably because it happened in a flash.

Urruti came from the Basque region of north-eastern Spain, signing for Barça in 1981, and was a popular figure at Camp Nou, respected by both team-mates and fans for his never-say-die spirit, and destined to play a major role in Barcelona's next attempt at winning the European Cup.

The final Barça player to be suspended was Marcos, following his sending-off for spitting at Villa's Mark Walters, who had been brought on as a substitute and was the only black player on the pitch. UEFA banned Marcos for five matches, a punishment which Nicolau Casaus, Barça's vice-president, was quoted as calling 'a complete exaggeration', adding, 'Even though we admit that he committed an ugly and unsporting act, this is normal on football pitches all over the world.'[7] This response, by a representative of a major football club, seems surprising today. Although it is not known whether race was the motive for the incident, it is worth pointing out that the official programme for the Super Cup carried no statement from UEFA about abuse, racial or otherwise, something that has become standard practice in recent times.

One of those who escaped further action was Migueli. Despite a difficult evening at Villa Park, 'Tarzan' deserves to be remembered as a Barça legend, and I was grateful for the chance to see him play. By the time Migueli retired in 1989 he had set a club record for the number of appearances, which stood until it was overtaken by Xavi in 2012. Another of the players that night who would make a large number of appearances for Barça was Carrasco. 'The Wolf' went on to play for the club for 11 years between 1978 and 1989, becoming one of the few players to make over 500 appearances. In future years, Carrasco went on to hold the record for the number of European Cup Winners' Cup triumphs, after adding a winner's medal in 1989 to the two he had received in the 1979 and 1982 tournaments.

After the Villa game the president of FC Barcelona, Josep Luís Núñez, said, 'The image of our club has been harmed. We are always labelled the animals, which is very upsetting.'[8]

---

7   'Barcelona get away with it again': official programme, Charlton Athletic vs Crystal Palace, 4 April 1983.

8   *World Soccer*, March 1983, p6.

3

Following the
Flight of the Sparrow

LATTEK BLAMED the opposition for some of the violence at Villa Park and also what he called the incompetence of the referee; however, a few weeks later on 3 March 1983 he was sacked. The damage to the club's reputation in the Super Cup and the German's poor relationship with Maradona were factors, with the final straw being defeat to La Liga's bottom side Racing Santander. Barcelona rarely played in England in those days and limited finances restricted my trips abroad, so because this is an eyewitness history a series of encounters with relevant football personalities from that era will be used to continue the story.

Sixteen days after Lattek's dismissal, I travelled down to London to see Leeds United away at Charlton Athletic in the old English Second Division. On the pitch that Saturday afternoon was a player who featured prominently in Lattek's initial success at Barcelona, Allan Simonsen.

Lattek's achievement of being the first coach to win all three European club competitions was later matched by Giovanni Trapattoni. However, Simonsen's record of being the first player to score in the finals of all three tournaments was never equalled and, after the demise of the Cup Winners' Cup, never will be. The Danish striker made his name playing for Borussia Mönchengladbach, joining the West German club in 1972. Three years later Lattek arrived at Mönchengladbach, replacing Hennes Weisweiler who left to coach Barcelona. Simonsen established his international reputation in 1977, scoring in that season's European Cup Final when his side lost 3-1 to Liverpool, and became the first Danish player to win the European Footballer of the Year award. After scoring the winning goal in the 1979 UEFA Cup Final for Lattek's Mönchengladbach against Red Star Belgrade, Simonsen joined Barcelona.

The Dane's time at Camp Nou occurred between two superstars, following the departure of Cruyff and before the arrival of Maradona. Consequently, Simonsen tends to get overlooked, but he was, briefly, the star player at Barça. In 1981 he teamed up once again with Lattek after the German arrived at Camp Nou and the two of them won the 1982 European Cup Winners' Cup, with Simonsen scoring in the final. However, both Lattek and Simonsen were to be unsettled by the arrival of Maradona a month after that final. The Argentinian superstar conflicted with Lattek's training methods and playing style, while Simonsen felt insulted by having to fight for his place, because at that time La

Liga regulations only allowed two foreigners in a team, meaning he would have to compete with Maradona and Schuster. Barcelona has an unfortunate tendency for its star players to leave under a cloud, and Simonsen was no exception, feeling so slighted by the arrival of Maradona that he asked for a transfer. Charlton Athletic offered £300,000 for Simonsen, outbidding the likes of Real Madrid, who also showed interest. Simonsen was happy to join Charlton and ply his trade at a smaller club with less pressure.

Still under 30 years old at the time of his transfer in October 1982, Simonsen was at his peak, and to say that signing him was a coup for the south London club would be a massive understatement. Charlton's home, The Valley, was once the largest club stadium in England, but by the time of Simonsen's arrival it needed extensive renovation. The last time The Valley attracted large crowds was for rock concerts, including 75,000 people who attended a 1976 gig in the stadium by The Who which set a record for being the world's loudest. Although the Dane doubled the gate for his debut, unfortunately this was only from 5,000 to 10,000.

On my visit to The Valley just 8,229 people turned up to watch Simonsen, who looked to me like a child footballer wearing an adult's kit, with a red shirt and baggy white shorts that were several sizes too big for him. Simonsen was only 5ft 5in tall (even shorter than Lionel Messi) which led to the Spanish nicknaming him '*El Pequeño Gran Danés*' ('The Little Great Dane'), while back in Denmark he was known as the '*Spurven fra Vejle*'

('Sparrow from Vejle'). Back in the 1970s and 1980s football was very physical, meaning that size was more important for players than it is today, and consequently Simonsen had to be even better to succeed in the game.

When Simonsen arrived at The Valley the first Charlton shirt he wore carried the sponsorship logo of FADS, the do-it-yourself decorating merchants. Sadly for Charlton, 'fad' can also mean a short-lived craze or impulse and by the time of the Leeds match the company's logo had gone, soon followed by Simonsen himself. The Dane turned out to have been something of an impulse buy for Charlton, and the club's financing of it proved to be like a botched DIY job. Charlton couldn't afford his transfer fee and wages, meaning the Leeds game turned out to be historic as it was the last of Simonsen's 17 games for the south London club. Simonsen created a couple of chances in the opening ten minutes, but both were wasted by his colleagues. After that, Simonsen was effectively marshalled by Leeds' teenage defender Martin Dickinson, who had been tasked with marking him. Simonsen played the whole 90 minutes but couldn't get on the scoresheet, although Leeds did in the second half, nicking a 1-0 win.

After the game, Simonsen activated a clause in his contract allowing him to return to Vejle, the Danish club where he played in his youth, on a free transfer. In the match programme for its next home game two weeks later, Charlton made the standard statement wishing Simonsen well for his future, but also published a full-page article entitled 'Barcelona get away with it again'.

Unsigned, therefore suggesting it was the view of the club and not just an individual, the article referred to what it called Barcelona's 'disgusting behaviour in the European Super Cup Final second leg at Villa Park' and criticised UEFA's decision not to ban Barça from European competition[9]. Such public attacks on other clubs are unusual, and it was possibly motivated by a dispute with Barça over Simonsen's transfer. Either way, Simonsen's signing contributed to a financial crisis that pushed Charlton into administration and forced the club to leave The Valley after struggling to pay for the stadium's upkeep.

Six months after the Leeds game, Simonsen scored the only goal from the penalty spot as Denmark beat England at Wembley in a vital European Championship qualifier that helped his country reach the finals at the hosts' expense, heralding a golden era for the Danish national side. In 1989 Simonsen retired from playing to embark on a coaching career, then in 2013 he re-entered the limelight in a rather unusual way, as we shall discover later in chapter ten.

After Lattek's sacking, Argentinian World Cup-winning manager, César Luis Menotti, became the new Barcelona coach, appointed partly to get more out of Maradona. However, he too failed to mount a successful challenge for major honours and was replaced in 1984 by Terry Venables. A former player with clubs such as Chelsea and Tottenham Hotspur, Venables followed his

---

9 'Barcelona get away with it again': official programme, Charlton Athletic vs Crystal Palace, 4 April 1983.

retirement in 1974 by becoming a successful coach at Crystal Palace and Queens Park Rangers.

Venables was not the first Englishman to coach Barcelona nor would he be the last, but his appointment still came as a surprise. On arrival, he claimed that expectations were low at Barcelona, with many at the club obsessed about beating Real Madrid, and more interested in moaning after defeats than celebrating victories. After reintroducing a positive attitude, Venables won La Liga in his debut season at Camp Nou, the club's first championship since 1974, and was nicknamed 'El Tel' by the English tabloids.

Venables' La Liga success qualified Barça for its first crack at the European Cup in 11 years. Barça knocked out Sparta Prague, Porto and Juventus to reach a semi-final against IFK Gothenburg. After losing 3-0 in Sweden, Barça pulled off a famous comeback in the second leg thanks to a hat-trick by Pichi Alonso (an unused substitute against Villa in the Super Cup) and a heroic performance by Urruti who made several vital saves in open play, before saving a spot kick and scoring one himself to help his team win the resulting penalty shoot-out.

Barça was firm favourite to win the 1986 European Cup Final in Seville against Steaua Bucharest from Romania. Before the final, no eastern European club had ever won the tournament. Furthermore, Romania was still a communist country and financial limitations combined with political restrictions meant that only a few hundred Steaua supporters were allowed to travel to the match, massively outnumbered by an estimated 50,000

Barça fans in attendance. However, what should have
been the greatest day in FC Barcelona's history became
one of the worst. Venables' team, including eight players
from the Super Cup in Birmingham, failed to break
down the Romanian defence, with Schuster particularly
ineffective. The West German was actually substituted a
few minutes before the end of normal time and stormed
out of the stadium, refusing to stay and watch the rest of
the game. After the final ended in a goalless stalemate,
it went to another penalty shoot-out. Urruti did his best,
saving Steau's first two penalties, but unfortunately for
him Barça missed all its spot kicks.

Schuster's replacement in the final was Josep
Moratalla, another midfielder. Moratalla played the
last five minutes of normal time and all of extra time,
although he didn't take any of the penalties in the
disastrous shoot-out. Born in Catalonia, Moratalla
was 27 at the time of the final. He had progressed
through the Barcelona youth system and played in the
1982 Cup Winners' Cup Final victory. Moratalla was
not a regular starter in his early career, but although
he missed the 1983 Super Cup at Villa Park our paths
did cross years later when he attended the PBL dinner
in Barcelona in 2015 as a guest speaker, in his capacity
as a leading member of the Agrupació Barça Jugadors
(literally 'Grouping of Barça Players'). The ABJ is the
Barcelona players' association, established in 1959 to
assist footballers during and especially after their careers.

Moratalla's own career at Barça ended shortly after
one of the most sensational episodes in the entire history

of the club, but before hearing about that attention will focus on a certain Diego Maradona.

In the season following the European Cup Final defeat, Barça finished sixth in La Liga and was knocked out of the UEFA Cup by eventual runner-up Dundee United in the quarter-final. A few months after the defeat to the Scottish side Venables was asked to coach a Rest of the World XI in a match against a Football League XI to commemorate the centenary of the English Football League. For the game, the Rest of the World team was made up of players, regardless of nationality, who played abroad, while the Football League side included those who played in England, again regardless of which country they were from. The match took place at the old Wembley Stadium on Saturday, 8 August 1987, and I was among the crowd of 61,000 to see some of the stars of world football, including several with connections to Barcelona. The Football League XI was coached by Bobby Robson, who would later perform the role at Barça. Venables' Rest of the World side included Andoni Zubizarreta, who had joined Barcelona after the 1986 European Cup Final defeat and replaced Urruti in goal, Julio Alberto who had played in the 1983 Super Cup at Villa Park, and Gary Lineker, who arrived at Camp Nou from Everton the previous year. However, undoubtedly the biggest star with Barcelona connections to appear in the exhibition match was Maradona.

Still a Barça player when Venables was installed as coach in May 1984, Maradona was sold to Napoli soon afterwards. The Argentinian star had financial problems and needed a big-money move, while Barcelona was prepared to sell him. The only time Maradona played for Venables was in that exhibition match at Wembley. Getting Maradona to feature proved to be extremely difficult and was a PR disaster, with disputes about the Argentine's appearance fee and doubts about whether he would actually appear being aired publicly in the media. Maradona was such a huge star at the time, having almost single-handedly won the World Cup for Argentina the year before and played a major role in Napoli's first-ever Serie A title only weeks earlier, that his appearance was essential to justify the team's billing as a Rest of the World XI. This, of course, increased Maradona's bargaining position, and his autobiography reveals that the English FA paid him $160,000 to play in the match and was so desperate it also provided a private jet to fly him from Italy[10].

From my position in the top tier behind the goal above the tunnel, Maradona looked distinctly overweight as he strutted on to the pitch in the all-red kit of the Rest of the World XI. Maradona showed a few glimpses of his ability, creating chances for others rather than threatening to score himself. Perhaps his pre-season fat was a hindrance to those trademark dribbles. Unfortunately, a large proportion of the crowd booed whenever Maradona got the ball. This was partly in protest at his handball goal against England in the previous year's World Cup quarter-final, and partly hostility to Argentina because of the Falklands War five years earlier. The match, which ended 3-0 to the Football League XI, was rendered farcical by

10 Maradona, D., *El Diego* (London: Yellow Jersey Press, 2000), p140.

multiple substitutions constantly interrupting the flow of the game, with a total of 35 players appearing. Maradona, despite being unfit, lasted the whole 90 minutes, providing my one and only view of the Argentinian superstar.

The month after the Football League centenary game, Venables left Barcelona following a poor start to the 1987/88 season, to be replaced by Luis Aragonés as caretaker manager. A few months later, the bulk of the Barça squad, supported by Aragonés, publicly rebelled against the club. FC Barcelona had tried to save money by reducing the amount of tax due on players' wages through paying some of the money as image rights which were taxed at a lower rate. The club issued players with two contracts, one with their full earnings which was kept secret, and a second with different figures which was declared to the taxman. When this was discovered the players were ordered to pay taxes and fines imposed by the authorities. The players felt that the club was responsible and should pay the bill.

On 28 April 1988 team captain Alesanco (a veteran of the Super Cup at Villa Park), supported by the rest of the squad including Moratalla but with the notable exceptions of Schuster and Lineker, read out a statement at the Hotel Hesperia publicly criticising Núñez, saying the players had lost confidence in him and urging him to resign. The rebellion became known as 'El motín del Hesperia' ('The Hesperia Mutiny') after the hotel where it took place. Despite many fans having misgivings about the president, most sided with him and turned against the footballers, regarding them as greedy and booing them on the pitch. After the 'mutiny' Aragonés was replaced by Cruyff and an incredible 14 squad members were moved on, including Moratalla. In some cases the cull was punitive, but not all, as shown by the fact that the rebels' spokesman Alesanco remained at the club.

Meanwhile, Venables returned to London and rejoined one of his former clubs, Tottenham Hotspur, this time as coach rather than player, and it was then that I had my closest encounter of an El Tel kind. In 1990 I was elected as a local councillor in Haringey, north London. The borough had considerable financial, political and social problems, with massive budgetary difficulties, the introduction of the hated Poll Tax and the danger of riots on the Broadwater Farm housing estate. Councillors also risked surcharge because of a multi-million-pound debt accrued at fire-damaged Alexandra Palace. However, despite these issues, being on the council did have one advantage, which followed Tottenham Hotspur's victory in the 1991 FA Cup Final. The White Hart Lane stadium was located within the borough, meaning that the day after Spurs won the cup Haringey Council, as the local authority, hosted a civic reception to celebrate the victory.

Around midday on Sunday, 19 May 1991 I reported to Tottenham Town Hall, situated within the Tottenham Central ward I represented, just under a couple of kilometres south of Spurs' stadium. Built in 1905, the town hall was designed in a baroque style and listed to preserve its faded glory in an otherwise rundown and deprived area. The mayor of Haringey, plus an assortment of councillors and council staff, joined people from the local community at the reception on the building's first floor. As was customary at such gatherings, refreshments were laid on. This was in an age before canapés arrived in the UK, turning finger snacks into an art form, so it was the usual fare of sandwiches, sausage rolls, potato crisps, and because Haringey was hot on diversity, samosas and bhajis (vegetarian of course). As it was a formal occasion I wore a suit, but decided to accompany it with my club's tie, which had a white rose badge and 'Leeds United FC' embroidered on it. I did it as a joke, but while we waited for the Spurs team to arrive, local MP Bernie Grant questioned me about the tie, while another councillor said it was 'disgraceful' to wear it on such an occasion.

According to local newspaper, the *Tottenham and Wood Green Journal*, it took the Spurs bus two whole hours to get down Tottenham High Road because over a quarter of a million people had filled the streets wanting to get a glimpse of their heroes and the FA Cup[11]. When the bus finally arrived, the Spurs party (including coaching staff, players, wives and girlfriends) got off and entered the town hall with the trophy. Venables was dressed in a navy blue suit with a lighter blue shirt and a navy blue tie, but all his players wore Spurs tracksuits.

Despite having just won the FA Cup, El Tel and his team looked miserable and gave off the impression that they didn't want to be at the reception. At the time I thought this was because of the duration of the journey and a consequence of the football club not having a very

---

11 *Tottenham and Wood Green Journal*, 23 May 1991.

good relationship with the council at that time. Football was then out of favour with the political world and would remain unfashionable until Euro 96 and the rise of Tony Blair a few years later. There had also been some disputes between Spurs and Haringey Council, not helped by me teasing Peter Barnes (Tottenham Hotspur's club secretary) during a visit to White Hart Lane some months before, when I suggested he sold star player Paul Gascoigne to raise money in order to pay the council for the cost of street cleaning on matchdays. However, I later learned that financial problems, a search for new owners and concern over the severity of an injury suffered by Gascoigne the day before, were the main reasons for the downbeat mood.

The Spurs contingent also left the spread of food untouched, possibly because they were going to their own celebration meal afterwards or had to obey rules about healthy eating. It would have been interesting to see what impact Gazza would have made on the tray of sausage rolls had he not been hospitalised.

I used another councillor's unwanted invitation to enable Dave, a friend from my Warwick University days, to join me at the reception because he was a big Spurs supporter. When Venables walked by, Dave simply said, 'Well done.' Venables could easily have said 'thanks' or smiled while passing, but instead he rudely ignored Dave. I was standing next to Dave at the time, so perhaps El Tel had spotted my tie? Certainly, when Venables joined Leeds 11 years later he was never 'tied' to the club, being sacked after only eight months in the dugout. The Spurs contingent then took it in turns to stand on the small balcony, displaying the trophy to thousands of cheering fans in the street below.

Although potato crisps were served at the civic reception, I don't know whether they were the ones that inspired Lineker to start advertising packets of Walkers four years later. Lineker had been a success in an otherwise disappointing 1986/87 campaign for Barça, scoring 21 goals. He missed the Hesperia Mutiny the following season, being away on England international duty at the time. After Cruyff arrived in 1988, Lineker famously spent a season played out of position on the wing because Julio Salinas was preferred as the central striker in a three-man attack. Lineker did, however, play in the 1989 Cup Winners' Cup Final triumph before leaving to rejoin Venables at Tottenham. At one stage I was standing near to Lineker at the civic reception and was surprised how young and fresh-faced he looked, despite being almost exactly a year older than me (he was born on 30 November 1960; I was born on 29 November 1961).

Apart from Venables and Lineker, there was another person with Barça connections at the civic reception. Of Moroccan origin, Mohamed Alí Amar, known as Nayim, had been recruited to Barcelona's La Masia youth academy at the age of 12 in 1978. When Menotti was coach in 1983/84 he selected talented members of the academy to take part in first team training sessions. Nayim was chosen and trained with the likes of Maradona and Schuster once per week, which made a huge impression on him. After being promoted to the first team by Venables, Nayim played a handful of games for Barça in the 1987/88 season. However, when Cruyff became coach, Nayim was deemed surplus to requirements and joined Tottenham, linking up with Venables again. Nayim become the first Muslim to play in the Premier League after it began in 1992. In the previous day's FA Cup Final, Nayim had replaced the injured Gazza before playing a part in both Spurs goals. Nayim later moved back to Spain to play for Real Zaragoza, where I saw him play against Chelsea in the semi-final of the 1995 Cup Winners' Cup. He will always be remembered for a last-minute long-range lob over Arsenal's David Seaman to win that tournament's final, a goal immortalised in the terrace song 'Nayim from the halfway line'.

Venables may have seemed rude at the civic reception, but as this is a book about football rather than manners, the real question is how should he be judged as a coach? Three promotions in the English leagues with relatively small clubs is not to be sniffed at, and neither is taking QPR to Wembley in the club's only FA Cup Final and securing UEFA Cup qualification for only the second time in its history. At Barcelona, Venables ended an 11-year drought to win La Liga and was only a penalty shoot-out from winning the club's first European Cup. In his autobiography, Venables explains how he encouraged his Barça team to press and play a high-tempo game, rather than a slower continental style, which may surprise those who have been led to believe that pressing was brought to Camp Nou only by his successors, such as Cruyff and Pep Guardiola, or has always been part of the club's DNA[12].

---

12 Venables, T., *Born to Manage: The Autobiography* (London: Simon & Schuster, 2015), pp267-268.

4

The Adventures of Tintin
and the Little Plastic Man

IN 1988 with the majority of the Barcelona squad in
public rebellion against the president in a financial
dispute while the team played in a half-empty stadium,
it was time for the return of Johan Cruyff, not as player,
but as coach. The Dutchman revolutionised the club,
introducing a new playing style with more emphasis on
quick touches and close passing centred around control
of the ball. Cruyff also imposed the same formation at
every level from the youth setup to the first team, making
it easier for players to progress through the ranks, while
at the same time clearing out those players who were not
capable of performing in the way that he wanted.

Cruyff's first season saw the club win its third Cup
Winners' Cup, but it had, of course, to wait until winning
La Liga before getting another crack at the European
Cup. In 1989 Cruyff signed the Danish forward Michael
Laudrup from Juventus and the Dutch defender Ronald

Koeman from PSV Eindhoven. The following year they were joined by a bullish striker from CSKA Sofia, Hristo Stoichkov, who completed the 'Dream Team'. These three foreign stars were joined by a number of home-grown players, such as Pep Guardiola, who came through the youth setup. Once assembled, the Dream Team won its first of four consecutive Spanish league titles in 1991, securing qualification for what was to prove to be the last European Cup in 1991/92 before being rebranded as the UEFA Champions League the following season. Of special interest to me was the fact that the final was scheduled to take place at Wembley. By then I had moved from Coventry to London, and lived less than 15km from the famous old stadium.

The first round saw Barça overcome East German side Hansa Rostock 3-1 on aggregate. Hansa had qualified in a rather unusual way, as the champions of the communist German Democratic Republic, a country that ceased to exist by the time the 1991/92 European Cup started. The second round was also against German opposition, but this time against Bundesliga champions Kaiserslautern, a match that entered Barça folklore. The first leg at Camp Nou was won 2-0 by Barça. However, the second leg two weeks later saw that advantage wiped out as the home side took a three-goal lead. Barça was heading out of the competition, but with only ten seconds remaining a header from José Mari Bakero snatched a crucial victory on away goals.

Having said that the 1992 European Cup was the last one before rebranding, one important change that would characterise the UEFA Champions League was actually introduced for the first time in the 1991/92 tournament. Whereas the European Cup had previously been knockout all the way through, the 1991/92 competition featured a group stage instead of a conventional semi-final. Eventually the Champions League would see the group stage, or sometimes stages, appear earlier in the competition, with knockout rounds later on, but the first time one was used was in place of a normal semi-final. Barça competed in a group with Sparta Prague, Benfica and Dynamo Kyiv. Each team played the others home and away, according to the old system of two points for a win and one for a draw (three points for a win, to encourage attacking play, was not introduced until later). Barça had six matches, the first on 27 November 1991 and the last on 15 April 1992. In other words it took nearly five months to conclude the semi-finals. It was a tight affair; Barça won four matches, but lost in Prague and drew away in Lisbon. Had Barça lost its final game at home to Benfica and Sparta Prague won in Kyiv, it would have been the Czechoslovakian side in the final. However, Barça won 2-1 to secure a date at Wembley.

The other group was even closer; Italy's Sampdoria edging out holders Red Star Belgrade. It was the Genoese side's first, and so far only, European Cup Final, but not its first European final of any kind, having reached the Cup Winners' Cup Final twice in 1989 and 1990. 'Samp' won the second of these, but lost the first to Cruyff's Barcelona. Would it be an omen?

Task number one was obtaining a ticket for the final, which in future years was to become more difficult and increasingly expensive. Wembley had previously hosted four European Cup finals, and at the last of these in 1978 over 92,000 tickets had been available. However, the Taylor Report following the Hillsborough disaster required Wembley to become all-seater, with its capacity reduced to 74,000. For the 1992 final Barça and Sampdoria were each given about 25,000 tickets and completely sold out their allocations. There were about 24,000 tickets left for neutrals along the sides of the stadium. Younger fans will be amazed to hear that in the weeks before the final you could simply ring up Wembley Stadium, order your ticket and pay by card over the phone. Yes, they were on general sale, you didn't need to be part of anything like 'Club Wembley' or have contacts at UEFA, anyone could get them. Too good to be true? What's the catch? The price? No, there was no catch. The price for a good seat along the side was £21 (about €23) including booking fee and postage! The previous year's European Cup Final had been a scoreless draw between Red Star Belgrade and Marseille, a match so tedious that it may have dampened demand from neutrals for Wembley and therefore made tickets easier to obtain.

In those days, the European Cup Final was always held on a Wednesday evening. It wasn't until 2010 that it changed to Saturday. The kick-off time was also slightly different, 7.15pm rather than the 7.45pm (UK time) which was established later. At 5pm on the day of the final, Wednesday, 20 May 1992, I left my dreadfully dull job working in a public library in Islington and headed up to Wembley on the London Underground. There weren't as many football supporters on the Tube train as I'd expected, because the turnstiles had opened at 5.15pm and many of the fans were already at Wembley. For both clubs this was an opportunity to win a first European Cup and make a competitive debut at the famous stadium, so the supporters were determined to make the most of the occasion and soak up the atmosphere. It took ages to struggle through the crowds down Wembley Way, pass the famous Twin Towers, reach the far side of the stadium and enter via turnstile A. By the time I took my seat in block 220, row 30, seat 134, it was just after 7.05pm, only a couple of minutes before the two teams walked out.

My seat was in the upper tier, on the south side of the stadium. The view of the pitch was perfect; however, I was too far back to see the Royal Box at the top of the famous steps on the opposite side of the stadium where the trophy would be presented because an extra mini-tier, called the Olympic Gallery, had recently been installed under the rim of the roof. To my left, behind the goal in the west end of the stadium were the Sampdoria fans, while those of Barça were congregated in the end to my right. Both sets of fans behind the goals had only a distant view of the action because of an oval greyhound track surrounding the pitch. Even though the stadium was all-seater, both sets of fans behind the goals and in the lower portion of the sides stood up throughout the match to get a better view. Only those in the top tier along the sides actually sat in their seats. I was located off-centre, nearer the Barça fans than the Genoese, so 'Cant del Barça' rang out louder than anything sung by the Italians, although, to be fair, both sets of fans gave terrific backing to their teams throughout the contest. It was a sunny evening in London, warmer than usual for the time of year, and the slightly humid conditions added to the intense atmosphere.

A recurring theme in this book is attempting to describe the formations of Barça teams, which is often difficult because of their fluid styles, particularly full-backs and sweepers pushing up, holding midfielders and forwards dropping deeper and players switching positions. However, Cruyff insisted his teams usually played 3-4-3, so I shall defer to this and list the starting line-up as Zubizarreta in goal, behind a back three of Ronald Koeman as sweeper surrounded by Nando to his right and Albert Ferrer to his left. Ahead of them were two wing-backs, Eusebio Sacristán on the right and Juan Carlos on the left, either side of Pep Guardiola as the defensive midfielder or pivot with Bakero as the more attacking midfielder. Laudrup, Julio Salinas and Hristo Stoichkov were the forwards.

Club captain Alesanco was the only survivor of the 1986 debacle in Seville (and the 1983 Super Cup), which shows the extent of Cruyff's transformation of the squad. However, the day before the final Alesanco had celebrated his 36th birthday, so was no longer a regular starter and only a substitute, meaning Zubizarreta captained the side.

Sampdoria was coached by its former player, the Yugoslav Vujadin Boškov, who had coached the likes of

Ajax and Barça's bitter rivals Real Madrid. The Italian side was arranged in a 4-4-2, with Gianluca Pagliuca in goal; Moreno Mannini, Pietro Vierchowod (an Italian international with a Russian-born father), Marco Lanna and Srečko Katanec (from the newly independent Slovenia) in defence; ahead of them Attilio Lombardo, Toninho Cerezo (a veteran Brazilian international), Fausto Pari and Ivano Bonetti; with captain Roberto Mancini accompanied by a curly haired Gianluca Vialli up front.

In the old Wembley the tunnel was behind the east goal, not in the centre of the north side as it is in the rebuilt stadium. This meant that the two teams emerged from the Barça end, with a colourful mosaic of red, blue and yellow cards held up by the fans behind the players. The two teams took their positions on the pitch, both wearing change kits. Sampdoria usually wore blue shirts with red, white and black detailing, so it was judged a colour clash with Barça's classic blue and red stripes. Sampdoria therefore wore white shirts with blue shorts and white socks, while Barça appeared in an all-orange kit.

As was customary with the European Cup in those days, the 37th final started as a rather cagey affair, both sides probing to discover the other's strengths and weaknesses. Barça attacked the goal to my left and had most of the early play, which interestingly tended to be initiated through Koeman's long balls rather than short passing, and standing off the ball rather than pressing. However, Koeman's long passes were proper passes, not the aimless hoofing common in English football at the time. Chances for both sides were at a premium, partly because Boškov had a clear game plan based on trying to contain Barça, closely marking key players and hoping to nick a goal on the counter-attack using the pace of Lombardo down the wing. Three opponents were identified for special attention. Stoichkov was watched by Mannini, and Cerezo was tasked with following Bakero. Cerezo may have been an adopted son of a clown, but Bakero wasn't laughing because Barça's normally attacking midfielder was so closely man-marked by the Brazilian that he made little contribution to the game, the two players cancelling each other out. Finally, Pari focused his attentions on Laudrup, which is also what I shall do in my account of this match.

Born in Denmark in 1964, Laudrup became famous at the 1986 World Cup finals in Mexico where he starred for his home country. By the time of the Wembley final he was a few weeks short of his 28th birthday. In 1993 the Danish director Jørgen Leth made a documentary film, *Michael Laudrup: En Fodboldspiller* (*Michael Laudrup: a Footballer*), about the player's time at Barcelona[13]. In the film Laudrup explained that when playing for other teams, including Juventus, he would instinctively dribble, the skill he was best known for, but at Barcelona he was required to play the ball around more, particularly if up against an opponent with pace. Laudrup added that in the Dream Team eight or nine of the outfield players had

---

13 *Michael Laudrup: En Fodboldspiller*, video, directed by Jørgen Leth (Zentropa Entertainments, 1993)

fixed roles, which tends to contradict the usual view that Cruyff's teams were based on 'Total Football' with players constantly changing positions. Laudrup told the film that he was one of those encouraged to move around and given a free role by Cruyff as a playmaker, creating attacks with sudden bursts, one or two touches and passes, which was the way to get the best out of him.

Laudrup began the Wembley final playing deep on the left of midfield, with his opening contribution coming after 11 minutes, flicking the ball to Salinas who was then fouled by Lanna, which led to the first decent chance when Pagliuca made a save from a Koeman free kick. Laudrup then played his team into trouble after 23 minutes while defending a Sampdoria corner by poking the ball into the path of Lombardo, who nearly scored with a shot from a tight angle. Immediately after this, Laudrup made a more positive intervention, participating in a move that led to a Stoichkov header which was saved by Pagliuca. For most of the opening part of the game Laudrup was closely marked by Pari; however, it was a foul by another opponent, Mannini, who scythed down the Dane six minutes before half-time, which led to the game's first yellow card. Surprisingly for a player normally given licence to roam, that was one of the very few times Laudrup had moved out to the right of the pitch.

In the final minutes of the first half the Sampdoria fans sung an Anfield-style rendition of 'You'll Never Walk Alone', complete with scarves held aloft, swaying from side to side. Soon after they lowered their scarves,

German referee Aron Schmidhuber blew his whistle and the traditional military band then marched four abreast on the pitch in their navy blue uniforms, to provide our half-time entertainment with the match still goalless.

Early in the second half Salinas, who until then had made little impression and looked clumsy and ungainly to me, was surrounded by three defenders in the penalty box. With surprising skill and close ball control he managed to evade them all and get in a shot which Pagliuca saved. Soon after that Laudrup made his first effective contribution of the second half, feeding the ball to Stoichkov. The Bulgarian hit a shot from a tight angle which led to Pagliuca pulling off a double save, blocking both that effort and one from Eusebio on the rebound. Following this, Mannini, already on a yellow card after his first-half foul on Laudrup, should have been sent off for a lunge at Stoichkov which deserved a second yellow, but the referee bottled it.

On the hour, there were two great chances at either end within a couple of minutes. First, Sampdoria, sitting back and hoping to nick something on the break, counter-attacked. Lombardo raced down the wing and crossed the ball to Vialli but his shot went over the bar. Then, Barça launched a break after Bakero supplied Laudrup, who moved forward over the halfway line before playing a superb cross ball to Stoichkov on the right. The Bulgarian beat Pagliuca with his shot, only to see the ball hit the inside of the far post and bounce out. The 25,000 Barça fans at that end let out a collective groan, and at that moment I started to believe the game would repeat 1986, end goalless and be decided by the dreaded penalties, with the same outcome.

A few minutes after Stoichkov's chance Cruyff made a substitution, replacing Salinas with an attacking midfielder, Jon Andoni Goikoetxea, who occupied the right flank. I expected Laudrup to move further forward, but what actually happened was that he remained in midfield as Barça went to more of a 3-6-1, with Stoichkov alone up front. Up until then Pari had marked Laudrup, but after the substitution he started to mark Goikoetxea, and for the rest of the game the Dane was followed by Vierchowod. Immediately after this change Laudrup's new companion made his presence known by fouling him and earning a yellow card. Sampdoria then had two chances in quick succession – first another breakaway saw a Vialli shot saved by Zubizarreta, then Mancini found Vialli on the right and his chip beat the Spanish keeper only to go fractionally wide of the far post. After a few more attempts at goal there was still no breakthrough, so the game went into extra time.

The tension in the stadium increased. As always, the players didn't get long to rest before the start of extra time, so didn't go down the tunnel and instead stayed on the pitch. As the teams received instructions from their coaches or treatment and massages from physios, the Barça fans behind the goal to my right held up their blue, red and yellow cards to recreate their mosaic from earlier.

Barcelona dominated possession during extra time to such an extent that the Sampdoria fans whistled continuously when their opponents kept the ball for lengthy spells. However, Cruyff's team didn't do much with this possession and both sides had a chance apiece in the first period, Mannini for Sampdoria, Stoichkov for Barça, but neither resulted in a goal. Sampdoria was awarded a bizarre free kick when Katanec leant into Nando and pushed him over. If anything it was a foul on the Spanish defender, but the referee gave a decision the other way. Interestingly, it was at the same end, and nearly on the same spot, that Barça would be awarded another contentious, but more significant, free kick in the second period. Sampdoria wasted the free kick when Mancini tried to lob the ball over the wall.

During the short interval between the two portions of extra time the Barça fans behind the goal rhythmically clapped, almost as if they were trying to relieve themselves of nervous tension, while Cruyff and his assistant Tonnie Bruins Slot gave out further instructions to their players. Laudrup had enjoyed his best spell of the match in the first 20 minutes of the second half, but after Vierchowod started marking him the Dane's influence faded. However, five minutes after the restart, Laudrup was involved in the build-up to one of the game's most important moments, playing the ball to Stoichkov in the D on the edge of the penalty area. The Bulgarian then laid the ball back to Eusebio who got into a tangle with Giovanni Invernizzi, a substitute for Bonetti in the second half. The referee should have ordered a drop ball or played on, because it was not clear who, if anyone, had fouled who, but instead he gave a free kick to Barça.

With only nine minutes remaining it was possibly the last big chance. Koeman was famous for his ferocious shots, and I could sense the crowd's anticipation and concentration as the Sampdoria wall got into formation. Barça had already been awarded several free kicks in the game which provided shooting opportunities. With three of these the Sampdoria wall had broken and some of the players rushed forward. This time Stoichkov played a very short pass to Bakero, who stopped the ball as Koeman ran up to smash it with his right foot. The tip-tap between Stoichkov and Bakero was done to slightly change the angle of the shot, but also encourage some of the defenders in the Sampdoria wall to once again rush out. It was a gamble, but luckily three broke and the ball didn't hit any of them. Koeman's shot flew past a diving Pagliuca into the corner of the net. The fans behind the goal erupted, with a sound that I can still hear today. It was only then, when many of the fans sitting nearby stood up to celebrate, that it became clear most of those who had purchased tickets in the so-called 'neutral' section supported Barça. Soon the end to my right was a noisy mass of scarves twirling around, while the opposite end was a complete contrast, totally silent and still.

Sampdoria did get one final chance five minutes from time when Renato Buso, who had replaced the disappointing Vialli in the first period of extra time, headed wide of the goal. With Sampdoria forced to search for an equaliser, Laudrup found more space and surged forward before crossing to Stoichkov. Unfortunately the Bulgarian failed to control the ball and Pagliuca blocked it.

There was so much noise coming from the Barça fans that I never heard the final whistle. Stoichkov and Goikoetxea were deliberately keeping the ball in the far corner to my right, wasting the last seconds, when suddenly they broke off to celebrate. Even after the final whistle Stoichkov, who had been in a belligerent mood for much of the evening, hadn't finished because he tried to snatch the match ball out of the referee's hands as a souvenir.

Amid all the excitement of the goal, I hadn't even noticed that Cruyff made a substitution immediately after it, replacing Guardiola with the veteran Alesanco who filled in at centre-back. This meant that, as club captain, he would collect the trophy. The Barça players then replaced their orange shirts with the traditional blue and dark red ones before receiving the cup. As mentioned earlier, the Olympic Gallery obscured my view of the Royal Box, so I missed the presentation of the trophy to Alesanco by UEFA president Lennart Johansson and also didn't see Stoichkov cheekily sitting on the counter in front of the dignitaries. However, it wasn't long before the players climbed down the steps with the cup, then starting a lengthy celebration in front of the Barça fans to my right, many of whom were chanting 'Campeones, campeones, olé, olé, olé' and 'Madrid, cabrón, saluda al campeón' ('Madrid, bastards, salute the champions').

Koeman was rightly judged to be man of the match, not just for scoring the winning goal but for directing much of Barça's play so brilliantly from the back. The team's other playmaker, the further forward Laudrup, didn't have a particularly good game by his own high standards, being closely marked, but still managed to be involved in Barcelona's two most important moves. Laudrup wore number nine on his shirt at Wembley, but was far from a conventional striker. The Dane is sometimes cited as an example of a player performing a 'false nine' role, a centre-forward who occasionally drops deep to support the midfielders, linking play between them and the attack. However, at Wembley he played on the left, deeper and often behind Stoichkov, particularly in the first half.

The Barça players and coaching staff eventually disappeared down the tunnel, so it was time to make my own way out of the stadium. My late arrival meant missing out on the chance to buy any souvenirs, and all I'd got was a match programme. However, as I walked back along Wembley Way to the Tube station there was an old guy selling pennants. I couldn't get a good look at his merchandise because it was dark by then and I was conscious of people crowding behind me, so I quickly just bought one. It was only after getting home just before midnight that I saw the pennant contained the predictable design of trophy, club badges, details of game and venue, but spelled Barcelona with two Ls, in other words in Italian. If anything this made it an even more interesting souvenir.

I was 30 years old when Barça won its first European Cup in 1992. In 2017, at the age of 55, I was honoured to be invited to take part in a special television documentary commemorating the 25th anniversary of that famous occasion, the greatest night in the club's history. The programme lasted for 45 minutes and was broadcast by Dutch television channel Ziggo Sport on 3 June 2017 immediately before that year's Champions League Final. Called *Bestemming Wembley* (Dutch for *Destination Wembley*), the documentary concerned Barcelona's trip to England for the final in 1992 and Ronald Koeman's winning goal. The programme was made by Wasserman and Captains Studio (Wasserman is also Koeman's management agency)[14]. I was invited to participate after the Dutch film-makers contacted FC Barcelona asking for fans who were at the game in 1992 to come forward. The football club then circulated this request to its international network of *penyes*, and as a member of PBL I got to hear of it and offered my help.

The programme wasn't just about what happened on the pitch, instead it adopted a more unusual approach looking at wider aspects of that famous occasion. As well as Wembley Stadium the documentary was filmed in other parts of England, at Sopwell House in Hertfordshire where the Barça squad stayed in 1992, and Manchester where Pep Guardiola (by then coach of Manchester City) was interviewed. Some of the programme was filmed in Holland where Richard Witschge (a squad member in 1992) and Tonnie Bruins Slot (Barcelona's assistant coach) made contributions. The two other locations were Genoa where Invernizzi, the former Sampdoria player, talked about giving away the foul which led to Koeman's goal, and Barcelona where a couple of team staff and three

---

14 *Bestemming Wembley*, Wasserman and Captains Studio, broadcast on Ziggo Sport (Dutch TV), 3 June 2017.

supporters featured. One of these was Joan Casals, who since the 1980s has adopted the appearance of Avi del Barça, a cartoon character from the club's early decades and its mascot. This modern Avi can regularly be seen at Camp Nou with his white beard, *blaugrana* striped shirt stretched over his pot belly and a maroon *barretina* (traditional Catalan hat).

At the designated time of 2pm on Thursday, 18 May 2017 I arrived at Wembley to find Koeman, the programme's presenter Jack van Gelder and some of the production crew waiting outside an entrance to the stadium's north stand. A Wembley official then took us in and along the side of the pitch. The producers told me beforehand that the plan was for Koeman to reproduce his European Cup-winning shot by kicking a ball into the same goal. When there are no matches scheduled, football stadiums usually dismantle the goalposts, so to help the documentary Wembley staff temporarily erected one of the goals. However, just as Koeman was about to go on the pitch to re-enact his famous kick, I pointed out that the specially erected goal had been positioned at the west end of the stadium, whereas the 1992 goal had been at the east end. As a result of my intervention it was decided to abandon the idea of Koeman recreating his shot on goal, and instead this part of the film just shows him walking out on to the pitch, talking about the magic moment.

As is always the case with filming, lots of footage was taken and most of it ended up on the cutting room floor. The part featuring me that appeared in the finished documentary was when I provided a brief summary of the game, particularly the moment when Stoichkov hit the post, and a fear that 1986 would be repeated. Like Guardiola, Invernizzi, and others not from the Netherlands who appeared in the film, the bit with me talking was broadcast with Dutch subtitles.

The young Dutch film crew were delayed by about three-quarters of an hour because of north London's notorious traffic. The delay meant that I was able to have a much longer than expected conversation with Koeman about the final, his goal and football in general, while we waited at the stadium for the film crew's arrival. To prepare myself and jog my memory, I had watched a recording of BBC television's coverage of the 1992 final several times in the weeks before the filming, and noticed a couple of interesting points.

Firstly, since the days of Guardiola's success as coach of Barcelona, Bayern Munich and Manchester City, it has been common to trace his philosophy of pressing to Cruyff's Dream Team. Yet the 1992 final was played at quite a slow pace, with minimal pressing. Terry Venables, Barça's coach in the club's previous European Cup Final, made a similar observation when asked by BBC presenter Des Lynam at half-time if Cruyff's team had played in the first half like his Barça side of a few years before. Venables replied that it was different, saying that Cruyff's side sat off the ball, whereas his own team had played more of a pressing game[15]. This reinforces the point made

---

15 BBC TV broadcast, 20 May 1992.

in the previous chapter that Venables played a major role in introducing pressing to Barcelona, and did it before the likes of Cruyff and Guardiola. The tactic is often associated with the Dutchman, but in the most important match of Cruyff's coaching career he didn't play a pressing game – it looked to me more like an Italian-style match.

I also noticed that the 1992 final was the last played under rules allowing the goalkeeper to pick up the ball following a back-pass from his own team. Consequently, there were quite a few back-passes by both Barça and Sampdoria. I mentioned this to Koeman when we met, telling him that my club, Leeds United, had been badly affected when the back-pass was banned, because the team's centre-backs struggled to play the ball under pressure as competently as defenders of other teams. Leeds went from reigning league champions to relegation candidates overnight, largely as a consequence of the rule being introduced at short notice with little time to prepare for the change. Koeman's reply surprised me as he said that in his opinion the ban on the back-pass wasn't too much of a problem for defenders, they just had to control the ball more. Instead, he believed it was a greater challenge for some of the goalkeepers, requiring them to play the ball with their feet. For a defender of Koeman's skill the new rule could be taken in his stride, but his reply possibly suggests he overestimated the ability to adapt of lesser players.

When I discussed the famous goal with Koeman his expression changed from a serious look to a smile, saying it was the most important one of his life. I imagine

Koeman frequently gets asked about the goal, but he clearly took great pride and pleasure from talking about it. I also mentioned to Koeman that the first time I had seen him 'in the flesh' was five years before the final, in 1987 at a Dutch league match between FC Utrecht and PEC Zwolle which I attended during a weekend break in Holland. At the time Koeman was 24 years old, a couple of years younger than me, and played for PSV Eindhoven. As a respected Dutch international, Koeman was asked to attend the Utrecht game so that he could urge fans to behave following recent hooligan violence in the country. I remember that it was a cold autumn evening and my breath was visible while speaking. Koeman walked on to the Stadion Galgenwaard pitch just before kick-off wearing a blue puffer jacket, holding a microphone, then made his announcement reading a prepared statement from a piece of paper, while the players stood around the centre circle. Interestingly, Koeman told me he had no recollection of the incident, although a YouTube film clip will confirm my story[16].

The production team asked me to bring along souvenirs connected to the final, so I chose my ticket stub, the Italian pennant with two Ls, match programme and some photos which Koeman kindly signed. Another thing I brought along was a player from Subbuteo, a tabletop game where you use fingers to flick miniature plastic figures on wobbly bases to 'kick' tiny footballs. Soon after the 1992 final I hand-painted a Subbuteo

16 youtube.com/watch?v=sCfdLbGZSBg.

team in the special orange kit worn that day, accurate in every detail including *blaugrana* stripes on the sleeves and top of the socks. The figure I brought along had Koeman's number four on the back and his distinctive mop of blonde hair on its head. At the time of the 1992 final Koeman had a short back and sides with thicker hair on top. The haircut earned Koeman the nickname 'Tintin' because of his resemblance to the character in Hergé's famous cartoon adventure stories, although by the time of our meeting a quarter of a century later, he sported a more conventional style. When I showed the 15mm-tall figure to Koeman, he looked at it but didn't comment. I think he thought the little plastic man was rather bizarre, perhaps like a stalked celebrity might feel when viewing an effigy of himself made by a creepy fan.

Apart from the fans in Barcelona, I was the only football supporter to feature in *Bestemming Wembley* and was very pleased with the finished programme and grateful to Koeman for being so generous with his time for our conversation. Three years after *Bestemming Wembley* was filmed, Koeman returned to Barcelona as coach and Wasserman and Captains Studio made a new documentary series called *Força Koeman* for Videoland covering the 2020/21 season. The little plastic man was not invited to participate.

5

Philosophical about Athens

INSPIRED BY the Wembley final, I decided to travel to Barcelona to see my first game at Camp Nou, selecting a fixture with Athletic Bilbao in November 1992. The trip started with an afternoon flight from London to Madrid, the plan being to stay in the Spanish capital for a couple of days then travel on to Barcelona. Coincidently, on the evening I arrived in Spain, Barça was playing at Camp Nou in the second leg of a tie against CSKA Moscow. The match was in the second round of the newly rebranded UEFA Champions League. Having already defeated Viking Stavanger in the first round, Barça was expected to progress after securing a 1-1 draw in Russia with an important away goal. Barça was also the holder of the trophy, while CSKA was not considered much of a threat. Watching in a tapas bar in Madrid I saw that Barça was 2-0 up after half an hour. Believing that the game was over, I left the bar, went back to my hotel and didn't catch the rest of the game. So it was a bit of a shock to open a Spanish newspaper the next morning and see that Barça had conceded a goal just before half-time, and then two more in a crazy four-minute spell on the hour. Barça lost 3-2, so exited the tournament 4-3 on aggregate.

Despite the loss to CSKA, Barcelona won Saturday's game against Athletic Bilbao, which although played in a subdued atmosphere after the midweek defeat later proved to be crucial in enabling Barça to retain its La Liga title in 1992/93 by a single point ahead of Real Madrid, so qualifying the team for another crack at the Champions League. To try and improve its chances of winning, Barcelona added a fourth foreigner, signing Brazilian striker Romario from PSV Eindhoven. After Romario's arrival Cruyff sometimes left Laudrup out, preferring to select Koeman, Stoichkov and the Brazilian as his permitted three foreigners.

In the first round of the 1993/94 tournament Barça was nearly knocked out for the second successive year by a team from the former Soviet Union, this time Dynamo Kyiv. A 3-1 defeat in Ukraine was only narrowly overturned when Barça won the home leg 4-1. The second-round opposition was Austria Vienna, and this time Barça cruised through, winning both legs and 5-1 on aggregate. This qualified Barça for the last eight, but instead of a quarter-final knockout round, there was a group stage. The eight surviving teams were divided into two groups of four, and each team played its three opponents home and away. Barça was drawn against Monaco, Spartak Moscow and Galatasaray, with the top two going through to a semi-final knockout round.

Barça topped its group with four wins and two draws, so earning a semi-final against Porto who had finished second in the other group. Strangely, the semi-final wasn't played over two legs, just one. Home advantage was given to the side that topped its group, meaning the tie took place at Camp Nou. It ended 3-0 to Barça, a game memorable for a terrific shot from Koeman which, unusually for him, followed a lengthy run with the ball from inside his own half. Milan topped the other group, so played at home against Monaco and, like Barça, triumphed 3-0. This set up a final between Barça and Milan in the Greek capital, Athens.

The weekend before the final in Greece, Barça narrowly clinched its fourth successive La Liga title, after Deportivo La Coruña missed a last-minute penalty in their match, while Milan had retained the Italian Serie A title a few weeks earlier. This meant the two top sides in Europe would meet in the final of the continent's major club competition. A couple of months earlier I had predicted that Barça would meet Milan in the final, and in anticipation of this fixture booked my flights and hotel accommodation in advance. Once again, I was able to secure a match ticket at face value. After the final I lost the ticket, but from memory I think it cost about £45.

There was a gap of three weeks between Barça's semi-final win and the final on 18 May 1994. During the wait between the two fixtures I remember looking forward to this particular final more than any other match, before or since. There was just time to post a letter to FC Barcelona (remember, no internet in those days) ordering a retro-style Barça shirt. I remember opening the package containing the shirt, but soon realised it wasn't suitable for the trip because it was made of heavy cotton and the temperature in Athens at the end of May would be boiling. This meant the shirt, which was worn 23 years later in the *Bestemming Wembley* film, had to stay at home and never made it to Greece.

I flew out from London on Tuesday, the day before the final, with the return flight arranged for Friday, providing two and a half days to take in the sights of Athens, a city I had never visited. After a flight time of just under four hours, I arrived in the Greek capital in the early afternoon. The Greek taxi driver who took me from Athens airport to my hotel was doing a roaring trade ferrying fans. He was clearly excited about his city hosting the game and fascinated that an English person should have travelled such a long way to see a team from Spain play one from Italy. The driver believed Barça would win because, in his words, 'They have fantastic strikers, Romario and Stoichkov, and Milan miss their defence.' He knew what he was talking about because Milan's Franco Baresi and Alessandro Costacurta were missing from the final through suspensions picked up in the semi-final against Monaco. Marco van Basten would also be missing, having sustained a long-term injury. Although the taxi driver thought Barça would win, as did most bookmakers on the continent, back in England Milan was the favourite.

My hotel was ideally located near the city centre, and judging by the colours of the flags hanging out of bedroom windows about one-third of its guests were Barça fans, one-third Milan, and the remainder ordinary holidaymakers or people on business trips. However, it was just as well that the heavy cotton Barça shirt remained at home because it was sweltering. During my stay in Athens I got up early to do sightseeing until 11 o'clock, then retreated back to the hotel to escape the midday heat, before popping back out after five when it cooled a little. It didn't give much time to see the many sights of Athens, but I managed to squeeze in a few, including the ancient Greek areas of the Agora and Plaka plus a visit to the superb National Archaeological Museum. Greece has had its economic troubles in the 21st century, but the piles of uncollected rubbish, social unrest and other signs of decay that recent visitors have told me about were not to be seen when I went there.

Another of the must-see attractions in Athens is the Acropolis hill that dominates the city with the Parthenon temple on its summit. The Greek word 'acropolis' means upper city, or area of high ground where people could seek refuge. The Parthenon at the top was built in the fifth century BC to celebrate the political and cultural achievements of Athens. About 200 years ago, when the city was occupied by the Turks, many of the marble sculptures decorating the Parthenon were in poor condition. The British Earl of Elgin controversially removed some of the sculptures for restoration, and despite repeated requests by Greece they have never been returned. About 15 years after my Athens trip I started work conducting tours in London, and one of my jobs was being the guide for Museum Mile London, showing people the Elgin Marbles on display in the British Museum. One Greek tourism website refers to the Parthenon as 'probably the most recognisable structure in the world next to the golden arches of McDonalds'[17]. Although classical architecture isn't usually associated with burgers, this description does make the point that the Parthenon is an iconic image for Athens, which is why it appeared on a pennant that I bought from a street seller, with the ancient temple depicted as a plinth for the European Cup trophy.

Anticipating that huge crowds would visit the Acropolis on matchday, I visited it on the evening of my arrival. On the day of the final thousands of fans from both Spain and Italy arriving on day trips covered its slopes like ants. Some of those who climbed it in the midday heat were among the 100 or so football fans who received medical treatment for breathing problems caused by the city's heat and poor air quality.

In those days the final wasn't the commercialised and corporate affair it has since become. The programme described it as the '39th Final European Champions Clubs' Cup' and there was no sign of the branding and logo used today, because in 1994 'UEFA Champions League' still only referred to the group stage. While walking around the city and taking in the atmosphere I spotted a street kiosk selling newspapers, including *Sport*, the Barcelona football daily. Although I don't speak any

17 athensguide.com.

foreign languages, you can always get the gist and look at the pictures, so I bought a copy. One picture was of Barça strikers Romario and Stoichkov under the heading 'Atenes sera un clam' ('Athens will be a cheer' or 'We'll be cheering in Athens')[18]. Like the caption writer and a Barça fan I met who translated it for me before the game, I confidently expected this to be the case later that evening.

The game was scheduled to kick off at 9.15pm local time, with Greece an hour ahead of western Europe. I didn't fancy getting the train out to the stadium at peak time, packed in a crowded carriage in the fierce heat, so decided to head out early to avoid the last-minute panic and rush of Wembley a couple of years before. This proved to be a good call, because my train was mainly empty and arrived at the stadium in plenty of time. It was too hot to do any sightseeing in the city, and I had decided not to drink alcohol to avoid feeling drowsy and missing any of the game.

Located on the outskirts of Athens, the Olympiako Stadio (Olympic Stadium) is a great venue, living up to the sporting reputation of the city and worthy of hosting the final. Built in 1982, it has since had a roof added, but back in 1994 was uncovered. Its cream-coloured plastic seats reflected the hot sun, making the stadium look like marble from ancient Greece. Built in two tiers, the stadium had a cut-away area behind each goal where huge scoreboards were mounted. The most distinctive features

---

18 *Sport*, 18 May 1994.

were four very tall floodlight pylons which leant over at a gravity-defying angle, looking like they were about to fall over. Even though it had a running track, meaning the fans were some distance from the pitch, the stadium managed to generate and maintain a great atmosphere.

As soon as the turnstiles opened I entered and was given a free match programme and shown to my seat by a middle-aged Greek lady, who then meekly asked for a few pennies, which I happily provided. Soon after, an Englishman arrived, a couple of years younger than me, from Lancashire in north-west England. I discovered he was from that county because of a Union Jack flag with 'Fleetwood' emblazoned across it, which he hung in the corner of the ground (clearly visible on television coverage of the game). When the Greek lady asked him for a few pennies for providing the programme and showing him to his seat, he reacted by shouting 'Fuck off!' at her. I find this type of behaviour embarrassing, completely unnecessary and the kind of thing that gives English football fans a bad name abroad. In any case, a few coins for the programme would have been a sensible investment for him, because by 2020 at least one online dealer was charging £150 for originals. Despite his behaviour, I decided to speak to him to pass the time before kick-off and discovered that he was a Liverpool fan who had decided to take in the final.

Another person I chatted to was a Greek man of around my age wearing that season's Leeds shirt, who had taken advantage of the final coming to his home city. Sitting a couple of rows behind me, he explained that he had decided to support Barcelona, mainly because of Milan's controversial defeat of Leeds in the 1973 Cup Winners' Cup Final, which had taken place not far away in Thessaloniki, northern Greece, after highly dubious refereeing.

My seat was in a neutral area along the side, towards one of the corners. Slowly the surrounding places filled up with fans, and it soon became clear from the red and black banners that most were Milanese. In fact, taking the stadium as a whole, they outnumbered the Barça contingent by about three to one. There were also quite a few empty seats scattered around the stadium, although the official attendance was given as 70,000. Two of the seats which had been empty were eventually occupied by Englishmen whose plane had been delayed, meaning they only got into the stadium with minutes to spare (the perils of the day trip). It was still hot when the final kicked off at the designated time. So far the trip had lived up to my expectations. The next 90 minutes were rather different.

Cruyff's line-up consisted of Zubizarreta in goal; Ferrer, Koeman, Miguel Ángel Nadal and Sergi at the back; Guardiola, captain Bakero and Guillermo Amor in midfield; then Aitor 'Txiki' Beguiristain, Stoichkov and Romario up front. It's difficult to compare formations, but very roughly the changes from the Wembley team of two years earlier were Nadal and Sergi instead of Nando and Juan Carlos in defence; Amor instead of Eusebio in midfield; and Beguiristain and Romario replacing Laudrup and Salinas in attack. If Wembley was 3-4-3, morphing into 3-6-1 in the second half, then Athens looked to me more like a variant of 4-3-3 on paper which developed into 4-4-2 because Beguiristain was pushed back.

Fabio Capello's Milan team was definitely a 4-4-1-1, with Sebastiano Rossi in goal; captain Mauro Tassotti, Filippo Galli, Paulo Maldini and Christian Panucci in defence; the Croat Zvonimir Boban, Demetrio Albertini, French player Marcel Desailly and Roberto Donadoni in midfield; then Montenegrin Dejan Savićević playing in the 'hole' behind Daniele Massaro.

The teams came out on to the pitch from an entrance on the opposite side to my seat, with Milan in an all-white change strip and Barça wearing the latest version of the traditional blue and dark red stripes, blue shorts and blue and dark red socks. One corner of the stadium was suddenly filled with blue, red and yellow cards spelling out 'BARCA' in large letters, held up in unison by supporters.

After nine minutes Milan, attacking the end to my left, put the ball in the Barça net following a header from Panucci. Although disallowed for offside, it was a warning of things to come. In the first half Barça had 56 per cent of the possession but more importantly its few attacks petered out or were intercepted by Milan on reaching the final third. Bakero had difficulty at Wembley with Cerezo man-marking him, but in Athens he would have even more trouble dealing with Desailly who began playing in the holding midfield position, before growing to dominate the whole of midfield with both his strength and technique.

A couple of moves that happened within minutes of each other in the middle of the first half rather summed things up. In the 20th minute, Romario played the ball through to Amor to give Barça a rare attacking opportunity, but Maldini made an interception in the nick of time. Three minutes later, Galli hit a long ball forward, Nadal headed it away, only for Boban to win it back and play a pass through to Savićević. The Montenegrin beat Nadal on the right, then crossed it for an unmarked Massaro who hit an accurate shot from a tight angle back across into the corner of the net. Whereas Milan's Maldini made a vital interception in the first incident, the nearest Barça player was a good eight metres away from the goalscorer in the second. Most of the stadium erupted with a number of red flares set off by the celebrating Italians.

Five minutes before the break, Bakero finally managed to evade a Desailly tackle and passed the ball to Stoichkov who slipped it forward to Romario in a central position. The Brazilian striker hit a right-footed shot which looked to have Rossi beaten, but Galli got across just in time to deflect it out for a corner. Had it gone in the game might have developed differently. As things turned out, it proved to be the nearest Barça got to scoring the whole evening, with Romario and Stoichkov starved of service.

As every follower of football knows, the worst time to concede a goal is just before half-time, but this is exactly what happened after two minutes of stoppage time. The move began with Rossi throwing the ball to Panucci, who then started a series of passes from the back to Donadoni,

Massaro, Panucci again, Maldini, Galli, out to Savićević on the right, then to Boban, to Savićević, back to Boban, Tassotti, Boban once more, then across to Donadoni out on the left who slid the ball back for Massaro to hit a left-footed shot from just inside the box into the goal. It has been described as one of the greatest goals in the entire history of the European Cup Final, although it's worth pointing out that it was helped by poor defending. Barça failed to get in a challenge and Zubizarreta could have done more than just get a hand to it.

In the stadium there was a row of Milan fans behind me. When the first goal went in they jumped up cheering, but I remained seated. That identified me. After the second goal one of the Milan fans grabbed me around the neck. No big deal, it didn't hurt or cause any injury, but was still out of order. Unfortunately, it wouldn't be the last unpleasant incident involving Milan fans, with urine thrown at me when Leeds went to the San Siro in 2000.

There was only just time for Barça to kick off again before the referee blew his whistle to end the half, amid more red flares from the Italians. Both goals had been scored by Massaro, a player blamed for Milan's defeat against Marseille in the previous year's final because of his missed chances. I was stunned by what I had witnessed, and wondered whether Cruyff's side could get an early goal in the second half to turn things around.

As the players re-entered the pitch after the break, Barça supporters held up their coloured cards, while the Milanese lit red flares. At this stage the fan choreography was a close contest. Just as well, it was the only thing that was.

If Barça still had a chance it evaporated a couple of minutes after the restart. Savićević dispossessed Nadal wide on the right, immediately in front of where I was sitting, and then, from the corner of the penalty area, brilliantly lobbed Zubizarreta, who had strayed off his line. This goal, which killed the game as a contest, was controversial. When Savićević challenged Nadal he had his left foot raised high. If players do this on the continent it is invariably given as a foul, so Nadal immediately stopped and appealed. However, the referee was an Englishman, Philip Don, and in England such challenges were tolerated (at least in the 1990s). So Don played on and the goal stood.

A few minutes after the goal, Cruyff, perhaps acknowledging that his line-up had been lacking strength in midfield, brought on Eusebio for Beguiristain, although the change didn't seem to make much difference. Nadal, who had been made to look foolish by the third goal, was furious. Seven minutes later he tried to take revenge, lunging at Savićević in a challenge that would definitely produce a red card today, but Don only got out a yellow. By now Desailly was winning everything in the middle of the park, Barça couldn't cope with him and Bakero and Sergi were both booked for fouls on the French player. Bakero was lucky not to be sent off when he should have received a second yellow for yet another foul on Desailly just after the hour, but once again Don let it go.

If there was any doubt that Capello had decided that in the circumstances attack was the best form of defence, then the proof came after 57 minutes when he got off his bench to shout and gesticulate at his players when they started to sit back at 3-0. His team responded by going forward and scoring a fourth. Milan was awarded a free kick and the ball came to Savićević, who eluded the Barça defenders before shooting against the post. Barça regained possession only to immediately lose it. Albertini then supplied Desailly, who burst through the defence to score with a right-footed shot. It was 4-0 with half an hour still to go.

If you arrived in the stadium late and just saw the final 30 minutes you'd think that it was a close game, with Barça just edging it. However, although Barça had lots of possession, the ball was just being passed around, all moves petering out when reaching the final third. Even Capello was satisfied now, and remained seated, letting his team see out the game. With just over quarter of an hour remaining Cruyff ordered on Quique Estebaranz as a replacement for Sergi. This was to be one of very few appearances for Quique at Barça, and the only time I saw him live. To be fair, he got quite a bit of the ball and looked lively attacking down the right, but by then the game was already lost.

The last event of note was the departure of Maldini five minutes from the end. Normally a full-back, he had played brilliantly as a makeshift centre-back, but had picked up a knock, so hobbled off to be replaced by Stefano Nava. Guardiola, who like the rest of the Barça team had struggled in the game, would later dedicate his first Champions League win as coach 15 years later to Maldini, with performances such as Athens in mind.

Like Wembley, the Greek stadium had a flight of stairs going up to a presentation area level with the halfway line on the opposite side of the pitch from my seat. After the full-time whistle Tassotti led his victorious players up the steps to collect Milan's fifth European Cup. By then, many of the Barça fans had left the stadium, with those that remained still and silent, except for a large blue, red and yellow flag, which waved defiantly. Strangely, this flag had the mouth and tongue logo of the Rolling Stones on it, proving that you can't always get what you want.

I also left pretty quickly after the end, taking a train back to the city centre. Most Milan fans stayed in the stadium to celebrate, so my carriage was filled with Barça fans and I got talking to one of them. From Barcelona, wearing a 1980s replica shirt, in his late 20s and, unusually for his part of Europe ginger-haired, he blamed Koeman's lack of pace for the defeat. I argued that Laudrup's omission had been a mistake. He shrugged his shoulders, suggesting it was possibly a bit of both and simply said, 'Anyway, that's Cruyff,' hinting at the coach's perceived stubbornness. Our mini post-mortem helped to pass the time, and soon we were back in the city centre. By now the temperature had cooled and I was starving. While sitting in a café in Athens having a snack and reflecting on the game, an elderly couple from Barcelona joined my table. The waiter came round to take their order, and suggested pasta. The Catalan lady replied to him in heavily accented English, 'No, no, no pasta! No, no, no Italian.' I resisted the temptation to suggest she ordered a quattro stagioni pizza, one part for each goal.

The atmosphere in Athens over all three days of my trip was fantastic, fitting for a city with such a sporting tradition, as the historical home of the Olympic Games. Despite the heavy nature of the defeat, the Barcelona fans behaved themselves and I didn't see any trouble as the two sets of supporters mixed freely in the city centre.

After retiring to my hotel room, I saw the copy of *Sport* magazine on the bedside table. What the Barça fan in the city centre hadn't told me was that 'Atenes sera un clam' can also translate as 'Athens will be a cry' or 'We'll be crying in Athens'. On the subject of crying, the ancient Greek tragedian Sophocles could easily have been referring to Barcelona's trip to Athens when he wrote in his *Theban Plays*, 'Home you'll come in tears, cut off from the sight of it all, the brilliant rites unfinished.' His statement encouraged me to consult Greek philosophers to try and understand what had happened in the 1994 final. Here are my conclusions[19].

'Which of these options is without bad implications?' (Aeschylus, *Agamemnon*)

In those days teams could field a maximum of three foreign players on the field at the same time. When Barça just had Koeman, Stoichkov and Laudrup there was no problem, but when Romario arrived it meant that one of the four would have to be left out, which created a

---

19 best-quotations.com.

dilemma. For Athens, Cruyff opted to omit Laudrup. This decision, described by Capello as a mistake after the final, deprived Barça of a creative source[20].

'Make the best use of what is in your power and take the rest as it happens' (Epictetus)

Capello decided that without both Milan's usual centre-backs, the best strategy was not attempting to rely on the traditional Italian tactic of defence or play the offside game with players less experienced in it. Instead, Milan resolved to win control of midfield, making attack the best form of defence. The absence of Laudrup, able to play deeper than Stoichkov or Romario, made it easier for the Italian side to do this.

'His foot is slow but quick his mind' (Euripedes, *Ion*)

The Barça defence consisted of skilful footballers, able to read the game well and initiate moves from the back, but not all of them were blessed with pace. Usually this didn't matter because opposing teams tended to sit back against Cruyff's side. However, if opponents were good enough to have a go instead, as Milan did that night, then they could inflict serious damage.

'The middleness in everything is more safe' (Menander)

Before the final Cruyff said that Barça was better than Milan, who he claimed was negative as shown by the

---

20   Balagué, G., *Barça: The Illustrated History of FC Barcelona* (London: Carlton, 2014), p100.

signing of solid midfielder Desailly in the summer of 1993 while he had bought an exciting striker, Romario, around the same time[21]. In the final Desailly was brilliant, fighting to win control of the middle of the pitch, while Romario hardly touched the ball.

'Avoid undue elation in prosperity, or undue depression in adversity' (Socrates)

Barça had won La Liga a few days before Athens and overconfidence crept in, with Cruyff underestimating Milan.

'Good actions give strength to ourselves and inspire good actions in others' (Plato)

Milan won in Athens partly because every member of its team performed at the very top of their game and outfought Barça in all areas of the pitch.

'Anyone can become angry, that is easy, but to be angry with the right person at the right time, and for the right purpose and in the right way, that is not within everyone's power and that is not easy' (Aristotle)

It was reported that on the coach back to Athens airport after the game Barça's goalkeeper, Zubizarreta, was told he was unwanted by the club and not to bother coming back next season.

If true, this seems a callous way to end the Barcelona career of someone who had helped the club to

---

21 'Barcelona v Milan revisited: The night in 1994 the Dream died,' theguardian.com.

unprecedented success, having won four successive league titles and the 1992 European Cup.

'Number is the substance of all things' (Pythagoras)
The decisive moment of the match was goal number two. The number of different Milan players involved in the build-up was nine, taking 39 touches of the ball and exchanging 14 passes between them, without a single Barça player getting near the ball. The goal was scored by Milan's number 11 with a shot from 12 metres. However, the most important number was 47, because the goal came after 47 minutes and was the culmination of a move that lasted exactly 47 seconds.

6

Long Pants

THE CRUSHING defeat in Athens started the break-up of Cruyff's Dream Team, beginning with Zubizarreta and Laudrup, who left the club at the end of the season. The following campaign saw Barça back in the Champions League courtesy of its last-minute clinching of La Liga. This time the group stage was moved to the start of the competition, and expanded from two groups of four, to four groups of that size. Barça was drawn against English champion Manchester United, Galatasaray and its 1986 semi-final opponent Gothenburg. Of most interest to me was the third of Barça's six group matches, away at Manchester United on Wednesday, 19 October 1994, providing an opportunity for my first visit to Old Trafford.

I took the train up from London and stayed in a budget hotel in one of Manchester's less salubrious districts. The charm of the hotel was shown by a sign on the toilet door which read, 'A fart is a turd's cry for help.' Better than Manchester's hotels was its transport system, including the first line of a tram system which had opened a couple of years earlier and provided the best way of reaching the stadium.

The game kicked off at the unusual time of 8.30pm, as requested by television broadcasters who were showing it live throughout Europe. The later-than-normal start provided an extra three-quarters of an hour to fill, so I decided to go and wait for the Barça team coach to arrive. I managed to get near the front of the crowd watching behind a metal barrier as the players and coaching staff got off, one by one, providing my closest-ever view of Johan Cruyff, Stoichkov, Romario and the rest.

My match ticket, bought at a face value of just £17, provided a good seat along one of the sides, near the famous Stretford End behind the goal to the right. The Stretford End had previously been a notoriously rowdy terrace, but a year earlier became all-seater to comply with the Taylor Report. It's strange to think that in those days Old Trafford had a capacity of less than 44,000, arranged in one tier, a bit like a rectangular oven dish, quite unlike the stadium it has since become. After entering Old Trafford I was surprised to see that the first few rows of seats all the way round the stadium were cordoned off, but later learned this was because UEFA required the installation of tall advertising boards around the perimeter of the pitch, obstructing the view from the lowest rows. Consequently, even though there was a huge demand for tickets, the crowd that night was restricted to 40,000, nearly 4,000 below normal capacity. This became normal practice at Champions League games, but that night was the first time I experienced what was an early sign of commercial greed taking priority over supporters.

These days, Manchester United has learned to be apprehensive about encounters with Barcelona, following several defeats which will be mentioned later. However, back in 1994 the English club was optimistic after triumphing over Barça in the two previous encounters (the Cup Winners' Cup campaigns of 1984 and 1991). Manchester United had also never lost at home in European competition, a run of over 50 games, encouraging a confident mood among the fans who took their seats around me.

The two teams emerged from a tunnel on the other side of the pitch in the corner to my right. The home side, in its traditional red and white, was without the suspended Eric Cantona and the injured Ryan Giggs, but the big surprise was coach Alex Ferguson's decision to replace his captain Steve Bruce with Paul Parker who was quicker and selected, it was widely assumed, in order to man-mark Romario. The visitors wore an all-mint green kit, with three changes to the line-up in Athens: Abelardo Fernández instead of Amor; Luis Cembranos Martínez deputising for the injured Ferrer; while Carles Busquets replaced Zubizarreta in goal. The three foreign players law meant there was no room for the big summer signing, Romanian World Cup star Gheorghe Hagi.

When the teams lined up before kick-off I looked around to spot the three players I hadn't seen before, Abelardo and Luis in defence and Busquets in goal. I'd never heard of Luis, but learned later that the 21-year-old was a midfielder who Cruyff had chosen to deploy as a kind of wing-back. The only thing I knew about Busquets was reading that Cruyff had decided the two-year-old ban on keepers picking up the ball from back-passes rendered old-fashioned shot-stoppers like Zubizarreta obsolete. Instead he wanted his keepers to be able to play the ball with their feet and initiate moves, rather like Stanley Menzo, his 'sweeper keeper' at Ajax. Barça reserve Busquets had been dubbed 'the goalkeeper with no hands', so when Zubi left after Athens Cruyff promoted him. When I saw this new goalie, standing in the penalty area, something looked odd. It took me a few seconds to realise what it was.

Busquets was wearing a yellow and purple top, horrible but not particularly unusual. The strange thing was his leg wear of black tracksuit trousers rather than shorts. I later discovered that Busquets was well-known for always avoiding shorts regardless of the weather, claiming he found trousers more comfortable and offered better protection from injuries. Goalkeepers in long pants are a rather select bunch and identifying the first in the modern era is problematic. One candidate with a Barcelona connection is Billy Thomson, who wore them in goal for Dundee United when the Scottish club played Barça in the UEFA Cup in 1987. However, those trousers might not qualify because they ended just below the knee, meaning his success in the tie might have to be judged a case of knickerbocker glory.

Busquets was certainly one of the early pioneers of full tracksuit bottoms, wearing them at least as early as

1991 when he made his competitive debut for Barça in the Cup Winners' Cup Final defeat to Manchester United, deputising for the injured Zubizarreta. For the 1992 European Cup Final at Wembley, Busquets had been an unused substitute. The other Barça subs wore orange shorts while sitting on the bench, but Busquets insisted on wearing black tracksuit trousers instead, despite the hot weather. He also climbed Wembley's famous staircase to collect his medal in his long pants and kept them on for the celebrations on the pitch, although I must confess to not noticing at the time.

In the Old Trafford game, Busquets had an early escape when a cross from Manchester United's right-winger Andrei Kanchelskis evaded him, only for Koeman to come to the rescue by preventing the ball reaching former Barça striker Mark Hughes on the six-yard line. The home side started much the stronger, particularly in wide areas. Cruyff's tendency to play midfielders in defensive positions backfired with Luis, who looked confident on the ball going forward trying to initiate attacks, but was most uncomfortable when Lee Sharpe repeatedly tore past him, and in the 20th minute this resulted in a goal, headed in by Hughes. Busquets could perhaps have done a bit better dealing with the cross, but this time it was more a case of Koeman not getting tight enough on the Welsh striker.

However, Cruyff wasn't the only coach to have made a dodgy selection, because Ferguson's choice of Parker to man-mark Romario also looked questionable. Just after the half hour Koeman hit a long pass to Bakero who then supplied Romario. If Parker was supposed to be marking Romario he completely lost him, enabling the Brazilian to finish a great move by shooting the ball into the net between the legs of keeper Peter Schmeichel.

At half-time Cruyff brought on Eusebio in place of the struggling Luis, who only made a few appearances for the Barça first team and left the club at the end of the season. That change, plus an earlier swap, with Nadal dropping back and Koeman moving further forward, meant that United's wingers no longer posed the same threat. A few minutes after the restart Barça went ahead. This time the goal was nearer to me, so I had an excellent view as Bakero controlled a long pass from Koeman superbly on his chest and half-volleyed it into the net, escaping the attentions of no fewer than four defenders surrounding him. So far there had been little opportunity for Busquets to demonstrate his ball-playing skills, but that changed when Sergi kicked a dangerous back-pass which the keeper was able to control and clear from Hughes's pressure.

With quarter of the game remaining, Cruyff brought on his 20-year-old son Jordi to replace Beguiristain, while Ferguson replaced Nicky Butt with a 19-year-old Paul Scholes, followed three minutes later by Steve Bruce coming on for the injured David May. The changes went better for the home side than for the visitors. Jordi took up a position on the left of the attack, but struggled to make an impact, losing control of the ball on a couple of occasions with poor first touches and conceding possession. Barça was only ten minutes away from becoming the first team to beat Manchester United at Old Trafford in European competition, but the home side kept its record intact partly thanks to the determination of Paul Ince, who drove forward and flicked the ball to Roy Keane out on the right. Keane then crossed the ball for Sharpe to back-heel it into the net, securing a 2-2 draw.

Although it was an exciting contest, there were few actual saves by either keeper because most attempts were either off target or blocked by defenders. Busquets' only save of note was stopping an Ince shot after 83 minutes. Despite not being particularly culpable for the two goals that were conceded, the long-panted goalkeeper stayed near his line both times rather than coming out to claim the ball, which is perhaps surprising for a 'sweeper keeper'. Arguably Busquets' biggest error was four minutes from time when he played the ball out with his feet to Nadal in a dangerous position just outside the penalty area, but fortunately the defender managed to clear the ball as Ince pressed.

Talking of mistakes, referees usually only get mentioned when they make them, so it's good to be able to report, as Glenn Moore did in the following day's *Independent* newspaper, that the match was 'excellently refereed'[22]. The match official concerned, Ion Crăciunescu, allowed the game to flow and got all the major decisions correct. The only controversy involved a penalty appeal for handball against Nadal six minutes from the end. Even then, the referee was perfectly positioned and television replays of

---

22 *Independent*, 20 October 1994.

the incident were inconclusive. Crăciunescu has a rather unusual story, being a former professional footballer who became a referee. In 1975, a year after winning the Romanian league title with Universitatea Craiova, Crăciunescu was sent off in a game for swearing at a match official. Despite being only in his mid-20s, Crăciunescu decided if you can't beat them join them, retiring to become a referee. After Old Trafford, Crăciunescu went on to officiate at that season's Champions League Final between Ajax and Milan, later becoming president of the Romanian Referees' Committee[23]. Footballers in the UK often complain that referees who have never played the game at a high level don't understand it, particularly in relation to fouls, tackling and handball, arguing things would improve if ex-players qualified as match officials. Sadly, Crăciunescu remains a rare example of a former relatively high-level professional footballer taking up the referee's whistle.

Two weeks after the game at Old Trafford came the return fixture at Camp Nou. The three foreign players rule encouraged Ferguson to drop Danish goalkeeper Schmeichel and replace him with Englishman Gary Walsh. Commenting later in *The Guardian*, Walsh admitted that before the game Mick Hucknall, singer of pop group Simply Red, joined in a practice session with the Manchester United team and actually scored against

---

23 'Interviu Ion Crăciunescu, fost arbitru internaţional: 'M-am făcut arbitru ca să mă răzbun' adevarul.ro.

him[24]. It proved to be a bad omen. Using Simply Red song titles to summarise the match, Barça opened up the red box, leaving Walsh a broken man and Ferguson a sad old red. A 4-0 win, inspired by Romario and Stoichkov, secured qualification from the group at the English side's expense.

However, that victory proved to be the Dream Team's last hurrah. Weeks later, Romario left Barcelona in favour of life on the beach in Rio, then a Real Madrid side featuring Laudrup thrashed Barça 5-0 on the way to securing La Liga, before a George Weah-inspired Paris Saint-Germain knocked Barça out of the Champions League in the quarter-final.

At the end of the season Koeman and Stoichkov followed Romario out of the club. Cruyff then started to build a new side consisting of survivors from the Dream Team plus new additions such as Luís Figo, Gică Popescu and Iván de la Peña. Losing its La Liga title meant that Barça had to compete in the UEFA Cup the following season, a campaign which ended in defeat to eventual tournament winner Bayern Munich in the semi-final. After a second season ended without a major trophy Cruyff was sacked in May 1996.

As for Carles Busquets, although he gathered a large haul of medals in his eight years at Barcelona, most of them were as a reserve. During his two-year spell as Barça's number one the team failed to win any silverware. Whereas Zubi had been an excellent shot stopper but not

---

24 '2 November 1994: Manchester United are thrashed in Barcelona,' theguardian.com.

particularly comfortable playing the ball with his feet, Busquets proved to be the exact opposite.

Cruyff's replacement was the person who had coached the Football League XI against the Rest of the World XI at Wembley nine years before, former England coach Bobby Robson. Other new arrivals included two Portuguese players, goalkeeper Vítor Baía who Robson brought with him from his previous club Porto to push Busquets back on to the bench, plus Fernando Couto to strengthen the defence. These were joined by Spanish attacking midfielder Luis Enrique from rivals Real Madrid and Brazilian striker Ronaldo Luís Nazário de Lima from PSV Eindhoven.

In 1996/97 Barça participated in the European Cup Winners' Cup after being runner-up in the previous season's Copa del Rey, because the victors Atlético Madrid had also won La Liga and therefore qualified for the Champions League. Wins against AEK Larnaca, Red Star Belgrade, AIK of Sweden and Fiorentina meant that Barça would play the holder of the competition, Paris Saint-Germain, in the final at Rotterdam.

After obtaining a couple of face value tickets costing about £45 each, I flew on the morning of the game, Wednesday, 14 May 1997, to Amsterdam's Schipol airport. A short train journey took me to Leiden where I stayed with John, a former university friend of mine who was working there and had kindly offered to put me up for the night and agreed to accompany me to the game. After a couple of hours exploring the picturesque city of Leiden and its canals, it was time to take a train to Rotterdam, about half an hour further to the south.

With a population of 600,000 Rotterdam is Holland's second-largest city, but unlike Leiden isn't a pretty place. Its blandness inspired English pop group The Beautiful South to compose the song 'Rotterdam (Or Anywhere)' a year before my visit. The city has a huge international port, with docks on the banks of the Nieuwe Maas, one of the waterways which emerge from the massive River Rhine as it spreads out before flowing into the North Sea. It was Rotterdam's strategic location, as a major port and crossing point over the river that contributed to the present appearance of the city in a tragic way when it was heavily bombed during the Second World War, killing nearly 1,000 people. Unfortunately, the post-war reconstruction of Rotterdam wasn't done in a sensitive style, with large modern concrete buildings replacing older ones.

During the invasion in 1940, German paratroopers landed at several sites in Rotterdam with the aim of capturing intact the bridges over Nieuwe Maas so Hitler's army could cross it. One of these landing sites was near the Stadion Feyenoord, about 3km south of the city centre on the other side of the river. The site was selected by the Germans because it was a large area of flat land suitable for a parachute drop and near the all-important bridges.

Built three years earlier in 1937, the Stadion Feyenoord was designed by Johannes Brinkman and Leendert van der Vlugt, two local architects known for their design of industrial buildings in Rotterdam. Brinkman and van der

Vlugt were influenced by Constructivism, an architectural style which developed in the Soviet Union in the 1920s emphasising functionality. For the stadium, Brinkman and van der Vlugt's design involved a lot of steel, rather than concrete, bricks or stone which were more common at the time. The steel girders supporting the stadium were deliberately left uncovered to demonstrate their purpose, rather than hide them with cladding.

Three months after the Dutch surrender, some Wehrmacht soldiers entered the Stadion Feyenoord and posed in its seats for a group photo. The presence of so much steel was nearly a death sentence for the football ground when the Germans considered dismantling it for scrap metal, but in the end chose not to. The Germans' decision had important consequences for FC Barcelona, because the survival of the Stadion Feyenoord enabled it to be, as Simon Inglis says in his book *The Football Grounds of Europe*, 'The model for several of the major stadiums nearly two decades later, Nou Camp in Barcelona being a prime example.'[25]

When I went to the Stadion Feyenoord in 1997, I didn't notice any resemblance to Camp Nou, because concrete was preferred to steel at Barcelona and both stadiums have changed over the years. The Stadion Feyenoord originally had two tiers curving around the pitch, with a cantilevered roof (a cover supported only by a single structure along one side, rather than pillars underneath or walls at each end). Soon, an additional

---

25 Inglis, S., *The Football Grounds of Europe* (London: Collins Willow, 1990), p143.

small lower tier was added, which although supposedly temporary, eventually became a fixture. Then in 1994 the stadium was refurbished, and the roof was extended to go all the way round. When Camp Nou opened in 1957, it also had two tiers curving around the pitch and a cantilevered roof along one side. When the stadium was redeveloped for the 1982 World Cup an extra tier was added at the top, although the roof remained unaltered, just covering one side. In other words, although Stadion Feyenoord and Camp Nou look quite different today, the basic shape of their original designs was much closer, both being two-tiered with a cantilevered roof along one side.

After the Second World War, Rotterdam threw its energies into building up its port, which by 1962 had become the biggest in the world aided by its proximity to the heavily populated centres of the German Ruhr and other parts of western Europe. In the programme for the 1997 final, Rotterdam's mayor claimed that it was still the largest port in the world. Although Rotterdam remains the largest port in Europe today, it has slipped down the world rankings to about tenth, largely because of the massive growth of Asian economies in the subsequent quarter of a century.

Although officially known as Stadion Feyenoord, after the area where it is located and the club it hosts, the stadium is commonly known by its Dutch nickname 'De Kuip', meaning 'The Tub' because of its shape like a big bathtub. It is quite compact and the proximity of the crowd to the pitch, together with the roof, helps maintain a great atmosphere. The stadium held 50,000 people and, unlike Athens, was full, being closer to the homes of the finalists. It's a popular venue which has often been used for internationals and European finals. Our seats were in the middle of the three tiers, on the side opposite the dugouts, providing an excellent view.

PSG, the reigning holder of the trophy, benefitted from a weekend off before the final, whereas Barça had to play a demanding match against Real Madrid only four days earlier. In a departure from Cruyff, Barça lined up in Robson's preferred 4-2-3-1 formation, with Baía in goal; Ferrer, Couto, Abelardo and Sergi at the back; Guardiola and captain Popescu in deep midfield roles; Luis Enrique, de la Peña and Figo ahead of them; with Ronaldo as the striker. Regular defender Nadal was missing through suspension. At the time of the previous game at Old Trafford, teams were limited to fielding three foreign players, but in 1995 the Bosman ruling meant that according to European law free movement of labour applied to football, so the cap was abandoned. Robson's team that night in Rotterdam now had only six Spanish players, with the rest made up of three Portuguese, a Romanian and a Brazilian. Another change since Old Trafford was that the players' shirts now displayed their names on the back above the number.

PSG's normal colours were blue and red, so both teams had change kits. Barça wore a minty green kit, similar to the one at Old Trafford, while PSG looked like Ajax, all-white with a broad red stripe down the front. The French side's team was a 4-3-1-2 of Bernard Lama in goal; Laurent Fournier, Bruno N'Gotty, Paul

Le Guen and Didier Domi in defence; Jérôme Leroy, Vincent Guérin and Benoît Cauet in midfield; then Raí in the 'hole' behind Leonardo and Patrice Loko.

The first major chance came nine minutes after kick-off, when Barça attacked the goal to my right in a move involving de la Peña, Sergi, Figo and Ronaldo. During the game Figo and Luis Enrique switched wings a few times, but this time the Portuguese wideman was on the left and played a one-two with Ronaldo, beating several PSG defenders, before shooting wide of the far post. With 24 minutes gone PSG's Loko was unlucky to be flagged offside when through on goal after a great pass from Leonardo. Replays later showed that Sergi had played Loko onside. Another dubious decision followed a couple of minutes later when a Barça corner, taken by Guardiola, was headed by Couto into the net, only to be disallowed for an alleged push by Popescu on a defender. I couldn't see anything wrong with the goal at the time, and television replays later confirmed that impression.

The breakthrough came ten minutes before half-time. A PSG attack broke down as Sergi won possession. He played the ball to de la Peña and the bald-headed young player passed it to Luis Enrique, who forwarded it down the left to Ronaldo. The Brazilian striker went on one of his trademark runs with the ball before being brought down by N'Gotty in the penalty area. The referee immediately pointed to the spot. It was practically the only time Ronaldo eluded the French defender. Ronaldo got up to hit his penalty straight down the middle after Lama moved to his right. There were no other major incidents in the first half, so it remained 1-0 at the break.

Barça used the interval to make a substitution, taking off the injured Popescu and replacing him with Amor. PSG had chances to equalise in the second half, with the closest effort following a Leonardo pass to Loko whose shot from the right beat Baía, only to bounce back off the far post into the path of Leonardo, who wildly smashed the ball high over the bar. PSG made a couple of changes, Dely Valdés replacing Guerin and Cyrille Pouget coming on for Loko. With seven minutes left Barça took off de la Peña and brought on Stoichkov, then just before the end replaced Luis Enrique with another attacking player, Juan Antonio Pizzi. Stoichkov had left Barça for a year in Italy at Parma before returning, and Rotterdam was to be my last sighting of the Bulgarian. The French side's final opportunity fell to Leonardo, but his poor first touch meant the chance was wasted, so the game finished 1-0.

A temporary circular platform was hastily erected near the centre of the pitch for the presentation of the trophy. At 60cm tall, the Cup Winners' Cup is slightly shorter than the Champions League trophy, but the main difference concerns the handles which are much smaller, like comparing the ears of African and Asian elephants. At the time few people, including me, were aware of one particular dark-haired man in his mid-30s who joined in the celebrations. Only after this individual led Porto to Champions League glory in 2004 and subsequently joined Chelsea did he became a household name in England. José Mourinho was present in Rotterdam as

Robson's translator and assistant. In later years Mourinho went on to develop a bitter rivalry with Pep Guardiola, so it is now highly amusing to watch a YouTube film clip which shows him on the Rotterdam pitch in a man hug with that very same Barça player and a soundtrack of romantic music[26].

John and I left the stadium to catch our train back to Leiden, and the following day I flew back from Amsterdam to London. The trip had been an enjoyable one, helped by its low cost, with cheap flights, face value tickets and free accommodation. The compact layout of the stadium helped create a terrific atmosphere, for which both sets of fans deserve credit. However, the Barça performance wasn't altogether convincing. Although the players had entered the pitch to the sound of the *Star Wars* theme, the force had not all been with Robson's team, which had less possession of the ball than PSG. At the end of the season Barça failed to catch Real Madrid in the race for La Liga, and despite winning the Cup Winners' Cup, the Copa del Rey and the Spanish Super Cup in 1996/97 Robson was replaced as coach by Louis van Gaal. Robson was harshly dealt with, although it was ludicrous for him to claim in his autobiography that he had given Barça its 'second best season in a hundred years'[27]. The five cups won in 1952 and Cruyff's European Cup/La Liga double in 1992 easily eclipse his achievement.

Rotterdam was Barça's fourth success in the European Cup Winners' Cup, after previous triumphs in 1979,

---

26 youtube.com/watch?v=ghvq7VwD6e4.

27 Robson, B., *My Autobiography* (London: MacMillan, 1998), p173.

1982 and 1989. The Cup Winners' Cup lost out with the expansion of the Champions League from 1997/98, because those victorious in domestic cup finals usually finished towards the top of their respective leagues and now entered the more lucrative competition. For this reason the Cup Winners' Cup was discontinued in 1999, meaning that Barça's record of four triumphs in the competition would never be surpassed.

On the flight home I read the match programme. Whereas the 1992 Wembley programme had been old-fashioned, and the Athens one downright amateurish, the Rotterdam offering was my first encounter with the kind of quality glossy publication that would become standard in UEFA finals, printed on high-quality paper and lavishly illustrated. Unfortunately, the written contents left something to be desired, specifically a two-page article by the German Gerhard Aigner, UEFA's then general secretary[28]. Written to coincide with 1997 as the European Year Against Racism, the piece was titled 'No racism in the game'. However, after reading the article I felt it inclined towards there *is no* racism in the game, as well as *no to* racism in the game.

Aigner asked a series of rhetorical questions, the first of which was, 'Where, exactly, do we find racism in football?' In answer to his own query, he implied it was mainly at school and park-level games, a bizarre assessment after many years of black players being abused by fans at professional football matches. Answering his

---

28 Official programme, UEFA Cup Winners' Cup Final 1997.

next question, Aigner denied that racism existed between team-mates, before moving on to ask if racial abuse sometimes came from opposing players, where he then said, 'The fact is that all of us who have played football know that some people use "verbals" in an attempt to put opponents off their game.'

Aigner argued that it would be better if players indulging in 'verbals' left ethnicity out of it, which was a good point to make, but he then added, 'Is it also too much to ask players not to use claims of "racial abuse" as an automatic excuse for their own indiscretions?' Bizarrely, Aigner then asked, 'How can we talk about racism in a continent which elected George Weah as its Footballer of the Year?' This comment was especially strange when we consider that Weah, one of Africa's greatest players, had previously complained about racism in European football, including an allegation that an opponent racially abused him during a Champions League match between his club Milan and Porto only six months before Aigner's article.

Aigner then considered the behaviour of spectators. 'So do we leave the pitch and look for racism among the public in the stands? Even here, the immediate answer is negative.' Presumably, the death threat I received, because of being mixed-race, from a couple of Leeds United supporters before an away match at Fulham in 1985, never happened. UEFA's general secretary cited examples of black players who were popular with their club's fans, to try and suggest racism wasn't much of a problem and added that when it did appear it was only from opposing supporters because their side was losing a match. Sadly, I witnessed Barcelona supporters targeting Roberto Carlos in a *clásico* against Real Madrid in 1998. The racial abuse continued throughout the match, which Barça won 3-0, and was therefore never losing at any time.

To be fair to Aigner, his article should be understood as reflecting attitudes of the time. Several years earlier, in the late 1980s, I attended a meeting in London organised by the Football Supporters' Association which was addressed by a speaker involved in making BBC's *Match of the Day* programme. He explained that the volume of racial abuse of players by spectators was routinely turned down when highlights of matches were broadcast so it couldn't be heard. Wanting to avoid viewers being offended is understandable; however, it should be pointed out that very little was done in those days to deal with the underlying issue of racism. Years ago, the authorities were inclined to minimise the problem rather than deal with it. On the other hand, it could be argued that some of the anti-racist activities at football these days have gone to the other extreme and have provoked prejudice as a result. Rather than pass judgement or preach either way, I would rather just highlight Aigner's article as an example of how football has changed in the last four decades.

On a lighter note, in Rotterdam PSG's Lama became the second goalkeeper in this chapter to wear long pants rather than shorts, appearing in a black pair for the final against Barça. Inspired by Carles Busquets, who was an unused sub in the game, a few keepers chose tracksuit bottoms in the second half of the 1990s, and I attended a couple of matches during this period where keepers wore them. The first was Mark Bosnich when his Aston Villa beat my Leeds United in the 1996 League Cup Final at Wembley. Then three years later it was the turn of Gábor Király to wear the trousers, with his infamous grey baggy long pants bringing chav fashion to the Champions League for Hertha Berlin at Chelsea. Mercifully, the fad proved to be temporary, and tracksuit trousers failed to reappear in any of the matches featured later in this book. Although chapter 13 will report a goalkeeper wearing leggings under his shorts in the 2015 Champions League campaign, for me they were more tights than trousers.

Despite the undoubted significance of Busquets' sartorial contribution to the history of FC Barcelona, it is not his major legacy at the club. That is his son, who was five years old at the time of the match at Old Trafford in 1994. Named Sergio, he would later grow up to become one of the most successful players in the club's history, and he always played in shorts.

7

Núñez the Wiser?

THE SEASON after Rotterdam, UEFA introduced major changes to the Champions League. Previously, only winners of domestic leagues and the reigning European Cup holders could enter the competition, but from 1997/98 onwards the runners-up in the top European leagues qualified for the tournament too. This meant that Barça would nearly always feature in the Champions League after that time, only missing out in 2003/04 because of poor performance in the previous La Liga season.

The arrival of Louis van Gaal at Barça was accompanied by the departure of Ronaldo to Inter and his replacement with another Brazilian, Rivaldo, changes which I was able to see at my first Barça versus Real Madrid *clásico* in March 1998. The 3-0 victory in that match helped van Gaal's team win La Liga, but although the Spanish title was retained in 1998/99 the Champions League proved more elusive, with Barça eliminated at the group stage both times. The following season saw La Liga lost to Deportivo La Coruña, but more progress was made in the Champions League. This included two games in London, the first of which was on 19 October 1999 against Arsenal, after the two clubs had been drawn in a group with Fiorentina and AIK Solna. Arsenal opted to play its group matches at Wembley because the old Highbury ground had a reduced capacity following the Taylor Report. The game was the fourth of six games in the group. Three weeks earlier Arsenal had earned a draw at Camp Nou and the Gunners were optimistic about the 'home' game, creating huge interest in it. Such was the demand, I was unable to get a ticket from an official source, forcing me to try my luck with a tout. At the time I worked in the constituency office of a Member of Parliament, and because there were no political crises that day I was able to leave early in order to get to Wembley several hours before kick-off to maximise my chances of getting one of the few tickets available. Touts set their price according to supply and demand. My ticket cost £90, which was a considerable mark-up on face value. It was a lot of money 20 years ago and, at that time, the most I'd ever paid for a football game. The tout looked at me suspiciously, cautiously took the wad of cash, then said as he handed over the ticket, 'If you're a copper, and take the rest of my tickets, I'll smash your fucking face in.' Lovely people.

The financial hit, and the threat of a physical one, proved to be worth it, because the game turned out to be a thriller. Van Gaal's side, in an away kit of silver with blue and red trimmings, contained no fewer than five Dutch players: Winston Bogarde, Michael Reiziger,

Phillip Cocu and Patrick Kluivert joined by Boudewijn Zenden, who appeared as a substitute; there were only five Spanish players in the starting line-up. I discovered that my black market ticket was for a seat in the upper tier behind one of the goals. The old Wembley was only a year away from closure, prior to demolition and rebuilding. Stadiums require constant upkeep, and Wembley now looked sad and neglected, a shadow of its former self. The teams entered through the tunnel at the far end, which seven years earlier had been packed with Barça fans, but now was full of Arsenal supporters. The small contingent from Barcelona among the crowd of 73,000 was tucked into a corner. Van Gaal took his place on the bench, at the foot of the famous Wembley steps. Sitting next to him was Ronald Koeman, having returned as Barcelona's assistant coach, seven years after being a hero in the same stadium.

For this game I shall focus on a player of enormous significance in the history of FC Barcelona, Pep Guardiola. By then aged 28 and team captain, Guardiola was the 'pivot' at the base of midfield and made an immediate impact on the game, but not in the way he would have preferred. After less than ten seconds the ball was passed back to him from the kick-off. Guardiola had plenty of time to deal with the ball, but dwelt on it unnecessarily and was dispossessed by Nwankwo Kanu. Guardiola then fouled the Nigerian, but fortunately for Barcelona the resulting free kick was successfully blocked by a defender.

With quarter of an hour gone, Cocu collected the ball and played a one-two with a colleague, then reached the edge of the penalty area at my end. Tony Adams attempted a tackle and Cocu went down over the defender's outstretched leg. It was debatable whether it was in the area, and even more doubtful whether there was any contact. When the referee pointed to the spot Arsenal defenders Tony Adams and Lee Dixon stood over the grounded Cocu, accusing him of diving. Arsenal's goalkeeper, David Seaman, guessed correctly, going to his left, but such was the power and accuracy of Rivaldo's left-footed penalty kick that it didn't matter as the ball was blasted just inside the post. Barça then went two up straight from the kick-off after Luis Enrique ran half the length of the pitch with the ball. Adams, normally such an effective defender, slipped as he was about to put in a challenge, meaning that Enrique was free to hit a right-footed shot into the far corner of Seaman's goal.

Midway through the first half, Barça goalkeeper Francesc Arnau pulled off a brilliant double save. Firstly Kanu, who was giving Bogarde a tough time down the Arsenal right, beat the defender and on reaching the byline crossed the ball to Marc Overmars. The Dutch forward, and future Barça player, shot from a central position, but Arnau saved it, pushing the ball to his right. Adams pounced on the rebound but Arnau somehow managed to get off the ground and touch the ball over the bar. Arsenal besieged Barça's goal towards the end of the first half, but just when it looked like the visitors would get to the break without conceding, they did. Kanu again evaded Bogarde and crossed for Dennis Bergkamp who scored one of his trademark goals, deftly controlling the ball with his right foot then slotting it with his left past Arnaù from about ten yards.

Arsenal's best opportunity early in the second half highlighted Guardiola's limitations in defence. With the London club now attacking my end, Bergkamp sent Guardiola the wrong way on the age of the penalty area, but having created room for his shot on the Arsenal left, the Dutchman's effort was saved by Arnau. Guardiola's pivot role involved protecting the defence, making interceptions and tidying things up. However, he hadn't made much of a creative impact on the game, with most passes played short or sideways. That changed from early in the second half when Guardiola started to hit several more direct and forward balls. The first three of these failed to result in anything, but it was fourth time lucky on 56 minutes. Guardiola gained possession just outside his own penalty area and advanced with the ball on the right before hitting a long pass from inside his own half towards Kluivert on the left. Dixon inadvertently provided an assist by playing the ball back across goal to Figo, who side-footed it past Seaman. Adams, the player nearest to Figo, had left him unmarked at the critical moment.

The Arsenal team, like its fans, didn't give up and continued to create chances. The better side of Guardiola's defending was shown after Kanu once again beat Bogarde on the Arsenal right. The ball came to Overmars in a central position, but his shot was blocked by the Barça captain. Then in the 70th minute Guardiola once again gained possession inside his own half and played another long diagonal pass, this time to Cocu, who hit it first time with his left foot from the edge of the penalty area across Seaman and into the net to make it 4-1. This goal ended the game as a contest and the stadium finally went quiet, so much so that you could now hear the small band of visiting supporters singing 'Cant del Barça'. The last 20 minutes saw both sides make substitutions. The visitors brought on Gabri for Luis Enrigue, while Arsenal's changes included an appearance by future Barça player Thierry Henry, who replaced Kanu. With six minutes remaining Overmars scored a consolation goal for Arsenal.

In the last minute van Gaal opted to replace Cocu with Zenden and bring on Frenchman Frédéric Déhu for Guardiola. It was to be my final sight of Guardiola as a player, injuries keeping him out of my Barça games in the next couple of seasons. In hindsight, it was strange to see Guardiola, with his subsequent reputation for coaching tiki-taka short passing football, hitting such long balls, albeit highly accurate ones. Although Guardiola had been fairly anonymous in the first half, he had considerable influence in securing victory in the second.

The game provided Barça with its first competitive win over an English side on English soil since defeating Wolves 5-2 at Molineux back in 1960. *The Guardian* headlined its report 'Arsenal blown away by Barça'; however, watching in the stadium at the time I thought it was closer than that[29]. The first crucial goal had come from a dodgy penalty, while Arsenal won 13 corners to Barça's one.

---

29 *The Guardian*, 20 October 1999.

The Arsenal game took place just a few weeks before the centenary of Barça's formation on 29 November 1999. I had wanted to make another trip to Camp Nou to celebrate the occasion, but when that proved not to be possible, this game became a more than acceptable substitute. The victory helped Barça top the group, while Arsenal finished third behind runner-up Fiorentina and therefore exited the competition. Barça then entered a second group stage which started at the end of November. Once again, Barça ended top, ahead of Porto, Sparta Prague and Hertha Berlin, meaning I was able to catch up with the club when it was drawn against Chelsea in the quarter-final.

On the night of the first leg on Wednesday, 5 April 2000, I took my place at the top of the three-tiered East Stand at Stamford Bridge. The new West Stand that faced me was still incomplete, with its top tier yet to be built, consequently the attendance was only 33,662. It was Chelsea's debut season in the Champions League yet surprisingly easy to get tickets, although the fixture would get bigger in the future when a rivalry developed between the two clubs.

Van Gaal lost a Dutchman on the bench after Koeman left to become coach at Vitesse Arnhem in January, but increased the number of his compatriots on the pitch from four against Arsenal to five against Chelsea (Ruud Hesp and Frank de Boer being the additions while Reiziger was omitted). However, van Gaal's starting 11 at Chelsea contained more Catalans than Cruyff's 1992 team at Wembley, including my first viewing of two who would provide enormous service to the club (defender and future captain Carles Puyol, approaching his 22nd birthday, and midfielder Xavi Hernández, then only 20). Despite that, it still felt strange to see so many Dutch players and it was no longer clear, post-Bosman, that this was a Barcelona team, whether Spanish or Catalan. It looked more like a Dutch Eredivisie side.

Wearing all blue, Chelsea's line-up had several connections to Barça's last couple of European Cup finals. The team was coached by Gianluca Vialli, who had played for Sampdoria at Wembley. At full-back was former Barça star Albert Ferrer, who had played in both the 1992 and 1994 finals, while alongside him was Marcel Desailly, who having been so devastating in Athens left Milan to join Chelsea following his success with France in the 1998 World Cup.

Barça's players wore the same silver shirts as they had against Arsenal. However, this time it was the home team who raced into an early lead, going three up after 37 minutes with a free kick from Gianfranco Zola, followed by a couple from Tore André Flo, a close-range finish after a cross from Zola on the right and a chip over the keeper following a lob from Didier Deschamps. All three goals, scored at the Shed End to my left, came as a shock because Barça had been in an impressive run of form before the game. At the start of the second half it looked like Chelsea was trying to shore up the lead, but just after the hour Barça grabbed an away goal. Cocu, in a central position, played the ball forward to Rivaldo on the left whose cross was converted from close range by

Figo. There were no more goals, so it ended 3-1 to the home side.

Figo's strike proved to be vital because in the second leg it was 3-1 to Barça at the end of 90 minutes, meaning that the tie went to extra time. Barça scored two more goals to win 5-1 and go through 6-4 on aggregate. However, Barcelona was then knocked out by Valencia in the semi-final, a defeat made worse by Real Madrid's progress to the final.

Barcelona has only played its great rival Real Madrid eight times in the European Cup/Champions League, all of them parts of two-legged ties: the 1959/60 semi-final, a second round in 1960/61, and semi-finals in 2001/02 and 2010/11. I would have loved to see a *clásico* Champions League Final, and had already planned a trip to Paris in the hope of watching one. However, all the Barça supporters I have spoken to don't want it to ever happen, believing that the potential prize of beating their rivals is far outweighed by a fear of losing to them. Some express more confidence about winning over two legs in, say, a quarter-final or semi-final, but worry about being unlucky or making mistakes and not having time to rectify things in a 90-minute final. When asked if he would like to see a Barcelona versus Real Madrid final, Geoff, a member of Penya Blaugrana London, said, 'No, because I don't want the chance for them to beat us. Even if there's a 99 per cent chance that we will win, still no.' Cesar, another member of the *penya*, added, 'I don't think we would ever get impartial refereeing in the case of a tight match.'

The importance of the Champions League to Barcelona was shown when Josep Lluís Núñez resigned as president a few days after the Valencia defeat. Two years earlier, while in Barcelona for my first Barça versus Real Madrid *clásico,* it had been impossible to miss posters plastered all over the city advertising a campaign promoting a no-confidence motion in Núñez brought by an opposition group called Elefant Blau ('Blue Elephant'). On arriving at Camp Nou I discovered that my match ticket was not for a seat, as had been ordered, but for the terraces. Rumours alleged that the vote of no confidence had caused this, with good tickets becoming scarce as a way of buying support. During the match against Real Madrid the president sat in the directors' box watching the game. Just before half-time Núñez was handed a slip of paper containing the result of the vote showing that he had survived, receiving 24,863 votes to the opposition's 14,358. Although the campaigners of Elefant Blau hadn't managed to oust Núñez in 1998, he felt unable to survive failure in a Champions League semi-final a couple of years later. Núñez was followed by Louis van Gaal who resigned in sympathy, both tired of being constantly criticised by the media.

In 1978 Núñez had become the first elected president of FC Barcelona after the Franco era. His rule was to last for 22 years, the longest in the club's history. Born a Basque, Núñez arrived in Catalonia at a young age, becoming boss of Núñez y Navarro, the biggest construction company in Barcelona. Despite having no significant links to the city's football club, Núñez decided to get involved and eventually became president. Before Núñez, the club had usually been run by businessmen with backgrounds in the textile trade.

Núñez was determined to sort out the club's finances and stop excessive expenditure on transfer fees and players' wages (although he did sign the world's costliest footballer, Diego Maradona). Consequently, Núñez had disputes with several star players, usually over money, contracts and tax. These included a row with Cruyff on his departure from the club in 1978, followed by quarrels with Neeskens, Maradona, Schuster, practically the entire squad in 1988, and then Rivaldo towards the end of his reign. Núñez also came into conflict with some of his coaches, particularly Cruyff, although some, such as Terry Venables and van Gaal, worked well with him.

Núñez's relationship with Barça's fans was mixed. On the one hand, he subsidised fans travelling to the 1979 Cup Winners' Cup Final in Switzerland and was a strong supporter of the supporters' clubs. During his presidency the number of *penyes* increased by over ten times, and the number of *socis* (club members) also rose significantly. Less positively, he indulged the ultras/hooligans of the Boixos Nois. Despite Núñez encountering opposition on several occasions, he survived all challenges and kept the support of most fans.

Núñez oversaw the expansion of the capacity of Camp Nou from 92,000 to 120,000 in time to host matches for the 1982 World Cup, some of the money being raised by increasing *soci* membership fees. In 1979 La Masia was established as the home of Barça's youth academy (following Cruyff's recommendation) and three years later the Mini Estadi was built to house the B team's fixtures. In 1984 Núñez presided over the opening of the club's museum, followed by a megastore in the 1990s. As well as these infrastructural achievements, Núñez's presidency saw the club achieve success on the pitch and financial health off it.

At the press conference to announce his resignation, Núñez surrounded himself with the large haul of trophies won by Barça during his reign, including the club's first European Cup, all four of its Cup Winners' Cups, two European Super Cups, seven La Ligas and six Copa del Reys. Núñez had become a victim of his own success, resigning after failure in a European Cup/Champions League semi-final. Before his presidency the club had only reached three semi-finals in the tournament, triumphing just once, whereas under him the club reached four semi-finals, winning three. Núñez also left the club with a financial surplus of €1.2bn, whereas it had usually been plagued by debt before his reign. After resigning as president Núñez had problems with the law over his business activities, but two decades after the end of his spell in office and a few years since his death in 2018 it is worth reconsidering his term of office in the light of recent regimes at FC Barcelona which have burdened it with massive debts.

One of those who overspent was Núñez's replacement, Joan Gaspart, his former deputy. Widely regarded as the best vice-president in Barça's history, Gaspart's three-year reign ended in resignation and his own admission that he had been the club's worst-ever president.

After quitting in the summer of 2000, van Gaal was replaced by Lorenzo Serra Ferrer, Barça's former technical director. Serra Ferrer was one of those rarities, a coach of a top club who had never played the game professionally. Also departing was Luís Figo, who stunned the football world by leaving Camp Nou, where he was not only captain but a crowd favourite, to join Real Madrid.

In the following season's Champions League Barcelona was drawn in the same group as none other than my club, Leeds United, together with Milan and Turkish side Beşiktaş. In the opening fixture at Camp Nou Barça crushed Leeds 4-0. The Yorkshire club's assistant manager, Eddie Gray, later commented in his autobiography that Leeds gave Rivaldo far too much space and could have lost even more heavily[30]. However, results in the next three rounds of games meant if Leeds beat Barça in the fifth match at Elland Road on Tuesday, 24 October 2000, the English team would qualify for the next stage. Barcelona needed at least a draw to maintain any hope of progressing, and would have to achieve it without three of their stars, Kluivert, Overmars and Guardiola.

Barça's line-up of 3-1-3-3 included yet another change of goalkeeper, this time Frenchman Richard Dutruel, and also provided my first sightings of Portuguese international midfielder Simão and Spanish striker

---

30 Gray, E., *Marching on Together: My Life with Leeds United* (London: Hodder & Stoughton, 2001), p220.

Alfonso Pérez. Then aged 28, Alfonso is one of the few footballers to have a stadium named after him while still playing. The ground concerned was the Estadio Coliseum Alfonso Pérez, home of Getafe, a club located in a suburb to the south of Madrid. The naming is even more unusual because Alfonso, although born in Getafe, never played for the club. The stadium decided to honour him in recognition of his performances for the Spanish national side.

The mini season ticket I had purchased for the three Leeds Champions League home games was for a seat in the East Stand, along one of the sides and so high up the players looked like ants. Barça appeared in a rather dull version of its classic kit, broad blue and red striped shirts, with black shorts and socks, while Leeds wore a Real Madrid-inspired all-white. Lee Bowyer appeared on the cover of the match programme, which proved prophetic when he scored after only five minutes. Following an Abelardo foul on Mark Viduka, Bowyer lobbed the resulting free kick from a tight angle on the Leeds left over Dutruel, who was badly positioned and caught way off his line. Far more impressive was his opposite number, Paul Robinson. Then just turned 21 years old, Robinson produced the finest goalkeeping display I've ever seen in what was, incredibly, only his tenth first team appearance. Most of Robinson's saves were from attempts by Rivaldo, but arguably his finest came after an hour. It followed a Luis Enrique cross from the right which was met by a firm header from the centrally positioned Alfonso, only for the Leeds keeper to push it over the crossbar.

With a quarter of an hour remaining the home side was perhaps lucky when second-half substitute Dani was clean through with only the keeper to beat, but the linesman flagged for offside. Being at the side of the pitch I had a good view of the incident, and when the flag went up Dani was miles offside. At the time I thought nothing more of it, and although Dani looked across to the linesman there was no further complaint. However, a film of the game shows that when the ball was played to Dani at the started of his run the former Real Mallorca striker was definitely onside. The officials that night were Norwegian, and the referee was Terje Hauge; more about him in six years' time.

For most of the match Leeds defended desperately, looking to clinch a place in the next round against a Barça side facing elimination. At 90 minutes it was still 1-0 and the officials added four minutes of stoppage time. The tension mounted, with most of the capacity crowd of 36,729 anxiously keeping one eye on the pitch and the other on their watches to the soundtrack of thousands of whistles. In what surely had to be the final attack, Cocu lobbed the ball into the box and Alfonso's header beat Robinson only to hit the upright. For a split second Barça's last chance seemed to have gone, but the rebound came straight to Rivaldo who finally beat Robinson, slotting the ball home with his left foot from near the penalty spot.

Elland Road erupted into boos and chants of 'cheat, cheat' directed at the officials. The match ended just over a minute later with a lot of pushing and shoving on the pitch between the teams. There was controversy about the goal, with claims that it occurred after the four minutes of added time. For example, the following day's *Daily Telegraph* reported 'the goal was timed by UEFA at four minutes 37 seconds'[31]. However, when I later watched a recording of the game I saw that the goal came after 93 minutes and 15 seconds. The referee blew his whistle to end the game after 94 minutes and 30 seconds, but the goal itself was well within the four minutes of added time.

The last-gasp equaliser kept Barça in the tournament, assuming the Catalan side beat Beşiktaş in the last fixture and Leeds lost in Milan. Two weeks later I was at the San Siro to see Leeds draw 1-1. This was the game where urine was thrown at me by Italian fans. I got off lightly; two other travelling supporters were stabbed in the city. The draw secured Leeds a place in the next stage even though Barça beat Beşiktaş. Despite a win and a draw for Barça in the two matches against Leeds, it was the English side that went through in second place after better results against the other teams. To this day, Leeds United remains the only club in European football history to meet Barcelona in more than one European Cup/Champions League campaign and knock Barça out every time (the other occasion being the 1975 European Cup semi-final).

When Leeds battled it out against Barcelona you might be wondering how I felt about it, did I have divided loyalties? The answer is no, Leeds United is the team I support and hoped would progress at Barcelona's

---

31 *Daily Telegraph*, 25 October 2000.

expense. When I go to see Leeds I want the team to win, if necessary by grinding out results, but frequently have to endure various degrees of anti-social behaviour from some of the club's supporters. However, I go to Barcelona matches to watch the team play and appreciate its style of football, while better conduct from the fans makes it easier to enjoy the whole occasion. Some people have 'first' and 'second' teams. I would prefer to say that Leeds United is the club I support, while having more fun following the fortunes of Barcelona as well as watching European football generally and lower league games in England.

Having finished third in the Champions League group, Barça was demoted to the UEFA Cup and eventually lost to Liverpool in the semi-final. Barça's La Liga results weren't much better, and towards the end of the season Carles Rexach took over as coach.

In the 2001/02 Champions League Barça had to negotiate two group stages, topping the first containing Bayer Leverkusen, Lyon and Fenerbahçe, and the second ahead of Liverpool, Roma and Galatasaray. A quarter-final victory over Panathinaikos was followed by defeat to rivals Real Madrid in the semi-final stage, which was doubly disappointing because the final was in Glasgow, about five hours away from London by train.

The following year, 2002/03, Barça started its European campaign with Louis van Gaal back in charge. After beating Legia Warsaw in a qualifying round (a game described in chapter 17) Barça faced two group stages, topping both. The first contained Lokomotiv Moscow, Club Brugge and Galatasaray, while the second comprised

Inter Milan, Newcastle United and Bayer Leverksen. Although successful that season in Europe, poor results in La Liga prompted van Gaal's departure for a second time. Former Luton Town player Radomir Antić took the side to the quarter-finals, where it was eliminated by Juventus. Barça then missed out on Champions League football altogether in 2003/04 because of a poor La Liga position. This meant participation in the UEFA Cup which lasted until a fourth-round defeat to Celtic.

Since Cruyff's sacking, Barça had got through six changes of coach in seven years: Bobby Robson 1996/97; Louis van Gaal 1997–2000; Lorenzo Serra Ferrer 2000/01; Carles Rexach 2001/02; Louis van Gaal 2002/03; and Raddy Antić 2003. By this stage the club wasn't even competing in the Champions League, let alone winning it. In the decade following Barça's 1992 Wembley triumph, Real Madrid had gone on to win the trophy three more times in 1998, 2000 and 2002, making nine in total since the competition began. During the same ten years between the 1992/93 and 2001/02 seasons, Barça had surpassed Real Madrid's performance in La Liga, by four titles to three, but increasingly it was European competition, not domestic, that provided the benchmark for success.

8

Doing it up Brown

IN AN attempt to halt three years of drift at the club, Barça members elected lawyer and one-time Elefant Blau activist Joan Laporta as president in 2003. Soon after taking office, Laporta appointed former Ajax, Milan and Holland star Frank Rijkaard as coach, Txiki Beguiristain as director of football, and Brazilian forward Ronaldinho was signed from PSG. The election of Laporta also saw greater influence from Cruyff as an unofficial advisor on footballing matters.

The club returned to the Champions League in 2004/05 and after negotiating a group including Milan, Shakhtar Donetsk and Celtic, drew José Mourinho's Chelsea in the round of 16. Barça won 2-1 in the first leg at Camp Nou, a game shrouded in controversy after Mourinho alleged that Rijkaard had spoken to the referee, Anders Frisk, at half-time with the implication that he attempted to influence the officiating of the game. Frisk subsequently received death threats after sending off Chelsea striker Didier Drogba and retired from refereeing. I managed to get a ticket for the return at Stamford Bridge on Tuesday, 8 March 2005, but this time sat high up in the West Stand, on the other side of the stadium to where I had been five years earlier. The West Upper was now complete, resulting in a higher attendance of 41,515.

When the teams appeared through the tunnel facing me, the most immediately noticeable thing was the Barça kit. Research to discover an exact description of the colour produced possibilities such as 'hessian', 'dubloon' and 'October harvest', but in the end I decided to settle on light brown. The kit provoked a mixed response from people. At first I hated the colour, but later changed my mind, probably because of what one player did while wearing it. The Barça team lined up in a 4-3-3, providing my first sighting of some players who were to play huge parts in the club's future success, including goalkeeper Victor Valdés, a 20-year-old Andrés Iniesta, Cameroonian striker Samuel Eto'o, plus two Brazilians, Juliano Belletti and Ronaldinho.

In an uncanny repeat of this fixture in 2000, Chelsea went 3-0 up early in the game. Goal number one came after only eight minutes when Frank Lampard dispossessed Xavi to launch an attack down the right led by Mateja Kežman. The Serb striker crossed the ball to Eidur Gudjohnsen, who took one touch bringing it under control before shooting past Valdés with his second. The next goal followed on 17 minutes, with another attack down the Chelsea right. This time Paulo Ferreira passed to Joe Cole whose shot deflected off a defender, and although Valdés managed to save it Lampard converted the rebound. The third goal came only a couple of minutes later. Cole, in the centre circle, hit a long pass forward to Damien Duff, and the Irish winger needed only one touch to slide a left-footed shot under Valdés.

Barça looked beaten, but just before the half-hour was awarded a penalty by referee Pierluigi Collina when Ferreira handled the ball under pressure from Eto'o. Although Petr Čech dived the correct way, Ronaldinho's firm, low shot beat him. Eleven minutes later Barça was awarded a throw-in midway inside the Chelsea half; Oleguer gained possession and lobbed the ball towards the Chelsea goal. John Terry headed the ball away, only for it to reach Iniesta, who immediately passed to Ronaldinho. Surrounded by several defenders, the Brazilian striker stood still with the ball at his feet, then wiggled his body from side to side like he was performing some dance moves, before suddenly, without any backlift, he shot with his right foot. Čech was clearly expecting Ronaldinho to either take an extra touch or pass the ball, so was totally fooled and left stranded as the effort flew to his right into the corner of the goal.

At half-time it was 3-2 to Chelsea, but 4-4 on aggregate with Barça going through on away goals. For much of the second half Barça dominated possession and nearly scored again from a Puyol header, followed by an Iniesta shot which hit the post before Eto'o blasted the rebound over the bar from close range. The miss was made to look costly when Chelsea scored soon after, Terry heading a corner from distance into the goal. The Barça players protested that Carvalho had impeded Valdés, but referee Collina controversially allowed the goal.

The game ended quarter of an hour later with no further goals, 5-4 to Chelsea on aggregate, meaning Barça was once again dumped out of Europe's premier competition. Apart from Liverpool's exhilarating comeback in the final in Istanbul, the Chelsea away game was widely considered to be the best in that season's Champions League. Barça had been unlucky because Chelsea's fourth goal should have been disallowed.

Born in 1980, Ronaldinho had started his career at Grêmio in his native Brazil before moving to Europe and joining Paris Saint-Germain in 2001. The following year he starred for Brazil, winning the World Cup, and then in 2003 arrived at Camp Nou, aged 23. At the end of 2005 Ronaldinho won both the FIFA World Player of the Year award and the Ballon d'Or, confirming that he was at that time the greatest player on the planet. Unfortunately, Ronaldinho's form tailed off towards the end of his five years at Camp Nou, as late-night partying took its toll. Of his four matches that feature in this book, he only performed to a high level in one, and even then there were none of his famous stepovers, flicks or no-look assists. However, the only demonstration of his outrageous skills that I witnessed makes up for all of that. I have watched replays of Ronaldinho's second goal against Chelsea many times on film and still can't decide whether it was a flick off the top or outside of his boot, as some commentators claim, or a toe-poke as others reported. In American slang the phrase 'doing it up brown' has two possible meanings, depending on the context. It can either mean doing something well, or an act of deception. Dressed in the all-brown kit that night, Ronaldinho managed both. It was the best Barcelona goal I have ever seen live.

Totally unnoticed to me at the time was the name on the back of the match programme of someone who would later score many goals rivalling Ronaldinho's. Among the squad members was listed Barcelona's number 30. Largely unknown in England, the player wasn't mentioned elsewhere in the programme and didn't even make the bench as an unused substitute. His name? Lionel Messi.

At the end of the season Barça won La Liga and re-entered the Champions League, and on Wednesday, 22 February 2006 had the opportunity to demonstrate its improvement in European competition and take revenge on Chelsea, with a repeat visit to Stamford Bridge. The fixture was the first leg in the round of 16, after Barça had topped a group containing Panathinaikos, Werder Bremen and Udinese. For Barça's third visit to Stamford Bridge in six years, I was back to the same place as for the last encounter, namely the West Upper. The first thing I noticed on entering the stadium was the state of the pitch, which was very muddy and cut up. It looked like a surface from the 1970s, perhaps deliberately prepared in this way to undermine Barça's slick passing style.

Wearing an away strip of luminous yellow shirts and socks with dark blue shorts, Barça's starting 11 had four changes to the one that appeared in the same venue a year before. Mexican defender Rafael Márquez, Edmílson and Thiago Motta were in midfield, and most significant was the wearer of that number 30 shirt, Lionel Messi. At the time of the game, Messi was 18 years old. Since then it has become a well-known story that he received treatment for a growth hormone deficiency in his native Argentina, then moved to FC Barcelona in 2000 at the age of 13, before making his first team debut three years later and becoming a regular starter in 2005/06.

Although Messi may have been a newcomer, Asier del Horno became acquainted with him extremely quickly. It was clear from the early exchanges that the Chelsea left-back couldn't cope with his pace. After 36 minutes Arjen Robben tried to stop Messi, who managed to evade him, but then del Horno lunged at the teenager, knocking him flying. Del Horno was shown a red card by referee Hauge, the man who officiated at the Leeds versus Barça game in 2000. The incident took place by the junction of the East Stand and the Matthew Harding Stand, in other words the opposite side of the stadium from my position, so it was difficult to judge it clearly. Over the years I've watched film clips of the incident a few times, without reaching a firm conclusion. Although del Horno looks to be out of control and would be sent off today, in 2006 the rules were slightly different. What people sometimes forget is that this was one of a series of fouls on Messi by del Horno, the worst of which had been a terrible challenge where del Horno raised his left foot high up and stuck his studs on to Messi's left knee. That foul alone should have earned del Horno a sending-off. Mourinho claimed Messi behaved theatrically, an accusation that would lead to Barcelona fans chanting

'Mourinho, go to the theatre' whenever he returned to Camp Nou.

Chelsea took the lead on the hour after Lampard launched the ball into the box and Motta, under pressure from Terry, put it into his own net. Just over ten minutes later came another own goal, this time at the other end when a Ronaldinho free kick glanced off Terry for the equaliser. Barça almost went ahead soon after the restart when Messi, who had been booed by the home crowd with every touch despite being repeatedly fouled, chipped the ball from the edge of the area on to the junction of bar and post. Ten-man Chelsea struggled to hold on, but with ten minutes left a cross from Márquez reached Eto'o, who headed in at the far post to snatch a 2-1 victory.

The controversy about the sending-off added to the bad blood between Chelsea and Barcelona which lingered from the previous year's encounter. The second leg at Camp Nou ended 1-1, so Barça progressed 3-2 on aggregate. A scoreless draw away to Benfica in the first leg of the quarter-final was followed by a 2-0 triumph at home. That set up a semi-final against Milan, where Barça won the first leg at the San Siro 1-0 followed by a goalless draw at Camp Nou to avenge Athens.

Paris was the venue of the final, only a short flight or Eurostar train journey away, on Wednesday, 17 May 2006. There was only one problem: the opponents would be a London team. In the first leg of the semi-final Arsenal had beaten Villarreal 1-0 at Highbury. In the final minute of the second leg Villarreal was awarded a penalty. However, former Barça player Juan Román Riquelme's spot kick was saved by Arsenal keeper Jens Lehmann. Arsenal having more supporters than Villarreal made match tickets considerably more expensive, while the fact that most would be travelling to Paris from London pushed up train and flight prices considerably.

There are four things needed to go to a European final abroad: time off from work; accommodation; travel; match ticket. The first of these was straightforward because I had changed jobs and having left politics in disgust now worked providing street security and information in central London. As long as you gave enough notice it wasn't difficult getting time off, so I had booked a couple of days' annual leave several months earlier in case it was possible to attend the final. The second was also easy, requiring just a phone call to a friend of mine called Faisal to arrange a stay at his house in Paris. However, the other two requirements turned out to be trickier. Arsenal's semi-final was the day before Barcelona's. I could have bought the Eurostar ticket earlier, and just hoped that Barça made it to Paris, but decided instead to wait until a place in the final was confirmed. This meant that the train tickets rapidly became more expensive and difficult to obtain because the Arsenal fans had an extra day to purchase them. I did manage to get a seat on an early afternoon Eurostar on the day of the final, but it had risen in price by about £200 while I procrastinated.

The match ticket situation was dire. I was reluctant to try and haggle with touts in Paris and hand over lots of cash for what might be a forgery, so opted to use a London ticket agency instead. In those days I lived in north London, not far from Arsenal's stadium, and had used one particular agency to get tickets for some of Arsenal's home games. I trusted the agency, so was prepared to use it to get a ticket for the final. Unfortunately, there were a lot of Arsenal fans who wanted tickets too, which inflated the price. In the end, I paid about £900 for the ticket, probably twice as much as if Villarreal had been in the final. I ordered the ticket over the phone, and when it arrived in the post a week before the final saw that the face value price was €60 (about £45 by the current rate of exchange). All in all, Lehmann cost me about £650 with his penalty save.

I don't like travelling to big games on the day of the match in case there are transport problems, but luckily there weren't on this occasion and the Eurostar train arrived at Gare du Nord on time. The Métro took me to Faisal's house where he explained his decision not to go to the game, preferring to stay at home and watch it on television. Faisal promised to make a traditional Tunisian dish of slow-roasted lamb and couscous to cook in the oven while he watched TV and have ready for us to eat on my return from the game. For the moment, we just had some bread and cheese, and although Faisal had a glass of wine I didn't, wanting to keep my head clear for the final. Kick-off was at 8.45pm and Faisal's home was only about three-quarters of an hour's walk from the stadium, so I decided to leave at six o'clock, giving me plenty of time. At just before six his phone went. It was a friend of his calling to say he had a spare ticket for the match, available at face value. Typical, I could have saved myself over £800, oh well!

On my arrival at the Stade de France it was already crowded. I instinctively followed the Arsenal supporters, but on approaching the turnstiles saw that they were entering the north end of the stadium. My ticket clearly said 'sud' (south) and gate Z, not the letters displayed in front of me. Feeling confused, I walked around to the south end and saw my entrance. All the fans were wearing Barça colours. The agency, even though it was based in north London and had previously supplied only Arsenal tickets and should have assumed I was a supporter of that club, had sold me a ticket in the Barcelona end. You might think I would be pleased. Well, no, at least not initially. I wasn't wearing colours and in those days didn't know any Barça fans. The turnstile staff were also asking people to show proof of ID, principally passports. My passport was a British one. The security would assume I was an Arsenal fan and not let me in. There were no Barça fans who could vouch for me. What could I do?

First, I went to a nearby merchandise stall and bought a cap and scarf in Barça colours. Secondly, I decided to delay my entry. As previously explained, I hate arriving late when it's crowded, but decided on this occasion to wait until 15 minutes before kick-off, anticipating that there would be a big queue of people going through the ticket and ID inspection, and hope that the security would abandon their checking and just let people in. At just before half past eight, that was precisely what happened. You still had to show your match ticket but they abandoned the ID check. So in I went.

My seat in block Z11 row 58 was not only in the Barça end but directly behind the goal at the very back of the lower tier and on an aisle. This prevented the need to squeeze past people, which was helpful because I don't speak Catalan or Spanish and it would be just my luck if some ultra-type heard me speaking English and concluded I was a Gooner. Inside the stadium it was humid and much warmer than in London, meaning my clothes, particularly a leather jacket which I stupidly brought, were unsuitable for the conditions.

The Stade de France is a fantastic ground, built for the 1998 World Cup finals with the secondary aim of regenerating the surrounding area of Saint-Denis, a depressed suburb in the north of Paris. However, the area would sadly remain a poor one, with high rates of poverty and unemployment. The stadium consisted of three tiers, covered by a space age-looking roof. It was lucky that my seat was at the back because in the second half it rained heavily and the pitch and lower rows got soaked. I found my seat just in time to see the conclusion of the opening ceremony, performed in front of a capacity crowd of 85,000.

The two teams came out on to the pitch from the entrance by the halfway line to my left. Many of the Barça fans surrounding me were wearing the luminous yellow shirts that the team had worn at Stamford Bridge, in anticipation of Barça being ordered to use its away kit. As it happened, the players wore their usual blue and red kit, but this time with red shorts and blue socks, and it was Arsenal who wore a change kit of yellow shirts and dark blue shorts and socks. It was strange that both teams were allowed to wear blue socks, because if a player was looking down it might have been difficult to distinguish between the teams.

The Arsenal end consisted of fans wearing yellow or white tops, to create huge bands alternating in those colours. From where I was sitting, at the opposite end, it looked rather boring, not at all imaginative. By contrast, in my end the Barça fans held up blue, red and yellow cards, just as they had done at Wembley and Athens. It was only when watching a film of the game later at home that I was able to see they spelt out 'BARCA' in big capital letters. Every seat also had a yellow covering advertising Mastercard saying, 'My seat from the UEFA Champions League final, Stade de France, 17 May 2006.' The covering was removable and so provided a nice souvenir, which I still have today. It was the only purpose served by the seats, because everyone in my part of the stadium stood up throughout the match.

The Barça team lined up in a 4-3-3, consisting of Valdés in goal; Oleguer Presas, Márquez, Giovanni van Bronckhorst and captain Puyol at the back; Mark van Bommel, José Edmílson and Deco in midfield; with Ronaldinho, Eto'o and Ludovic Giuly up front. Messi was absent through injury, while Xavi, who had also been injured, was only fit enough for the bench. Arsenal's formation, at least to start with, was 4-5-1, made up of: Lehmann; Emmanuel Eboué, Kolo Touré, Sol Campbell and Ashley Cole in defence; Alexander Hleb, Cesc Fàbregas, Gilberto Silva, Robert Pires and

Freddie Ljungberg in midfield; with their captain Henry up front.

Both teams were in excellent form in that season's Champions League. Barça was the competition's top scorer, while Arsenal had only conceded two goals all campaign, so the game was set up perfectly. What could go wrong? Unfortunately, the referee chosen for the final was Terje Hauge, the man who officiated in the Leeds versus Barça fixture at Elland Road in 2000 and was also involved in the Messi–del Horno controversy at Stamford Bridge in the first knockout round a few months before. Before the match one of the designated linesmen, another Norwegian, had to be replaced after being photographed in a Barcelona shirt, which was not a good omen.

The game began with Arsenal attacking my end. The London side started the stronger and within three minutes Henry had two attempts on goal, both producing great saves by Valdés. With 18 minutes gone my end erupted when everyone thought Giuly had scored, but the goal was disallowed. The incident took place at the other end of the pitch, so there was considerable confusion about what happened and it was one of those situations where the armchair viewer is better off than fans in the stadium. It transpired that immediately before Giuly put the ball in the net, Eto'o had been fouled just outside the penalty box by Arsenal's keeper. The referee immediately blew for a foul just before Giuly kicked the ball into the goal. Lehmann was then sent off, so becoming the first player to be dismissed in a European Cup Final. Hauge should have waited a moment to see if he could play an advantage, which would have given Barça a goal and allowed Lehmann to stay on the pitch, but once the referee blew his whistle it was too late.

Arsène Wenger immediately brought on substitute goalkeeper Manuel Almunia, while Pires was the unlucky player to be sacrificed to make way for him. Both sides felt aggrieved – Arsenal because of having to play over an hour with ten men, losing an attacking outlet in Pires and changing formation to a 4-4-1, while Barça was frustrated because the goal was disallowed. Barça's sense of injustice was increased when the resulting free kick came to nothing.

After about 35 minutes the controversy switched to my end. Hauge awarded Arsenal a free kick after a blatant dive from Eboué. Henry took the free kick, crossing to Campbell who headed powerfully into the net. My end, which had been a sea of twirling scarves before, suddenly went quiet and it was the other end making all the noise. After recovering from the shock of conceding, Barça laid siege to the Arsenal goal for the remainder of the half. First, a Ronaldinho pass found Eto'o who shot against the post, then the Cameroonian had another effort turned on to the woodwork by Almunia.

At half-time I spoke to a Barça fan standing next to me, who was dressed in a 1980s replica shirt. He was surprised to find someone from London, but friendly enough. His English wasn't brilliant but it was good enough to tell me that the only Barça European Cup Final he had attended was in 1986. As he looked about 30 years old he must have gone to Seville as a child. With his team behind in this one too, I immediately felt sorry for the bloke.

Given how the game was poised at half-time, it was probably a case of next goal wins. If Arsenal scored it would probably give their players the strength and cushion to hang on for victory, but if Barça got it the full-strength team could be expected to beat its outnumbered opponents. In the event, the match would be transformed by the substitutions made by Rijkaard. Iniesta had recently been injured and was not considered fit enough to start. He was the first Barça substitute, coming on at half-time to replace Edmílson. Both players were midfielders, but Iniesta was more attacking and soon made an impression, bursting forward after 52 minutes and hitting a shot, forcing a save from Almunia.

By now it was raining heavily and the pitch was greasy. The next change took place on the hour when Larsson replaced the disappointing van Bommel. Just under ten minutes later, Oleguer committed a foul and became the first Barça player to be booked. From the resulting free kick, the ball came to Hleb in the middle of the pitch. The Belarusian slipped the ball through to Henry who raced in on goal, only for Valdés to pull off another great save. Had Henry scored, I felt Arsenal would have won. Another highly significant moment followed immediately, when the cautioned Oleguer was replaced by Juliano Belletti.

Eto'o and Ronaldinho had been swapping positions during much of the game. To start with, Eto'o was on the left and Ronaldinho in the centre, then after Barça went behind it changed to Eto'o in the middle and Ronaldinho roaming. Now Eto'o moved back out on the left, and with just under a quarter of an hour remaining he collected the ball from a Larsson flick before shooting past Almunia. This goal added yet more controversy, as replays showed Eto'o to be marginally offside when the ball was played to him. The equaliser had been at the Barça end, and the fans celebrated wildly, letting off several red flares. Fortunately, the smoke cleared in time to see another goal at the same end four minutes later. Belletti picked this moment to score his first goal for Barça, beating Almunia with a shot from wide on the other side. Again, Larsson supplied the assist. The rain was torrential but it didn't impede the celebrations as Belletti's team-mates piled on top of him, amid more red flares and smoke.

By now the Arsenal players were exhausted and Barça concentrated on retaining possession for the last ten minutes of normal time and the three minutes of added time. The game ended with Barça winning 2-1 and securing the club's second European Cup, which was presented on a podium built by the halfway line, accompanied by blue and red ticker tape and firecrackers.

It had been a bad night for referee Hauge. To sum up: he failed to play advantage for the Lehmann foul, meaning that the keeper was sent off in the biggest game of his career; Barça unnecessarily had a goal disallowed; Arsenal's free kick which led to the opening goal followed a blatant dive from Eboué; Barcelona's equaliser was offside. I couldn't help feeling sorry for Arsenal, but it had still been a great occasion, really exciting, with a terrific atmosphere.

By the time I had walked back to Faisal's it was past midnight. He'd already gone to sleep, so I was left alone to enjoy the food with a glass of red wine waiting for me on the dining room table. The meal was delicious, even if it was a rather quiet way to celebrate a European Cup win. My journey home illustrated one of the consequences of the growing commercialisation of football. Sitting in front of me on the Eurostar train from Gare du Nord back to London Waterloo was an Arsenal supporter, who for the best part of an hour kept up a very loud and annoying conversation on his mobile phone about moving millions of pounds of investments around the world. Overhearing him provided further evidence that football events, such as the Champions League Final, were ceasing to be a working-class pastime.

9

Gladiators

A FEW months after Paris, Barça was drawn in the same group as Chelsea, Werder Bremen and Levski Sofia to start its 2006/07 Champions League campaign. The fixture at Stamford Bridge on Wednesday, 18 October 2006 was on matchday three of the group.

There were three main changes to Barça's starting line-up in Paris. Eidur Gudjohnsen, a summer signing from Chelsea, returned to play against his former club instead of the injured Samuel Eto'o. The other two changes of note were the return of Lionel Messi and Xavi from injury. Going into the tie most people expected Barça to win, partly because the club had secured victory on its last visit to Stamford Bridge, but mainly after it became known that Chelsea would have to field its third-choice goalkeeper. Bizarrely, both Petr Čech and reserve keeper Carlo Cudicini had been seriously injured by challenges from opposing players in the same Premier League game the Saturday before, meaning José Mourinho was forced to select 30-year-old Henrique Hilário in goal.

If anyone thought that the sound of the third-choice keeper's name would result in a hilarious performance, they were quickly proved wrong after Hilário pulled off good saves from Messi and Xavi in the first half. In fact, the decisive goal was a Chelsea one. It came after the restart, with Didier Drogba turning to shoot past Víctor Valdés from just outside the penalty area. The assist came from Ashley Cole, who had played for Arsenal in the final at the Stade de France before crossing London to sign for Chelsea. The home team defended solidly, while Barça enjoyed plenty of possession but with little end product. Among the few good chances were a header missed by Messi and an attempt from Deco a couple of minutes from the end when Hilário made another save.

That night, Barça wore a change kit of all-orange and across each player's chest was the logo of UNICEF, the United Nations agency for helping children. This was the first time I had seen a Barça shirt carrying an advertisement. In a charitable gesture, instead of selling the space to a company for money, the club had paid UNICEF €1.5m per season to carry the logo. FC Barcelona's partnership with UNICEF also included projects aimed at helping vulnerable children abroad, with the first to benefit being those at risk from poverty and disease in Africa. Cynics like me suggested at the time that Barça did this partly as a way of abandoning its principled opposition to shirt sponsorship through a gesture that would cost money in the short term, but prove lucrative in the long run when the arrangement with UNICEF expired and the club sold its shirt sponsorship for megabucks. Sadly, I was proved correct in 2011 when Barça's shirts appeared carrying the logo of the Qatar Foundation and then Qatar Airways, organisations linked to a dubious Middle Eastern regime.

The Qatar sponsorship was reportedly worth €150m over the course of its five-year contract. In other words during the five years it lasted, the UNICEF deal cost Barcelona €7.5m but this was more than offset by the €150m received from Qatar. I am not suggesting that everyone who supported the deal with UNICEF was part of a plot to introduce commercial sponsorship, because there were some who supported the former but were against the latter. Johan Cruyff, for example, applauded the shirt deal with UNICEF but criticised the one with Qatar[32]. However, I suspect commercial sponsorship was the long-term aim for some back in 2006. Of course, many will say that Barcelona has to compete with rivals who have shirt sponsorship, but perhaps the club could have been more honest and selective about its choice.

The logo wasn't the only shirty incident at the game. I was sitting down in a part of the stadium reserved for Chelsea supporters. Watching a game in the opposition's section has its own code of conduct. Firstly, and most obviously, never wear colours that identify you as supporting the 'wrong' team. Secondly, avoid interacting with fans sitting around you. If they do speak to you, let them think you are either a supporter of their club or at least neutral. Thirdly, if your side scores, never celebrate

---

32 'Barcelona legend Johan Cruyff criticises club's shirt sponsorship deal with Qatar Foundation': goal.com.

in any way. Finally, if the opposition scores then stand up, because everyone around you will. You don't have to go native and pretend to smile, clap or cheer, but do stand up and show no sign of dissent or frustration. However, on this occasion, when Drogba scored I remained seated. This identified me as not supporting Chelsea and was the cue for the yob sitting behind to strike me on the head. I ignored his assault and pretended that I'd assumed it was done accidentally in the excitement of the moment, but we both knew otherwise. It was a harsh lesson, and now I religiously stand up whenever the opposition scores if watching in the 'wrong' end.

I left Stamford Bridge slightly bruised and disappointed that the game had lacked the excitement or intensity of the previous contests with Chelsea. At the time I put it down to the fact that this was a group match, not a knockout one. I later realised that it was because of deeper reasons.

Barça went on to finish second in the group, but was then eliminated by Liverpool on away goals in the first knockout round. Barça lost La Liga by the slenderest of margins, pipped by Real Madrid's superior head-to-head record. Eto'o, who had been injured at the time of the Chelsea game, returned after a lengthy spell to publicly criticise the atmosphere in the dressing room and, in particular, Ronaldinho, who it was alleged was more interested in partying than playing. Some suggested the absence of former assistant coach Henk ten Cate, who had moved to Ajax in the summer, had led to a lack of discipline in the squad.

In the following season's Champions League Barça did slightly better, topping a group containing Lyon, Glasgow Rangers and Stuttgart, then beating Celtic and Schalke in the knockout rounds, before being eliminated by Manchester United in the semi-finals. However, the drift was really shown in La Liga where Barça finished nearly 20 points behind champions Real Madrid, leading to the departure of Frank Rijkaard at the end of the season.

José Mourinho was the preferred candidate of some to succeed Rijkaard, but in the end Pep Guardiola, then coach of Barça B, was appointed. It was felt that Guardiola, although inexperienced, was better schooled in Barcelona's traditions and playing style, and that Mourinho's media performances would be bad for the club's image, leaving the Portuguese coach free to join Inter in Italy.

Guardiola's arrival prompted the departure of Ronaldinho and Deco. Eto'o was on the verge of leaving when the new coach had a change of mind. Several players arrived, including Dani Alves from Sevilla, plus the return of Gerard Piqué who had risen through the youth system at Barça before going to Manchester United. In Guardiola's first season in charge, Barça had to play a qualifying round in order to enter the Champions League group stage after only finishing third in La Liga the previous season. The opposition, Polish side Wisła Kraków, was dispatched 4-1 on aggregate, qualifying Barça for the group stage. Unfortunately for Guardiola, his first La Liga fixture in the 2008/09 season didn't go so well, with Barça losing 1-0. It was the first screening of a Barça match at Bar & Co, which became PBL's base in London.

The owner of the venue, Jorge, later told me, 'For our first match we lost versus Numancia. There were only a handful of people there and I remember one member shouting, "Guardiola is useless, why didn't we sign Mourinho?"'

Things soon recovered, and Barça successfully negotiated the Champions League group containing Sporting Lisbon, Basel and Shakhtar Donetsk. Wins against Lyon and Bayern Munich in the knockout rounds led to yet another tie with Chelsea in the semi-final. The first leg ended in a goalless draw at Camp Nou. I wasn't able to get a ticket for the second leg at Stamford Bridge and decided to watch a screening in a north London pub in order to save my money for the final.

One of those who did manage to attend the second leg was Tom, a former work colleague of mine from Islington Council. A veteran Chelsea supporter, his first live game at Stamford Bridge was Chelsea versus Stoke City in the old Second Division in 1963. Future Barcelona coach Terry Venables played for Chelsea, while the legendary Stanley Matthews appeared for the visitors. In more recent times, Tom had attended many of his team's fixtures in the Champions League, including the 5-1 defeat to that evening's opponent Barcelona in the quarter-final at Camp Nou in 2000, plus a trip to Moscow to see a penalty shoot-out defeat to Manchester United in the previous season's final.

Shortly before the 2009 semi-final began, Tom arrived at Stamford Bridge to claim his season ticket place in the West Stand lower tier. Chelsea started well, going ahead through a spectacular volley by Michael Essien after about ten minutes. The home fans were buoyant, but Tom was more cautious, saying, 'I felt Chelsea needed to score another to provide protection against a Barcelona away goal. We had four good claims for a penalty, and if any of them had been awarded and converted it would probably have sealed the victory.' The first of these was during the first half when Florent Malouda was fouled by Alves. Replays suggested it was inside the penalty area, but referee Tom Ovrebo awarded a free kick outside the box. Then Drogba claimed he had been fouled by Abidal but the referee waved away the appeals. Early in the second half Barça was reduced to ten men when Abidal was sent off, but Chelsea's lead was still far from secure.

With wild hair and an unkempt beard, Tom had a ferocious appearance, reminiscent of Gandalf from *Lord of the Rings* or Tormund from *Game of Thrones*, although in reality he was usually calm and peaceful as you would expect from a former library assistant. However, as the author David Gemmell once said, 'Each man has a breaking point, no matter how strong his spirit.'[33] For Tom, that breaking point came after Chelsea was denied a penalty for the third time, following a handball by Piqué. Watching from his seat in the ninth row from the front and next to the aisle, a furious Tom then got up and

---

33   Gemmell, D., *Legend*, quoted in psychologytoday.com.

walked down the steps towards the pitch to protest. He later told me, 'I was the only person in the stairway. I felt moved to do it although I knew the referee couldn't hear me shouting at him. We were still ahead and maybe that was the time for someone to remonstrate with the ref and draw attention to what was going on, rather than doing it after we lost.' Tom also told me that some of the Chelsea fans near him thought he was over-reacting because their team was still ahead. Tom, however, had a bad feeling about what might happen next.

Continuing the story, Tom told me, 'In the third minute of stoppage time, with the final whistle approaching, Messi passed the ball to Iniesta who cruelly dashed our hopes, scoring from just outside the area. It was a superb goal, particularly considering the high stakes being played for.' Incredibly, there was still time for a fourth penalty appeal when Michael Ballack's shot appeared to hit the arm of Eto'o in the area. Ovrebo was then chased by a furious Ballack after refusing to award a spot kick. Seconds later, the final whistle blew and Barcelona was through to the final and Chelsea eliminated. Tom later said, 'We looked on in disbelief and with a sense of injustice which remained so strong that not even an FA Cup Final win over Everton at Wembley days later could compensate. Losing the previous year in Moscow added extra pain to the defeat against Barça, a feeling which continues to the present day.'

Later, someone posted a film on YouTube of Ballack running after the referee, speeded up with a soundtrack of the chase music from the 1970s Benny Hill comedy show[34]. It's hilarious, but I think the film clip would have been even funnier if footage of Tom going up and down the stairway, incandescent with rage, had been included.

Having failed to obtain tickets for the semi-final, I was determined not to miss out on the final in Rome. By this time the authorities were clamping down on touts, and it had become illegal in the UK to sell tickets unless you were an authorised source, although it was not illegal to buy tickets from such a source. The north London agency used for Paris was no longer operating, so I had to look elsewhere. An internet search uncovered a company charging £3,000 for a pair of tickets. After some thought, I rang to order and pay for the tickets over the phone. The following day I discovered the scheduled delivery date for the tickets was just after my wife Josie would be flying to Rome to start a two-week-long residential Italian language course. I rang the agency again to ask if it was possible to receive the tickets a bit earlier. To my horror, the telephone number used the day before now answered, 'Sorry, the number you have dialled is no longer available.' I went into shock, it looked like a con.

After a lot of digging around on the internet, I found the geographical address of the company, which was near London Bridge, and went there at the first opportunity. It was a massive relief to find that it was an actual business address, occupied by people working for the agency. I told them their telephone number was faulty and wasn't reassured by the evasive answer; nor was I happy when

---

34 youtube.com/watch?v=0klY3vlHDy8.

they told me that it wasn't possible to speed up the delivery of the tickets. Much to my relief, the tickets did finally arrive, in the form of a wrapper containing a credit card-style bit of plastic, rather than a paper ticket. The face value of each ticket was €140, about £100 by the exchange rate of the time, so a markup of 15 times.

I flew out from London on Monday, 25 May 2009, two days before the game. As with the Paris trip I misjudged the temperature in Rome; it was sweltering, so while travelling by train from Fiumicino airport to the city centre I took off the jacket I had been wearing. Its pockets had contained my passport and the match tickets. I left the jacket on the train, and only realised about an hour later. Luckily, I had transferred the passport and tickets to my trouser pocket just before removing the jacket.

We had been to Rome before, to see a Lazio game, and had stayed in a cheap hotel in the touristy centre. This time my wife decided to stay somewhere different, so she rented an apartment in Prenestino, a bohemian quarter to the south-east of the city. The apartment was ideal, with a rooftop area for eating and viewing the city. The match was to be the last Champions League Final on a Wednesday evening. From 2010 it was moved to Saturdays, ostensibly making it easier for fans to attend, but I suspect the television companies had a hand in the decision too. My wife's language course was every weekday afternoon, meaning we had to do our sightseeing in the mornings.

On matchday I was excited, but also apprehensive about the game and the journey to it, continuing to hate arriving late and struggling through crowds. I planned that we should take a 20-minute walk from our apartment to Arco di Travertino station on Metro line A. That line goes straight through, or rather under, the city centre to Ottaviano San Pietro station, where we could get off, and walk about 40 minutes up to the Stadio Olimpico. My plan had three advantages. First, it avoided changing trains during what would be Rome's rush hour. Secondly, there'd be more chance of getting a seat as we were starting from the other side of the city. Thirdly, we'd completely avoid Ponte Duca d'Aosta, a bridge over the River Tiber which was a notorious ambush point for Roma and Lazio hooligans. At a rough estimation, this route would take just over an hour and a half to travel from Prenestino in the east of the city to the Stadio Olimpico in the north-west. I agreed this route with Josie, and also that we should leave as soon as she arrived back at the apartment at 5.30pm, with a few minutes' turnaround for her to dump the language course materials.

However, although my wife arrived back at the apartment promptly, she then decided that the quick turnaround was *not* going to happen. It had been a very hot day and she wanted to shower and change. I protested that this was not a good idea, but she insisted. Consequently, we eventually left the apartment at 6pm, half an hour later than planned. I was fuming. We didn't speak to each other during the whole walk to Arco di Travertino. As we approached the station at 6.20pm I finally said, 'Bet the Metro's heaving now and we won't get a seat.' There was no reply. When we entered the

Arco di Travertino station it was practically deserted. A train came after a few minutes; it too was nearly empty and we easily found a seat. Still no words from my wife. The Metro went through Parco dell'Appia Antica, Furio Camillo, Ponte Lungo, Re Di Roma and S. Giovanni stations. A few more passengers boarded on the way, but there was still plenty of room on the train. Only then did my wife finally say, 'You fuss too much. There was no need to panic or rush and leave so early. I'm glad I took no notice and had that shower.' The Metro carried on through Manzoni and Vittorio stations, still uncongested. I felt like a fool.

Seconds later, our train entered Termini station and the windows were suddenly filled with a sea of red, or more accurately red for those wearing replica shirts and sunburnt pink for those who had decided to remove them. Yes, the platform on the busiest station in Rome was crammed with Manchester United fans, and worse still they then poured into our carriage, filling it to bursting. Sweaty, naked beer bellies and armpits were thrust way too near your face for comfort. We had to endure the predictable drunken rendition of songs heralding the Busby Babes, Georgie Best, Eric Cantona, and one which contained the lyrics, 'We are the pride of all Europe, the cock of the north. We hate the Scousers, the Cockneys of course (and Leeds).' At that time Leeds languished in the third tier of English football, so it was good to know that my club wasn't forgotten. However, I didn't identify myself as a Leeds supporter, and just sat in silence, the odds not being favourable.

What was happening on the train was par for the course when English clubs play a big match abroad – too much beer, too much noise – but what happened next was appalling. Already sitting in that train were Italian commuters coming home from work, minding their own business. Some of the Manchester United fans then started to expose themselves by 'mooning', pulling down their trousers and underwear to bare their backsides in front of the locals, many of whom were female. I saw at least one of the English fans expose his front side and wave his penis right in front of elegantly dressed, middle-aged Italian women. The fans were certainly not the pride of all Europe, in fact I felt embarrassed and ashamed to be from England, but there was no doubt that we'd seen the cock of the north. The behaviour of the Manc fans did, however, vindicate my plan to travel early to the game, and my wife never complained about doing so ever again.

After about another half a dozen stops, the train finally reached Ottaviano San Pietro station. The packed train in the heat had been an ordeal, so it was a huge relief to get off. We joined the throng walking northwards to the Stadio Olimpico and finally arrived about 7.45pm, an hour before kick-off.

The Stadio Olimpico was built in 1953 near the Foro Mussolini, a sports complex created during Mussolini's fascist rule in between the wars. You can still see a white obelisk carrying the dictator's name on the approach to the stadium. Constructed for the 1960 Olympic Games, the stadium was originally uncovered, but a roof was added ready for it to host the 1990 World Cup Final. Our entrance was gate 28, and it was reassuring to see that everyone else in the queue also had the red credit card-style tickets. It's always a worry buying tickets from an unauthorised source, so it was a huge relief to wand the ticket at the automatic entry system and be greeted with a beep and a flashing light, meaning that the tickets were genuine. We were in!

It wasn't difficult locating our seats in block 28BD, along the seventh row from the front of the Tribuna Tevere grandstand, along one side of the pitch. Our seats were very low down. I prefer to sit higher up and get more of a panoramic view, but at least we'd be close to the action, and the most important thing was to be there at all. We were on the far left-hand side, immediately next to the Barça fans massed behind the goal. The other end, to the right, was occupied by the Manchester United supporters, while the stand opposite housed the tunnel, dugouts and trophy presentation area. The Stadio Olimpico is a featureless bowl and on my only previous visit to see a Serie A fixture it had been half-empty and quiet. However, the atmosphere inside it this time was electric.

It's worth remembering that before kick-off Manchester United was most people's favourite to win, for a number of reasons. Firstly, the club was the current holder of the title; secondly, it had beaten Barça in the previous year's semi-final; thirdly, Barça's coach Guardiola was still in his debut season as a top-flight manager, whereas Alex Ferguson possessed far more

Pennant from the 1992 European Cup Final. Barcelona is written with an Italian spelling.

My seat cover from the 2006 Champions League Final at the Stade de France.

The author with the Holy Grail, the European Cup trophy, photographed at UEFA's 2010 Champions Festival in Madrid's Retiro Park.

The Barça motto 'More than a club' on the seats at the famous Camp Nou stadium.

The Champions Festival in Hyde Park before the 2011 Champions League Final. Barça captain Carles Puyol is pictured with the trophy he would win later that week.

Cake decorated with the Barça badge at the supporters' club dinner before the 2011 Champions League Final.

'We Love Football' mosaic in the Barcelona end at Wembley, 2011 Champions League Final.

Bar & Co, the boat on the River Thames that's home to Penya Blaugrana London.

Group photo of penya members in the Barça Fan Zone in Berlin, before the 2015 Champions League Final.

The Champions League trophy (left) displayed at the dinner to celebrate the 30th anniversary of Penya Blaugrana London in Barcelona in 2015. The trophy on the right is for winning La Liga, the Spanish championship.

Xi wearing his Barça shirt at the penya dinner in 2015, pictured with the author, after completing an epic motorbike ride from China to Barcelona.

BENVINGUTS
A LIVERPOOL!

ENTRADA GRATUÏTA I MÚSICA
EN DIRECTE DURANT
TOT EL DIA.

*The Cavern Club welcomes Barça fans before the ill-fated
semi-final second leg in Liverpool.*

The evolution of football: a paper ticket for the Wembley 1992 final which cost £21.50, a credit card-style ticket for Rome 2009 and a lanyard for Berlin 2015 which both cost rather more.

experience, having been at Old Trafford for 23 years, plus a successful spell at Aberdeen before that. The final reason was because Barça had been forced into fielding a makeshift defence, with Alves and Abidal both suspended and Márquez injured. Puyol was moved to right-back, the reserve Sylvinho was selected at left-back at the age of 35, and Yaya Touré was played out of position at centre-back. The only member of the defence deployed in his usual position was Piqué. The rest of the Barça line-up, to complete its 4-3-3, was Valdés in goal; a midfield of Sergio Busquets (son of long-panted Carles who kept goal for Barça at Old Trafford in 1994) alongside Xavi and Iniesta; then up front Messi, Eto'o and Henry, who had joined Barça a year after losing to the club in Paris. Manchester United's starting team, also in a 4-3-3, was Edwin van der Sar in goal; John O'Shea, Rio Ferdinand, Nemanja Vidić and Patrice Evra in defence; Ryan Giggs, Michael Carrick and Anderson in midfield; Wayne Rooney, Cristiano Ronaldo and Ji-Sung Park up front.

The opening ceremony was a bizarre pageant, consisting of dozens of women parading on the pitch wearing weird green and red costumes and what looked like black swimming caps covering their hair. Two huge square banners laid on the pitch featured the crests of the finalists, together with a round one in the centre circle displaying the maroon 'Roma Finale 2009' logo. As the players marched out the fans at both ends held up cards to create mosaics. The Manchester United one to our right read 'For Sir Matt' in white letters on a red background, honouring the man who coached the club at its first

European Cup triumph in 1968, while the Barça end was a colourful mixture of blue, red and yellow, although I couldn't make out any messaging from my position.

For the fourth time in a row, Barça's opposition in a Champions League Final had to wear a change strip because of a colour clash, so Manchester United wore all-white. Barça appeared in a new version of its classic kit, this time blue-and-red-halved shirts, as opposed to stripes, blue shorts and red socks.

In the previous season's semi-final Ferguson had packed United's midfield with five players to crowd out Xavi and Iniesta, but this time he set his team out in an attacking formation, possibly encouraged by Barcelona's makeshift defence. For the first few minutes this looked a wise decision, with United starting brightly and much the better team. The English club could easily have scored early on when Ronaldo took a free kick from 35 yards, Valdés spilled the ball and Piqué made a crucial intervention to clear the danger. Ronaldo then had three shots on goal before Messi had really touched the ball.

Against the run of play, Barça then scored from its first attack. In Paris, Arsenal had to deal with Ronaldinho and Eto'o swapping positions. Three years later in Rome it was Manchester United's turn to cope with something similar. This time Henry started on the left, Eto'o in the centre and Messi on the right. Then just before the first goal Eto'o moved out to the right, with Messi moving inside to take up a 'false nine' position. Iniesta fed the ball to Eto'o out on the right, and he cut in, beat Vidić and scored. I didn't get a very good view of the goal, being low down and at the other end, so, as is sometimes the case, I had to rely on film replays to discover the details.

The whole game changed with this goal; up to that point Manchester United had been on top. After taking the lead Messi settled into the 'false nine' role, joining attacks where possible in the middle of a front three, with Henry to his left and Eto'o to the right, but also slipping back to support Busquets, Xavi and Iniesta, occasionally building a midfield four which later took control of the game by outnumbering Manchester United's midfield three, to say nothing of the difference in quality. It was a masterclass in passing and keeping possession which helped promote tiki-taka beyond Spain.

The 'false nine' was invented by the Hungarian national side who famously thrashed England 6-3 at Wembley in 1953, deploying Nándor Hidegkuti in that position. In chapter four we heard how Johan Cruyff had sometimes deployed Michael Laudrup as a 'false nine' in his Dream Team in the early 1990s. Guardiola had also tried the tactic a few weeks before Rome in a *clásico* where it worked spectacularly as Barcelona thrashed Real Madrid 6-2. However, after that *clásico* Messi went back to playing on the right and didn't play again as a 'false nine' until Rome, so it came as a nasty surprise to Ferguson's team. It seems appropriate that the goal came in the ninth minute.

It has become quite common for commentators to say that this game was one-sided after the first goal, but as I remember from watching in the stadium at the time the outcome seemed very much in doubt until the second. At half-time the possession statistics showed Barça with 54 per cent and Manchester United on 46, so hardly overwhelming, while the English club had twice as many attempts on goal, eight compared to Barça's four.

In the second half Barça attacked my end, providing a better view of the action. The only change in the line-ups was for United, who brought on Carlos Tevez to replace Anderson. Soon after the restart Henry had a couple of runs and efforts on goal, running down the Barça left just in front of me. Then ten minutes into the second half Iniesta burst through, before being fouled. The resulting free kick, just outside the penalty area, was taken by Xaxi, who curled the ball around the wall, beating van der Sar, only to hit the keeper's left post and bounce out.

Ten minutes later Dimitar Berbatov replaced Park. The decisive goal came on 70 minutes, and I had a superb view of the flight of the ball from Xavi's cross on the way to a totally unmarked Messi, who leapt to head the ball over van der Sar and into the net. Ferdinand was several inches taller than Messi but got caught out of position and was unable to stop the header. Speaking ten years later on BT Sport about this goal, Ferdinand explained that he had gambled on Xavi not being able to beat him at the near post, but had underestimated his opponent[35].

---

35 Manchester United vs Barcelona, BT Sport commentary, 10 April 2019.

Messi rarely scored from headers, but for the second time in the final Manchester United's central defence had, like their fans on the Metro, been exposed. As Messi scored the goal his blue right boot fell off and he ran celebrating with it in his hand towards the corner where I was located.

Messi's header was greeted with an even louder roar than the opening goal, possibly because the fans now believed the game was won. The fact that it wasn't became clear when Manchester United nearly scored straight from the kick-off, after Giggs found Ronaldo in a crowded penalty area, only for Valdés to pull off a great block from the Portuguese. It was one of Giggs' last actions before being replaced by Paul Scholes. Barça also made a substitution of its own, with striker Henry being replaced by holding midfielder Seydou Keita to secure the lead.

Barça nearly made it three when Xavi crossed the ball from a free kick on the right to Puyol, who although totally unmarked, failed to score. With a minute to go Barça brought on Pedro for Iniesta. Then aged 21, it was my first sight of Pedro, who had played for Guardiola the previous season at Barça B and moved up with him to the first team. Pedro had little time to make an impact on this Champions League Final, but was to play a big role in a future one.

After three minutes of stoppage time, the referee blew the whistle, which was a cue for tall inflatables in Barça colours to pop up behind the goal, accompanied by flares. The presentation took place on a temporary stage, located near the tunnel entrance on the other side of the pitch, with ticker tape falling as Puyol received the prize. The Barça players then brought the trophy to the end where their fans were congregated, giving me a really close view of it.

This was my fourth sight of Barça in a European Cup Final. Two of the previous three had involved major refereeing controversies, Schmidhuber awarding Barça the decisive free kick instead of a drop ball at Wembley, and the many mistakes of Hauge in Paris. This time there were no such problems, which surprised me because the official was Massimo Busacca, a Swiss referee who made a whole series of dubious decisions in a Swiss league game I attended at Young Boys Berne the previous year.

A lot of the Reds fans departed the stadium soon after the final whistle, leaving huge swathes of empty seats behind them. This meant that when we left, after the celebrations on the pitch had finished, the journey back was much better (no mooning). Fortunately, the previous day I had done some research and found a bar near our apartment in Prenestino that would be open late and where we could enjoy a quiet beer.

During our stay in the Italian capital we visited the opera to see a performance of Leoncavallo's *Pagliacci*, which is Italian for 'clowns'. Instead of dwelling on whether that opera described Manchester United's defending, I shall move on. While Greek philosophers had helped me understand Barcelona's crushing defeat in Athens, the 2009 final prompted thoughts of that other centre of classical antiquity, ancient Rome.

Although the origin of the name 'Barcelona' is disputed, one theory is that the Carthaginian general Hamilcar Barca decided to call the settlement 'Barcino' in the third century BC. Hamilcar Barca was the father of Hannibal, who became famous as Rome's greatest enemy, invading the Italian peninsula with his army of soldiers and elephants.

However, the connection between the final and ancient Rome that I prefer to focus on concerns gladiators, men who fought in armed combat for public entertainment.

Invented by the Etruscans of northern Italy around 250 BC as public games, gladiatorial contests were copied by the Romans, who initially held them as part of funeral ceremonies to honour the death of the rich and powerful. Gladiators were usually slaves, although sometimes people volunteered in return for payment, but apart from that, and the gruesome endings for many of them, their 'sport' had some similarities to modern-day football. Firstly, gladiatorial bouts evolved into the mass popular entertainment of their time. Secondly, the contests were used to demonstrate the prestige of the organisers and to keep the masses happy. Thirdly, like today's footballers, gladiators received strenuous physical training, special diets and medical attention, which cost a lot of money but were necessary to make them effective performers. In another similarity, the most successful gladiators became celebrities, rather like modern sports stars. Gladiatorial duels also had rules which were overseen by umpires, precursors of modern referees. Finally, special arenas had to be constructed to accommodate the huge audiences that watched gladiators fighting.

It didn't take long for me to encounter a connection between gladiators and football on my trip, because the first thing I visited on the Tuesday was the UEFA Champions Festival. One of the few positive outcomes of the commercialisation of European football, the Champions Festival had started in Paris for the 2006 final, and was a free event containing things like small football pitches, advertising and merchandising stalls, to give local people without tickets an opportunity to sample the atmosphere of the big game. For Rome, the festival was located by the famous Colosseum. Built around AD 75 from stone and concrete, the Colosseum was originally known as the Flavian Amphitheatre. At the time it was the largest amphitheatre in the Roman Empire. As well as hosting gladiatorial contests, the arena also held mock sea battles, animal hunts and executions. After the end of the Roman Empire it ceased to be used for entertainment. Renamed the Colosseum in the Middle Ages, it was damaged by storms, fires and earthquakes, and some of the stone was removed to build the Vatican. However, much of the Colosseum survives, and in recent years it has been described as the most visited tourist attraction in the world.

Being a large bowl which emphasises its size and the crowd, the Stadio Olimpico reminded me of the Colosseum. Both had similar capacities: the Colosseum accommodated up to 80,000 spectators, while the Stadio Olimpico had an attendance of 67,000 for the final. In many ways, the amphitheatre became the precursor of modern football grounds, or as Simon Inglis described it in his book *Football Grounds of Europe*, the Colosseum was 'the daddy of all stadiums'[36].

The opening ceremony in the Stadio Olimpico concluded with Italian tenor Andrea Bocelli singing 'Il Gladiatore', a song based on music from the film *Gladiator*. Released in 2000, *Gladiator* was directed by Ridley Scott and told the story of Roman General Maximus who was betrayed by Commodus, son of the Emperor. Forced into slavery, Maximus became a gladiator searching for revenge. Immediately before Bocelli belted out his song, but unknown to spectators at the time, in the Barça dressing room Guardiola was busy showing his players a seven-minute-long film. Specially made for the occasion, the film consisted of highlights of the team's season alongside scenes from *Gladiator*. Contributors to the fascinating DVD *Take the Ball, Pass the Ball* explain that the film, intended to be a motivational tool, backfired as it made some of the players emotional, reducing them to tears with little time to prepare properly for the match, possibly explaining their poor start[37].

Sections of the media had also busied themselves billing the game beforehand as a gladiatorial contest between the best two players in the world: Cristiano Ronaldo, the holder of the 2008 Ballon d'Or, against his challenger Messi. However, there was only one winner.

---

36 Inglis, S., *The Football Grounds of Europe* (London: Collins Willow, 1990), p7.

37 *Take the Ball, Pass the Ball*, DVD, (Zoom Sport International, 2018).

In the words of *The Guardian*'s report, 'As gladiators clash in Rome, Messi emerges as champion.'[38]

---

38 *The Guardian*, 29 May 2009.

10

Strictly Football

BARÇA'S CHAMPIONS League win in 2009 was one of six trophies the club collected that calendar year, alongside La Liga, Copa del Rey, Spanish Super Cup, UEFA Super Cup and the FIFA Club World Cup. In other words Barça won every competition it entered in 2009, an unprecedented achievement, all the more remarkable given that it was Pep Guardiola's first season as a top-flight coach.

Barcelona's big signing in the summer following Rome was Swedish striker Zlatan Ibrahimović, who arrived in a swap deal with Inter which involved the Italian club receiving Samuel Eto'o plus €46m in return. After Eto'o's evaluation of €20m is taken into account the Swede cost €66m, the second highest transfer fee in world football at the time. Ibrahimović began the 2009/10 season strongly with goals in each of his first five matches. Barça topped a Champions League group containing Inter, Rubin Kazan and Dynamo Kyiv, and it was Ibrahimović who got a valuable away goal in Stuttgart in the first knockout round to secure a 1-1 draw. Barça beat the German side 4-0 at Camp Nou in the second leg to progress to the quarter-final where the club was drawn against Arsenal.

By the time of the first leg in London on Wednesday, 31 March 2010, I lived less than 20 minutes' walk from Arsenal's Emirates Stadium. Once again, match tickets were at a premium. Since Arsenal moved to its new ground in 2006 I had become a Red Member as it provided more chance of obtaining tickets for big games. However, Barça was such an attraction that Red Membership, one of the lowest levels, was not enough to get a ticket, which meant using touts. By 2010 the authorities had further tightened their measures against touting, so not only had the north London agency I had used for Paris disappeared, so had the London Bridge one used for Rome. It was now a question of either accepting defeat or going back to touts hawking tickets outside the ground. On my previous visits to the Emirates Stadium there had been no sign of touts operating. Further enquiries revealed that the touts were old guys who preferred to continue operating from near the old, now abandoned, Highbury ground, several minutes' walk from the Emirates. So three hours before kick-off I went to Avenell Road, spotted a tout and parted with a wad of cash in return for a ticket.

On all my previous visits to the Emirates Stadium, Arsenal fans used plastic cards to open electronic turnstiles at the gate, but for the Barça game in 2010 my ticket was a paper one, so I suspected it was issued as a temporary means of admission for visiting supporters. The seat was in the top tier of the Clock End, the end allocated to away fans, and when the first person to sit next to me inside the stadium was a Barcelona supporter from Spain I jumped to the conclusion that this was the visitors' section. A later arrival, occupying the seat on the other side, then overheard me saying that I wanted Barça to win. When the stand filled up it became clear that the Barça fans were two tiers below me and I was in an Arsenal section. The Emirates Stadium is very strict about ejecting fans in the 'wrong' area, so I was lucky that the Arsenal fan next to me was relaxed about it and didn't grass me up.

Going into the game Arsenal stood third in the Premier League, while Barça was level on points with Real Madrid at the top of La Liga. Playing in a change kit of yellow shirts, blue shorts and yellow socks, Barça lined up in Guardiola's usual 4-3-3, with five changes from Rome: Dani Alves and Maxwell replacing Yaya Touré and Sylvinho in defence; Keita replacing Iniesta who had a hamstring injury in midfield; with Ibrahimović and Pedro taking the place of Henry and Eto'o up front.

By the time of the game, Ibrahimović was 28 years old and his relationship with Guardiola had deteriorated. In his highly readable autobiography *I am Zlatan Ibrahimović*, the striker claims that Guardiola couldn't handle strong personalities such as himself, preferring the better behaved graduates of La Masia, such as Xavi, Iniesta and Messi[39]. Shortly before the game at Arsenal, Guardiola decided

---

39 Ibrahimović, Z., *I am Zlatan Ibrahimović* (Penguin, 2013), p281.

to use Messi in a more central role, which resulted in Ibrahimović being deployed on the right.

In the first half Barça attacked the end away from me, and despite being some distance from the action, sitting high up still provided a good enough view to see Barça dominating the game, but failing to score. One reason for this was Arsenal's goalkeeper, Manuel Almunia, who had been partly to blame for both Barça goals in Paris but this time made several great saves in the first half. The other reason was Ibrahimović having a bit of a nightmare and wasting several good chances. By his own admission, the Swede was surprised to stay on for the start of the second half[40].

What happened next was a perfect example of why you shouldn't take long getting half-time refreshments, because quite a lot of the 59,572 crowd hadn't retaken their seats before there was a goal. After only 25 seconds of the second half, Piqué gained possession inside his own half and lobbed the ball down the Barça right. The ball bounced once and Ibrahimović, seeing that Almunia had raced off his line, sent a perfectly executed lob of his own, with his only touch, over the advancing keeper and into the far corner of the goal. A quarter of an hour later, Xavi played another ball up the Barça right and once again Ibrahimović, eluding the offside trap, beat Almunia from a similar position to his first goal, albeit with a lower shot. My seat provided a brilliant view of both goals, which made it five in four games for the Swede and 20 so far that season.

---

40 Ibrahimović, Z., *I am Zlatan Ibrahimović* (Penguin, 2013), p287.

However, the game changed when Theo Walcott came on after 66 minutes and three minutes later burst down the flank to score, shooting past Valdés, suggesting Barça's defence might be vulnerable to pace. Maxwell didn't exactly cover himself in glory with his weak defending at left-back. Six minutes later Guardiola took off Ibrahimović, replacing him with Thierry Henry, making his first competitive return to the Emirates Stadium. It looked like Barça would hold on to its lead until five minutes from time when Puyol fouled Fàbregas in the box. The Barça captain was sent off, meaning he'd miss the second leg. Fàbregas got up to convert the penalty only to injure his foot in the act. Guardiola responded to the sending-off by replacing Messi with another Argentine player, defender Gabriel Milito, to secure the draw. There were no further goals and it ended 2-2.

In the return fixture, Nicklas Bendtner stunned Camp Nou by putting Arsenal 1-0 up and ahead on aggregate, but four goals from Messi took Barça into the semi-finals. The prize, a place in the final, was even bigger this year because the showpiece occasion was in Real Madrid's own Estadio Santiago Bernabéu. The host club wouldn't be in the final following a first knockout round elimination by Lyon. The chance to see Barça win European club football's biggest prize in its bitterest rival's stadium was a unique opportunity, unlikely to be repeated in my lifetime.

Before the first leg of the semi everything for the final was secured: return flights to Madrid, a week's accommodation in an apartment not far from the famous Prado museum, and match tickets for the Bernabéu obtained at face value from UEFA. All that was needed was for Barça to overcome its semi-final opponent, Inter (now coached by José Mourinho). The two sides had already played twice in the group stage earlier in the season, with Barcelona drawing 0-0 away and triumphing 2-0 at home. As the semi-final approached Mourinho tried to pile on the pressure by claiming Barça was 'obsessed' with winning the Champions League in its rival's stadium.

However, it wasn't mind games that disrupted Barça's preparation for the first leg, but eruptions from an Icelandic volcano. Fear that ash blown into the atmosphere would damage aircraft and cause crashes resulted in all European flights being temporarily suspended. Consequently, the Barça squad was forced to travel overland by coach to get to northern Italy, a journey that took 16 hours and left the players exhausted. Despite scoring an early goal, Barça then conceded three as tiredness took its toll. The 3-1 defeat meant that Barça required a 2-0 victory at Camp Nou to progress. Before the second leg Ibrahimović had suffered a calf injury and hadn't fully recovered or regained match fitness. Guardiola gambled by selecting the Swedish striker, but this proved to be an error as he was ineffective against his former club. Inter, down to ten men after the sending-off of former Barça player Thiago Motta, defended stubbornly and survived a late Barça goal to progress 3-2 on aggregate.

Mourinho then took his Inter team to Madrid where it triumphed over Bayern Munich. Although Barça was absent from the final, the trip did provide me with a chance to be photographed with the trophy during the Champions Festival in Retiro Park. Mourinho must have liked the Bernabéu, because immediately after the final he left Inter to become the new Real Madrid coach.

Although Barça won La Liga again, setting a new Spanish record with 99 points, the defeat in the Champions League semi-final and the consequent missing out on the chance to win the trophy in the Bernabéu cast a shadow over a season which ended with Ibrahimović being loaned out to AC Milan. The deal later became permanent with a transfer fee of €24m, meaning that Barça lost a whopping €42m through his signing. The decision to sign Ibrahimović and then fail to integrate him into the team was arguably Guardiola's biggest setback as Barcelona coach. The situation was rectified in the summer of 2010 when David Villa was signed from Valencia to replace Ibrahimović and Henry. A Spanish international, Villa was more of a team player and the perfect fit for this Barça team, better suited to playing out wide.

Boosted by Villa's arrival, Barça was highly fancied to regain the Champions League trophy in 2010/11 and easily topped a group containing FC Copenhagen, Rubin Kazan and Panathinaikos. In the first knockout round Barça drew Arsenal for the second year running, with the first leg also at the Emirates. After my Red Membership again failed to deliver, it was time to make a repeat visit to the old geezers on Avenell Road. Going in to the game, on Wednesday, 16 February 2011, Arsenal was doing well, positioned second in the Premier League behind Manchester United.

This time my ticket was for the other end of the stadium, in the lower tier near the corner. It was also near the front and too low to get a decent view, which was why all the fans stood up throughout the match. Barça, sporting a smart new away kit with green shirts, a *blaugrana* horizontal band across the chest, dark blue shorts and green socks, made three changes from the previous season's trip to the Emirates. Abidal replaced Puyol in defence; Iniesta returned to the midfield at the expense of Keita; with Villa instead of Ibrahimović in attack.

In front of another capacity crowd, there were early chances for both sides, Valdés saving from Robin van Persie, then Messi unusually hit an easy chance narrowly wide. It looked like it might not matter when Barça took the lead after 26 minutes. Messi slipped a pass through to Villa, who slotted the ball past the outrushing Almunia, before celebrating by jogging backwards while gesturing for his colleagues to join him near the corner, right in front of where I was standing.

Another Messi miss in the second half, with a shot into the side netting, later proved costly. With 68 minutes gone both coaches made changes; Guardiola brought on Keita for Villa to try and protect the lead, while Wenger brought on Andrey Arshavin and Nicklas Bendtner. However, it was Wenger's changes that proved to be the game-changing ones, when with just over ten minutes remaining Gaël Clichy chipped the ball to van Persie down towards the left-hand corner, very close to my position. Valdés expected a cross, but van Persie smashed a shot from a tight angle and beat him at the near post. Arsenal then scored a second goal within four minutes. Man of the match Jack Wilshere initiated a move which ended with Arshavin scoring with a shot from inside the box. Barça had a couple of chances to grab an equaliser in the remaining seven minutes, but without success, meaning the English club took a 2-1 lead to Camp Nou. For the second year running Barça had wasted chances early on then surrendered a lead at the Emirates.

In the second leg Barça was winning 3-1 (and 4-3 on aggregate) but with three minutes of normal time remaining a cross from Wilshere found Bendtner. It looked like there was only the goalkeeper to beat, but at the last moment Javier Mascherano slid in to make a tackle. Without Mascherano's interception Bendtner would probably have scored to make it 4-4 on aggregate and send Arsenal through on away goals.

In the quarter-final Barça comfortably beat Shakhtar Donetsk to set up a semi-final against Mourinho's Real Madrid. Famously, this meant the teams would play each other not once, but four times in a period of only 18 days. On 29 November 2010 I had celebrated my birthday (and that of FCB) by travelling to Barcelona for the first Pep versus José *clásico* at Camp Nou. That match ended 5-0 to the hosts and was such a terrific occasion that I decided to also attend the second one at the Bernabéu in April 2011. A much-improved Real Madrid got a 1-1 draw, although the result practically handed La Liga to Barcelona. Next up was the Copa del Rey Final in Valencia, which Madrid won by a single goal. The third of the four was the opening leg of the Champions League semi-final which Barça won 2-0 away with a wonder goal from Messi. The second leg followed a week later and ended 1-1, meaning Barça won 3-1 on aggregate to secure its place in the final, and another, after a 19-year interval, at Wembley.

The opposition in the final was Manchester United, meaning that many of its fans would be desperate to attend the match, only a two-hour train journey from their home city. The new Wembley held about 90,000 people. The two finalists were each allocated 25,000 tickets, and the remaining 40,000 were taken by UEFA, the English FA and Wembley Stadium to distribute, with many going to sponsors, football federations and corporate hospitality. FC Barcelona received nearly 100,000 ticket applications for the final, a club record, and I was too new a member of PBL to have any real hope of getting a ticket from the limited allocation. I was also aware that any black market tickets would be extortionate because the agencies I had previously used had all been forced out of business by tighter laws and enforcement on the resale of tickets. The prospects looked bleak. Back in 1992 a simple phone call to Wembley Stadium secured a cheap ticket for the European Cup Final. What would happen if I tried nearly 20 years later?

More in desperation than expectation, I made the phone call to Wembley. The woman who answered politely told me that they didn't have any tickets for the final available from the box office (surprise, surprise) but then added, almost as an afterthought, that I could try corporate hospitality, and gave me a telephone number. I had heard of corporate hospitality, but never experienced it and assumed it was just for sponsors and big businesses taking groups of clients. I dialled the number immediately. The man who answered told me, to my surprise, that anyone could buy a single ticket for the Champions League Final as part of a hospitality package – he'd just have to check that there were some still available. After being put on hold for a couple of minutes, he returned and said there were still a few remaining. I asked how much was the cheapest package available. He replied that it would be '£3,480 per person'. I gulped, told him I'd think about it, and possibly ring back.

Wow! A ticket for the European Cup Final bought over the phone in 1992 cost £21. In 2011 a ticket for the same fixture at the same venue was £3,480, over 165 times as expensive. That's football inflation for you. I took 45 minutes to walk round the block and mull it over, before deciding to go for it. I rang him back and did the deal.

My build-up to the big game included a visit on the Thursday to the now customary Champions Festival which this year was held in Hyde Park, then on the eve of the final I attended a fantastic dinner organised by PBL at a posh central London hotel. On the day of the match, Saturday, 28 May 2011, it was time to discover what £3,480 bought for me. The answer was access to 'Platinum Hospitality' at Wembley Arena.

Built in 1934 for the British Empire Games to house swimming events, it was originally called the 'Empire Pool' before the name changed to Wembley Arena. Located adjacent to the stadium, Wembley Arena is the second-largest indoor venue in London after the O2, and if seating inside is required it can accommodate 12,500. As well as sporting events, Wembley Arena has hosted other forms of entertainment. My first visit to Wembley Arena had been in 1993 to see The Velvet Underground during the veteran American rock band's reunion tour. Four hours before kick-off, it was time to head down to Wembley Arena and discover, in the words of a couple of Velvet Underground songs, what goes on with hospitality and whether we're gonna have a real good time together.

The hospitality opened at 4pm, with unlimited refreshments consisting of a selection of high-quality buffet-style food, champagne, wine and beer. For the final, Wembley Arena was decked out in the colours and logo of that season's Champions League, navy blue with red lettering and a silver trophy surrounded by lions. The vast space was decorated with names of previous European Cup winners, while signs hanging down from the ceiling displayed UEFA logos and pictures of the trophy. Small tables and chairs were scattered around the floor of the arena to enable people to enjoy the refreshments and watch the entertainment, which included competitions you could enter as well as screens showing football highlights.

By far the best part was a lively panel discussion on a raised stage previewing the evening's match. Compered by the smooth John Inverdale, it included two former Chelsea players, Gianfranco Zola and Ray Wilkins, and a couple of Liverpool European Cup winners, Alan Hansen and Phil Neal. I had never attended any form of corporate hospitality event, and was worried that it would be all posh businessmen in suits. While there were suits, with companies entertaining their clients, many of the people there were just ordinary fans who, like me, used it as a way (albeit an extremely expensive one) of getting to the game. One of the celebrities I spotted was Welsh actor Jonathan Pryce, who played the baddie in the 1997 James Bond film *Tomorrow Never Dies*. Given the cost of admission it should have been *Goldfinger*, or maybe *Diamonds Are Forever*.

At 7pm people were encouraged to leave the arena and take the short walk over to the stadium, through the Bobby Moore Entrance, and find their places. My seat was in block 208, row 14, located in the middle tier that runs around the stadium. I had been told in advance that the dress code for Platinum Hospitality was smart business attire, and definitely no football shirts or colours. To me, this was a sure sign of how the establishment was taking over football. Nevertheless, I decided to conform, which was just as well because my seat, although in a neutral ring, went between the upper and lower tiers in a corner, meaning that below, and more importantly above, there were thousands of Manchester United fans.

I took my seat in plenty of time to watch the opening ceremony, which was the usual bizarre pageant with dozens of people parading on the pitch in costumes. This time many of them wore business suits, bowler hats and carried umbrellas. Is this what some people think London or football is all about? Perhaps you needed to be a stockbroker to afford Wembley tickets?

Back in 1992 at the old Wembley, the tunnel had been behind one of the goals. Now, the teams entered via an entrance on the north side, where the famous Twin Towers used to be before they were replaced by the arch. The players entered the pitch walking past four military guardsmen dressed in red coats with black busbies. When the teams lined up I couldn't see what the Manchester United fans were doing because they were right on top of me, but did get an excellent view of the other end where the Barça fans held up red, blue and yellow cards to form a memorable mosaic reading 'We Love Football'.

Both clubs arrived at the match as newly crowned winners of their domestic leagues. For the fifth time running Barça's opposition in the European Cup Final was forced to wear a change strip, with Manchester United in white shirts and socks with black shorts. Barça wore yet another variation of their classic kit, this time blue and dark red striped shirts, with yellow trimmings, dark red shorts and blue socks.

The Barça line-up was the usual 4-3-3: Valdés in goal; Alves, Mascherano, Piqué and Abidal in defence; Busquets, Iniesta and captain for the day Xavi in midfield; with Pedro on the right of the attack, Villa on the left, and Messi as a 'false nine'. The four departures from the starting line-up in Rome two years earlier were Sylvinho, Touré, Henry and Eto'o. Puyol, who had also started in Rome, was on the bench at Wembley. The only notable change from my knockout round game at the Emirates was the selection of Javier Mascherano at centre-back. Normally a midfield player, and less than 5ft 9in tall, it was a bold call to select the Argentinian as the replacement for the still unfit Puyol.

Manchester United adopted a 4-4-1-1 formation with van der Sar in goal; Fábio, Ferdinand, Vidić and Evra at the back; Antonio Valencia, Carrick, Giggs and Park in midfield; and Rooney in the so-called 'hole' behind Javier Hernández. United's three changes from Rome were the absences of O'Shea, Anderson, and most importantly Cristiano Ronaldo, who had moved to Real Madrid.

The 2011 final began with Barça attacking my end. Manchester United, as in Rome, started the better of the two teams. Then after ten minutes Barça settled into a passing rhythm and used its large share of possession to probe the opposition and try to exploit any openings. Whenever they lost the ball the Barça players pressed quickly, high up and in numbers, to win it back. This, of course, is well-known as the trademark style of Guardiola's team, although it seemed to me to be more apparent at this final than in 2009.

The first real attempt on goal came after 18 minutes when Xavi picked up the ball from Messi, then played a short pass to Villa who hit a right-footed shot just wide of van der Sar's left post from about 20 yards. This was followed within a couple of minutes by another attempt, which van der Sar saved. The breakthrough came seven minutes later. Barça gained possession and Xavi moved forward with the ball. While there were a number of defenders present they all seemed to be watching Messi, leaving Pedro unmarked on the right to fire a shot past van der Sar.

Unlike Rome, Manchester United equalised seven minutes later. Rooney played a one-two with Giggs before shooting in with the side of his right foot past Valdés. Although I'd had a great view of the first goal, which was near me, this second goal was at the other end. Consequently, I didn't see that Giggs was marginally offside when the ball was played to him, so it should have been disallowed. In the first half Barça had 67 per cent of the possession and eight goal attempts compared with just two for the opposition. During the interval I overheard some Manchester United fans on the concourse expressing concern that their team was being outplayed.

The second half started with Barça dominating the game. After 51 minutes Alves made one of his attacking runs down the right, ending with a shot on goal which was saved by van der Sar. Two minutes later this was followed by what turned out to be the winner. Messi gained possession of the ball in a central position and dribbled forward. The defenders, possibly thinking of what had happened when they conceded the first goal, this time did the opposite. Instead of worrying about Messi, and leaving other players unmarked, they backed off him, holding their positions. They possibly expected

Messi to continue dribbling or pass to a colleague, but instead he hit a left-footed shot. Van der Sar also seemed to be taken by surprise, and should perhaps have done better, as the ball flew past him and into the back of the net. The goal was greeted by a tremendous roar at that end followed by the twirling of thousands of Barça scarves.

After 68 minutes Ferguson replaced Fabio with Nani. This change rapidly backfired when Messi was dispossessed down the right, because it was Nani who immediately lost the ball; Busquets then slipped it back to a waiting Villa to curl a brilliant right-footed shot into the top corner. Given that Manchester United had managed an equaliser in the first half, I felt watching at the time that victory was only secured with this third goal.

A few minutes after Villa's goal, Barça had another of their lengthy spells of possession. An elderly man a few seats away from me, perhaps trying to impress the teenager accompanying him, rose out of his seat and shouted in foreign-accented English 'Xavi, to Iniesta, to Messi, it's all choreographed' and made hand signs as if he was conducting an orchestra. Soon after his announcement he decided that the game was over and left the stadium, taking the youth with him. I was shocked that someone would spend £7,000 on a pair of tickets, then leave with a quarter of an hour still to play. There were thousands of fans of both teams who would have loved to have been at this special game and stayed to the end. It suggests that corporate hospitality enables the wrong kind of people to come to matches.

Scholes replaced Carrick after 77 minutes, then shortly before the end Barça made three changes, Keita came on in place of Villa, while Puyol and young Dutch player Ibrahim Afellay replaced Alves and Pedro respectively. The game finished with Barça even more dominant than in the first period, having 68 per cent of possession, 13 attempts on goal to the opposition's two, and six corners with none conceded[41]. The last statistic is particularly interesting as Guardiola identified Manchester United as being a threat from corners, and told his players not to concede any, an instruction which they clearly carried out precisely.

The famous old Wembley staircase from 1992 had been replaced by a new route, which took players up to the top of the lower tier, before they briefly vanished from sight to go under the lip of the second tier, then reappeared as they walked along the front row to collect the trophy. Although Puyol received the captain's armband when he came on a couple of minutes from the end, he decided to give it to Eric Abidal for the presentation. This was because about a month after I had seen him play in the first leg of the round of 16 tie at the Emirates, Abidal had been diagnosed with a tumour on his liver. He underwent surgery to remove the tumour, but then recovered sufficiently to play all 90 minutes of the final only 71 days later.

The Barça players descended the other flight of steps to go back on to the pitch and celebrate. 'Cant del Barça'

---

41   Opta Sports data, theguardian.com.

and 'Madrid cabrón saluda al campeón' rang out from the opposite end, just as in 1992, while my end emptied of Manchester United supporters as quickly as it had in Rome. The last act of note was Piqué cutting off the net from the goal at the other end to take away as a rather unusual souvenir.

After the players finally left the pitch, I walked back to Wembley Arena which reopened for post-match analysis by our pundits plus more food and drink, a far more preferable option to joining the massive queue to get into Wembley Park Tube station. Inverdale, Wilkins, Zola, Neal and Hansen took it in turns to eulogise Barcelona's performance in the game they had just witnessed. This was the start of 'Barçamania' where tiki-taka became the flavour of the moment, with some commentators calling the team the best club side in the history of football and one newspaper describing it as 'a high point in football's evolution'[42]. It is, of course, extremely difficult to compare teams from different eras, with changes to the rules on back-passes, offside and tackling, new equipment such as lighter boots and balls, better pitches, the varying standard of opposition that the different great sides had to compete against in their day, plus the impossibility of seeing players from different generations play each other. When dominating games with its possession, passing and attacking football, Guardiola's Barça arguably played some of the most entertaining football ever seen. However, defensively it was not so strong, and for that

---

42 *The Guardian*, 29 May 2011.

reason it might be an exaggeration to call the team the best in the history of football.

On the subject of entertainment, one of the events that Wembley Arena hosts annually is *Strictly Come Dancing Live*, a roadshow where celebrity contestants and professional dancers from the popular television programme tour the country giving viewers the opportunity to see performances in the flesh (sometimes quite a lot of flesh). For the show, celebrities learn a series of dances, from the tango to the Charleston, practising moves which must be performed according to the choreography taught by their professional dance instructors. The judges and television viewers then vote to decide the winners. After the game, while enjoying a few beers back in Wembley Arena, scene of so many *Strictly* routines, I thought about what the old man had said, 'Xavi, to Iniesta, to Messi, it's all choreographed,' and wondered if the match that had just ended was a bit like *Strictly Come Dancing*, with Guardiola's team performing carefully rehearsed routines?

Strictly is the UK version of a series of reality television dancing shows with a similar format across the world, where celebrities such as actors, singers, comedians and sports personalities compete. Among the latter have been some retired Barça footballers, who appear below, in order of increasing dance performance. Get out the hairspray, fake tan and sequins, it's time for CAMP Nou!

Miguel Angel Nadal played for Barça in a couple of games described in this book during the early 1990s. After retiring in 2010 Nadal participated in the eighth series of the Spanish version of *Strictly*, which was originally called *¡Mira quién baila!* (*Look Who's Dancing!*) before being rebranded as *¡Más que baile!* (*More Than Dancing*). In the 1994 Champions League Final in Athens, Nadal had been outdone by Dejan Savićević's raised leg, and footwork may also have been a problem for him on the dance floor. Nicknamed 'The Beast' during his football career as a tough and rugged defender, Nadal proved to be a rather less formidable dancer, finishing last out of eight entrants[43].

Julio Salinas looked ungainly for most of the hour he was on the pitch in my only view of him at the 1992 European Cup Final, before suddenly and unexpectedly demonstrating great agility to beat several Sampdoria defenders and get in a shot on goal in a crowded penalty area. Barça's former centre-forward tried to be similarly quick-footed in the seventh series of *¡Mira quién baila!* in 2008, but only managed to finish fifth out of eight[44].

In 2005 former Barça superstar Diego Maradona entered the second series of *Ballando con le Stella* (*Dancing with the Stars*), the Italian version of *Strictly*. Enduringly popular in Italy because of his achievements at Napoli, Maradona did well in the early weeks, demonstrating what one reviewer called 'surprising dance floor prowess'[45]. Being good in hold was to be expected of someone with the 'Hand of God'. However, a punishing

43 'Mira quién baila 2010: Nadal, primer expulsado – Que Me Dices,' quemedices.es.

44 'Manuel Bandera gana la séptima edición de *¡Mira quién baila!*' abc.es.

45 italymagazine.com.

schedule involving weekly flights between Buenos Aires and Rome took its toll and Maradona was forced to retire from the show following medical advice.

It's fair to say that by the time of my musings in Wembley Arena in 2011 Barça hadn't exactly excelled on the dance floor, but two years later that changed. Welcome back former European Footballer of the Year Allan Simonsen. In chapter three we heard how Simonsen's time at Barça ended with a shock move to London, where I saw his last game for Charlton Athletic in 1983 before he returned to Denmark. After retiring from football management, Simonsen entered the tenth series of *Strictly*'s Danish equivalent, *Vild Med Dans* (*Wild With Dance*) in 2013.

Simonsen is only 5ft 5in tall, and during his playing career in the 1970s and 80s football was a much more physical game than it is today, meaning that size was an important issue. Height can also be a significant factor for dancers; advantageous in ballroom, but less important in Latin. Aged 60 at the time of the contest, the 'Sparrow from Vejle' proved popular with the public and was voted through to the semi-final where he danced a Viennese waltz followed by a pasodoble. Despite being tipped to progress, Simonsen failed to reach the final, ending the series in third place. However, his performance was more than enough to win this glitter(foot)ball contest, following a successful transition from Charlton to Charleston[46].

---

46 'Then it went no further: Allan Simonsen out of Wild with Dance,' billedbladet.dk.

One of the publications eulogising Guardiola's team was Graham Hunter's *Barça: The Making of the Greatest Team in the World*, which tells us that Dani Alves brought 'dance moves' to Barcelona[47]. In 2018 a DVD based on Hunter's book was released called *Take the Ball, Pass the Ball*, where Alves says that the football under Guardiola wasn't all 'robotic', because although 60 per cent of the team's play was planned in advance, the remaining 40 per cent was left to the players' own initiative and improvisations[48]. This suggests that some of the football was choreographed, but not all, so the old man at Wembley wasn't entirely correct, strictly speaking.

47 Hunter, G., *Barça: The Making of the Greatest Team in the World* (BackPage Press, 2012), p174.
48 *Take the Ball, Pass the Ball*, DVD, (Zoom Sport International, 2018).

11

Babunski's Badges

THE MANNER of Barça's success in the 2010/11 Champions League, playing some of the best football ever seen in the history of the sport, made the team strong favourites to retain the trophy the following year when the final was in Munich. However, although Barça would play in a final in Germany, that would be three years later in Berlin. The next time I saw Barça live was in a match that did much to explain why the club never made it to Bavaria.

In the Champions League Barça topped a group containing Milan, Viktoria Plzeň and BATE Borisov. In the first knockout round Barça thrashed Bayer Leverkusen 10-2 on aggregate, then defeated Milan in the quarter-final, setting up a semi-final against Chelsea. As in 2000 and 2006, but unlike in 2005 and 2009, the draw dictated that Barca should play the first leg away at Stamford Bridge on Wednesday, 18 April 2012.

After initially struggling to get a match ticket, I was luckily able to borrow a season ticket from Tom, the Chelsea supporter mentioned in chapter nine. On the eve of the game I attended the customary dinner for PBL members plus visiting Barça officials. The mood was buoyant and a cake iced in Barça colours was served alongside Cava in anticipation of a good result the following day.

Tom's season ticket was in the lower tier of the West Stand, level with the halfway line, which meant that when the teams lined up I had a close view of the Barça team which included four changes from Wembley. In defence, Puyol replaced Piqué, while Adriano came in for Abidal who had undergone a liver transplant a week before. Up front, Alexis Sánchez and Cesc Fàbregas replaced Pedro and Villa, the latter still recovering after breaking a leg just before Christmas. Both Sánchez and Fàbregas had been signed the previous summer, but while the former was a striker, the latter was a midfield player. A product of the Barça youth system, Fàbregas had gone to Arsenal early in his career where he played against Barça in three games featured in this book. In 2011 the club decided to bring him back. The team that night is usually described as 4-3-3, but because Alves attacked up the wing and there was only one out-and-out striker it frequently looked more like 3-6-1.

Roberto Di Matteo had replaced Chelsea's former coach André Villas-Boas following a bad result away to Napoli earlier in the knockout stages, and the Italian opted for a 4-1-4-1 formation against Barcelona. The home side wore its usual all blue while the visitors appeared in an all-black away kit with my first view of the dubious Qatar Foundation shirt sponsorship.

Barça started the game attacking the goal on the left. The Barça fans, including a contingent from PBL, were in the far corner to the right. As usual, Barça dominated possession, but on this occasion was wasteful in front of goal. The worst offender was Fàbregas, missing two chances which highlighted the limitations of playing midfielders as attackers. Some say Fàbregas was brought back to Barça as the long-term successor to Xavi, but that night he played further forward. Sadly, things did not work out for Fàbregas back at Barcelona, and he would be sold to that evening's opponent a couple of years later.

With all the pressure, it looked to be only a matter of time before there was a goal, but when it happened it came for Chelsea. Towards the end of the first period Messi was dispossessed inside his own half by Lampard. The England midfielder played a diagonal pass to Ramires on the left. Ramires advanced then crossed to Didier Drogba, who steered his shot into the corner of the net from near the penalty spot. Chelsea's counter-attack exploited the fact that Alves was in an advanced position at the time instead of defending the right flank. The West Stand around me erupted when the goal went in, with fans desperate to avenge the 2009 semi-final. By now it was pouring with rain, although I was just far enough back to remain under cover. The second half saw more Barça chances, all either missed or saved by Čech. Pedro, Thiago Alcântara and Isaac Cuenca came on as substitutes, but still there was no breakthrough. The tension mounted in the closing moments, with everyone in the crowd of 38,039 remembering Iniesta's decisive injury-time goal at the same venue three years earlier. With one minute of normal time remaining Messi played the ball to Busquets, who back-heeled it only for Terry to deflect it across to Pedro on the left. His shot beat Čech and bounced back off the far post to Busquets, but with the Chelsea keeper prone and helpless on the floor the holding midfielder blasted his shot way over the bar.

The game finished soon after that glaring miss. Busquets could have snatched a priceless away goal, but instead the London club held the advantage going into the second leg despite having only 28 per cent possession, managing just a single attempt on target whereas the visitors had six, and completing only 169 successful passes compared to Barcelona's 743[49].

Di Matteo used a similar counter-attacking strategy in the second leg at Camp Nou, securing a draw with a couple of breakaway goals, meaning it was Chelsea who headed to Munich for the final, 3-2 on aggregate. Worse was to come, because soon after the semi-final defeat Guardiola announced his resignation, explaining at a dramatic press conference that he was worn out and needed time off to regain sufficient energy to motivate players. At the end of the season Tito Vilanova, the assistant coach who had sat to Guardiola's right in the dugout at Stamford Bridge, took over as coach.

A few months after the defeat to Chelsea, another Barça football team arrived in London, namely the

---

49 uefa.com.

Barcelona Juvenil A side who had come to participate in the NextGen Series, a European competition for under-19 teams which had started the previous year. On 13 September 2012 I joined a small contingent of PBL members on the short journey up to Tottenham Hotspur's White Hart Lane stadium for the game.

After winning 2-0 one of the Barcelona players, David Babunski, came over to the 30 Barça fans in our corner and, speaking in perfect English rather than Catalan or Spanish, said, 'My coach has asked me to give you some "pins" to thank you for supporting our team.' The coach concerned was Jordi Vinyals, who had been a Barcelona youth player 30 years earlier. I happened to be at the front, and as the person nearest to Babunski, he handed the packet to me. After opening it I found 20 'pins', kept one and distributed the remainder to other PBL members. Before the match I had not heard of Babunski, or any other members of the Juvenil A side, but subsequent research revealed a young player with a fascinating family history and highly unusual interests.

David Babunski was born in 1994 in Skopje, Macedonia, shortly after the break-up of Yugoslavia. His great-great-grandfather, Jovan Stojković, was one of the most famous Serbian military leaders in the early part of the 20th century, fighting in various Balkan conflicts and the First World War against the Bulgarians and Ottoman Turks. After Stojković's death in 1920 at the age of only 41 a monument was erected in his memory, although that was destroyed by the Bulgarians when they occupied the area during the Second World War[50]. Stojković adopted the name Babunski as his *nom de guerre* and it was then used by his descendants. Football then took over from fighting in the family, with David's father, Boban Babunski, representing Macedonia at international level and playing for clubs in several countries, while his younger brother Dorian was a youth player at Real Madrid.

David joined Barcelona's La Masia in 2006 at the age of 12. By the time of our game at Tottenham Babunski was 18, and at the end of the season gained promotion to the Barça B squad. UEFA's website described him as 'a playmaker with eye-catching technical skills, vision and a killer pass'. UEFA also mentioned that Babunski was nicknamed 'The Philosopher' because of his interest in the subject which caused him to claim, 'Philosophy is the only path to achieve all the goals in life.'[51] The website goal.com once speculated whether Babunski was 'the world's most intelligent footballer' after discovering he was reading a book about neuroscience[52]. However, despite around 50 appearances for Barça B and following his father by becoming a full Macedonian international, Babunski never made it into the Barça first team and was transferred to Red Star Belgrade at the end of January 2016, before later playing in Japan and Romania.

Had I been aware of Babunski's interest in philosophy, I might have gone all existential and asked him if the

---

50 'David Babunski for *Informer*: I am proud to be the grandson of the Chetnik Duke!' informer.rs.

51 uefa.com.

52 goal.com.

'pins' he gave me really were pins or whether they merely appeared to be so and were actually something else. However, all I managed to say was 'thanks' before opening the packet to find some metal pin badges, each of them about 13mm across. Despite their tiny size, the badges Babunski distributed contained all the details of Barça's crest and colours, both of which will be examined here.

Firstly, the club's badge. For the first few years after its formation in 1899, FC Barcelona used a version of the city's coat of arms as its emblem. This included a diamond shape containing Catalonia's Senyera (literally 'flag') made up of four red horizontal stripes on a yellow background, one of the oldest flags in Europe. The coat of arms also contained a red cross on a white background, sign of the local patron saint Sant Jordi (St George), surrounded by branches, topped by a crown and a bat. The bat was a heraldic symbol of the Crown of Aragon (which used to rule parts of eastern Spain including Catalonia) and remained on Barcelona's coat of arms until it was removed in the early 20th century.

In 1910 it was decided to design a badge, unique to the football club. Barça's official centenary book, *Barça: Centenario de Emociones*, says that after much arguing over the design someone 'settled the matter by saying, "If this is a loony bin, the best thing is for our club shield to be shaped like a bin." And that is how the current design, that has been maintained and has spread with outstanding success for almost a century, came into being.'[53]

---

53 Vilagut, M. (ed.), *Barça: Centenario de Emociones* (Barcelona: FC Barcelona, 1999), p280.

The chosen design was one by Santiago Femenia, a medical student who played for the club (FCB wouldn't turn professional until the 1920s). The 'bin' design he produced consisted of Sant Jordi's red cross on a white background in the top left; the Catalan Senyera in the top right; the club's initials 'FCB' below this; then a lower portion made up of three dark red vertical stripes surrounded by four blue ones with a football in the middle. This has remained the basic design throughout the club's history, with occasional alterations such as different colours (white, yellow or black) for the central bar where the letters are positioned.

However, bigger changes came after Franco's rise to power, with the dictator opposing Catalanismo ('Catalanism') and separatism. In 1941 his regime ordered the removal of the Senyera from the top-right corner of the club's badge, to be replaced by two red bars and three yellow ones looking more like the Spanish flag. However, the Senyera was restored to the badge in 1949 to mark the club's 50th anniversary. The club was also forcibly renamed from 'Futbol Club Barcelona' to the Castilian title 'Club de Fútbol Barcelona', which meant the badge letters were changed to 'C de FB' from 1941 until 1974.

In 2002 the dots between the letters 'FCB' were removed to supposedly modernise the crest. In 2018 a revised design appeared that proposed removing the letters 'FCB' from the badge altogether and reducing the number of blue and dark red stripes. Club members stood up for the club's history and traditions and rebelled against this 'simplifying' or 'tidying up' exercise, causing the changes to be scrapped, or should we say binned.

Far less clear is the history of Barça's famous *blaugrana* colours. Two weeks after Barça was founded in 1899 it selected *blaugrana* for the players' shirts. 'Blau' easily translates as 'blue', but 'grana' is variously described as 'maroon', 'claret', 'grenadine', or even 'carmine'. However, in this book I have generally called it dark red. The reason for the choice of *blaugrana* is uncertain, with several theories to explain it.

One theory is that the colours were suggested by the mother of Carles Comamala, who played for the club. However, Comamala didn't make his debut until 1903, so that probably isn't true. Another possibility is that the colours were chosen to copy those of the Barcelona Lawn Tennis Club, which had just been formed. A third suggestion is that the colours originated from France following the revolution of 1789, an idea mentioned in the match programme for the 2011 Champions League Final and in Phil Ball's book about Spanish football, *Morbo*[54].

Even FC Barcelona has come up with at least four different explanations over the years. In 1999 the official publication, *Barça: Centenario de Emociones*, argued that Joan Gamper chose blue and red because they were the colours of the Swiss canton where he originated[55]. Ten

---

54 Ball, P., *Morbo: The Story of Spanish Football* (London: WSC, 2003), p106.

55 Vilagut, M. (ed.), *Barça: Centenario de Emociones* (Barcelona: FC Barcelona, 1999), p280.

years later another official club publication, *Universal Barça*, put forward a different view that Gamper selected the colours to copy FC Basel[56]. However, Gamper is said to have been closer to other Swiss clubs such as FC Zürich or Excelsior than to Basel, so that idea might also be false. A third official club publication, Guillem Balagué's more recent *Barça: The Illustrated History of FC Barcelona* from 2014, adds to the mystery mentioning the strange idea that the scheme came from the blue and red pencils used by accountants[57]. More recently the club's official website promoted yet another possibility, saying the club now believed its colours originated from the Merchant Taylors School in Liverpool[58]. Two brothers, Arthur and Ernest Witty, were educated at that school, and participated in FC Barcelona during its early years. This theory had been promoted by Jimmy Burns in his 1999 book *Barça: A People's Passion*, which quoted a letter from the school's headmaster as evidence[59].

Whether the club's colours were chosen because of a player's mum, a tennis club, the French Revolution, other football clubs, Swiss cantons, an accountant's pencils or an English public school, we do know that the whole football kit was not fully developed at the start. Initially, the shirt had blue and dark red halves, with the famous stripes not appearing until 1910. The players' shorts were originally

---

56 Finestres, J., *Universal Barça* (Barcelona: Angle Editorial, 2009), p48.

57 Balagué, G., *Barça: The Illustrated History of FC Barcelona* (London: Carlton, 2014), p13.

58 fcbarcelona.com.

59 Burns, J., *Barça: A People's Passion* (London: Bloomsbury, 1999), p78.

white before becoming black in the 1910s, then blue in the 1920s, while the socks were black until changing to blue (sometimes blue and dark red) from 1920. In other words it took 20 years for the club to adopt its classic kit of blue-and-dark-red-striped shirts, blue shorts and socks. After that, the kit remained more or less the same, with minor variations such as differing stripe width, until manufacturers started introducing regular alterations for commercial reasons.

In 1981 Meyba became the first company contracted to produce Barça kits. Meyba is a sportswear company from Barcelona formed by two men, José Mestre and Joaquín Ballbé, who took the first two letters of their surnames to create the name of their company, 'Me-y-Ba' ('Me and Ba'). Established in the 1940s, Meyba started with swimwear and then expanded into manufacturing other sports clothing, before securing the Barça contract and then also supplying other La Liga teams[60]. This was around the time that football kits changed from cotton to man-made fibres, but otherwise Meyba stuck closely to the traditional design of the kit, with the addition of its curly 'M' logo opposite the club's badge on the front, and a zigzag pattern running down the edge of the blue sleeves replacing the older broad dark red stripe. Meyba produced Barcelona's yellow away shirt for the first game in this book, the 1983 Super Cup, and also the change kit for the second match, the 1992 European Cup Final, which was mainly orange with *blaugrana* stripes on the

60 meyba.com.

sleeves, a glorious and truly iconic kit befitting the most famous day in the club's history.

However, after Wembley the Italian sportswear company Kappa took over. The first Kappa Barcelona shirt was highly controversial because it included a white stripe running down the edge of the sleeve, with about a dozen images of the company's logo featuring a man and a woman sitting back-to-back. It wasn't the silhouette of the woman's breasts that was controversial, but the use of white, the colour of bitter rival Real Madrid. Those Barça fans who objected to white didn't have history on their side because the club had played in white shorts in its early years, and had used an all-white away shirt as recently as 1979. Personally, I loved the first Kappa kit; after all, white didn't bother me because it was Leeds United's colour, and it was the one Barça wore on my first match at Camp Nou in 1992.

However, after that Kappa's kits, in my opinion, went downhill with a series of increasingly garish designs, culminating in the company's horrible final Barça shirt for 1997/98. Having ridden the crest of the wave with the fashion for wearing sportswear in the 1990s, which included pop star Sporty Spice regularly seen in Kappa gear, the brand then suffered a potentially fatal blow when Matt Lucas appeared in a bright pink Kappa tracksuit acting the part of Vicky Pollard, an obnoxious chav teenager from Bristol, in the BBC television comedy programme *Little Britain* in 2003.

Barça had avoided any association with Ms Pollard by replacing Kappa with Nike five years earlier. The

American sports giant's first Barcelona shirt in 1998/99 appeared for the club's centenary season, reviving 1899's blue and dark red halves instead of the usual stripes. Since then Nike has continued to manufacture Barcelona's shirts, some stylish and faithful to traditional designs, some (such as 2015's hoops and the Croatian pattern from 2019) less so. The names of sponsors also appeared on the front of the shirts from 2006 onwards, as previously mentioned. In 2018 Barcelona started a ten-year deal with Nike, one of the most lucrative kit deals in the history of football, earning the club a whopping €155m per year.

In 2020 Barça discovered that the latest version of the famous *blaugrana* colours bled when wet and its replica shirts had to be withdrawn from sale, costing a considerable sum in lost merchandising revenue[61]. Philosophers like Babunski might have reacted to the bleeding by exploring the metaphysical issues raised, such as whether colours are part of a mind-independent reality and if theoretical problems about colour are fundamentally conceptual or empirical.

---

61 'What Barcelona's bleeding shirts tell us about the pandemic': ft.com.

12

Careless Hands

IN THE 2012/13 season, Barça won La Liga with a record-equalling 100 points, only to fail spectacularly in the Champions League. After topping a group containing Celtic, Benfica and Spartak Moscow, warnings signs came in the first leg of the round of 16 when Barça was defeated 2-0 in Milan, although this was overturned by a 4-0 triumph at Camp Nou. Paris Saint-Germain was defeated in the quarter-final on away goals, setting up a semi against Bayern Munich. After a spell out through injury, Lionel Messi was selected for the first leg in Bavaria. Despite completing the 90 minutes, Messi was clearly not fit and unable to play to his normal standard. Worse still, his side lost 4-0. Still injured, Messi was not selected for the second leg at Camp Nou, when Bayern scored three times without reply to win the tie by an astonishing 7-0 aggregate. The defeat to Bayern was an extreme example of what was called *Messidependencia*, a dependence, or excessive reliance on the Argentine player.

In the summer Tito Vilanova resigned as coach after cancer that he had been suffering from returned. It would sadly be the cause of his death in April the following year. Tito was replaced by Argentine coach Gerardo Martino, and in an attempt to deal with *Messidependencia*, Brazilian superstar Neymar was signed. Neymar's transfer was reported by FC Barcelona to be €57m. However, a Barça club member challenged the accuracy of this figure, claiming that the real amount paid was considerably higher and asking questions about what happened to the extra money. Barça's president Sandro Rossell later resigned in January 2015 after a Spanish court decided to investigate the allegations.

In the 2013/14 Champions League Barça once again topped its group, this time containing Milan, Ajax and Celtic. In the first knockout round the club was drawn against Manchester City, but work commitments meant that I couldn't make the tie at the Etihad Stadium. Barça progressed but was then eliminated by Atlético Madrid in the quarter-final. Atlético also won La Liga, denying Barça on the final day of the league season, an outcome that led to the departure of Martino.

For 2014/15, Barça's new coach was Luis Enrique, the player who had scored that breakaway goal against Arsenal in the Champions League group match at Wembley back in 1999. Other new arrivals included Uruguayan striker Luis Suárez from Liverpool, Croatian midfielder Ivan Rakitić from Sevilla, and two goalkeepers to replace the departing Víctor Valdés, the Chilean Claudio Bravo and the young German Marc-

André ter Stegen. It was decided to field Bravo in La Liga matches, while ter Stegen would feature in the Copa del Rey and Champions League.

Barça once again topped its Champions League group, ahead of Paris Saint-Germain, Ajax and APOEL of Cyprus. The first knockout round saw a return to Manchester City, but for the second year running I wasn't able to get time off work to attend the game. However, after Barça overcame City, I got lucky in the quarter-final draw when the club was paired with PSG on Wednesday, 15 April 2015 and I managed to squeeze in a quick trip to the first leg at the Parc des Princes between work commitments.

Face-value tickets for the game were extortionate, costing me €200 through the official PSG website, although I later discovered that they were being sold on the black market for much more shortly before the game. The Eurostar train was scheduled to get into Paris at about 7pm local time, providing an hour and three-quarters to get to the stadium for kick-off at 8.45pm. It would be okay as long as the train was on time. Frustratingly, 20 minutes into the journey my Eurostar stopped somewhere in Kent and the driver announced that his train had developed a fault and he didn't know what it was. I started to think that my expensive train and match tickets had not been very sound investments. Luckily, without any explanation from the driver, the train eventually restarted and reached its destination. After hopping on a Métro at the Gare du Nord, I made it to the Parc des Princes with only a couple of minutes to spare.

My seat was high up in the top tier near the corner and provided a superb view of the action. By the corner had been a good choice, because those behind the goal were a long way from the pitch. Also, the away fans at the other end had to put up with a dirty opaque screen obscuring their view, as *penya* members who had been in that part of the stadium before warned me. The stadium was full, with 45,713 fans inside and the atmosphere was expectant. PSG had spent heavily building its squad, was unbeaten in 33 home European ties and already defeated Barça 3-2 in that season's group stage.

Barça appeared wearing a fluorescent lime-coloured strip, lining up in a 4-3-3 of ter Stegen in goal; Martín Montoya, Piqué, Mascherano and Jordi Alba in defence; Busquets, Iniesta and Rakitić in midfield; with the attacking trio of 'MSN' (Messi, Suárez and Neymar) up front. This was a full-strength team, with the exception of Montoya replacing Alves at right-back.

PSG was coached by former Barcelona player Laurent Blanc. The Frenchman had been at Camp Nou for just one season, 1996/97, but missed Barça's victory over PSG in that season's Cup Winners' Cup Final through injury. At the Parc des Princes Blanc's team wore a dark blue kit, arranged in a 4-3-3 formation, with a couple of enforced changes. David Luiz was on the bench having sustained a hamstring injury only ten days earlier, while Marco Verratti and Zlatan Ibrahimović were both suspended. However, the Swede's friend Maxwell, who I had seen in a Barça shirt away to Arsenal a few years earlier, featured at left-back.

In the first half Barça attacked the goal to my right, and for much of the game played with just two defenders, Piqué and Mascherano, because the full-backs, Montoya and Alba, occupied advanced positions. After 18 minutes, a quick break saw Iniesta play the ball from the left to Messi running in a central position. He passed to Neymar, who steadied the ball and then hit a right-footed shot past goalkeeper Salvatore Sirigu. Despite the very warm and humid weather, the keeper had strangely opted for lurid green tights matching the colour of the shorts he wore over them. Soon after the opening goal, Thiago Silva had to go off with an injury and was replaced by Luiz, a change that proved to be very significant as Luiz was clearly unfit.

The best of the action came in the second half, at my end. Following a tackle by Javier Pastore, Iniesta was stretchered off and replaced by Xavi. PSG came more into the game and could have scored from a couple of shots which were both saved by ter Stegen. However, when the next goal came it was for Barça. After 67 minutes Montoya attacked down the right, supplying Suárez who put the ball between Luiz's legs, then followed this nutmeg by beating Marquinhos and Maxwell, before hitting a shot that went in by the near post. A quarter of an hour before the end Barça replaced Rakitić with Jérémy Mathieu, and five minutes later scored a third. Concluding a move involving ten passes, Suárez nutmegged Luiz for the second time in the match before curling a superb shot into the top-right corner of the goal. Film footage after both of Suárez's goals shows a miserable-looking Luiz probably wishing he'd stayed on the bench. Immediately after the third goal, Montoya was replaced by Adriano. PSG got a goal back soon after the change when a shot from Gregory van der Wiel was deflected in off the left foot of Mathieu.

The 3-1 final score was PSG's first defeat on home soil in European competition for nine years. Although I had seen plenty of the new Barça on TV, this was my first sight of the team live, post-Pep. Luis Enrique's side played a slightly different style, still with more possession of the ball, but not as much as it once enjoyed. When Barça did have the ball the playing style was slightly more direct, partly because of the replacement of the ageing Xavi by Rakitić. The Croat's passing wasn't as accurate as Xavi's and he played more forward balls, even at the risk of losing possession. Also, Barça didn't press to win the ball back as quickly or as high up the pitch as they used to (conceding possession more would make this too tiring).

In addition, Messi no longer played as a 'false nine'; instead he was back out on the right of the attack, with Neymar on the left and Suárez in the centre, as part of Barça's attacking trident. Messi was famous for his dribbling skills, but the addition of Neymar meant that the new MSN attack tended to dribble with the ball more; previously there was greater emphasis on passing and movement.

I stayed that night with Faisal in the suburbs of Paris, and after returning home saw that someone had posted an image on Facebook of David Luiz's head and torso superimposed on a picture of the Eiffel Tower with its legs apart, mocking the double nutmegging he received from Suárez. A week later Barcelona beat PSG 2-0 at the Camp Nou in the second leg to progress 5-1 on aggregate.

For the semi-final, Barça was drawn against Bayern Munich, while Juventus was paired with Real Madrid. This raised the possibility of the first *clásico* Champions League Final, but before that the two clubs would have to overcome the German and Italian champions respectively.

In the semi-final first legs Real Madrid lost 2-1 to Juventus in Turin, while the next day Barça beat Bayern Munich (now coached by Guardiola) 3-0 at Camp Nou. The second legs took place a week later. This time Barcelona played first, and despite losing 3-2 in Bavaria still qualified for the final, 5-3 on aggregate. With Barcelona's place in the final secured, I was now hoping Real Madrid would get a result against Juventus the following evening. Having scored an away goal in Italy, a 1-0 win would be enough for the Spanish side. Things were going to plan after Cristiano Ronaldo scored a first half penalty. However, with just over half an hour left, former Real Madrid player Álvaro Morata scored to secure Juve's place in the final. It was to be the closest I have got to my wish of attending a *clásico* Champions League Final.

Since 2010, all Champions League finals had been held on Saturdays, so Josie and I booked flights to arrive in Berlin on the Wednesday before the game. People sometimes ask which was my favourite Champions League Final trip? It's difficult to give a definite answer, but Berlin has to be up there, with so much to see and do. We stayed for a week, travelling around what was the old East Germany, visiting stunning modern architecture at Magdeburg, a Napoleonic battlefield near Leipzig, the home of a famous composer in Halle, and the birthplace of the Reformation at Wittenburg. On the days we stayed in Berlin we explored some of the places connected to Berlin's recent past, including the fascinating Stasi Museum, located in the original headquarters of the notorious East German secret police.

On the eve of the game we went to the opera to see a production of *La Traviata* (*The Fallen Woman*) at the Schiller Theatre. This Italian opera by Giuseppe Verdi tells the story of Violetta, a famous courtesan, meaning she may have been a prostitute and because of her fame, quite possibly an older one. Juventus is known as 'la Vecchia Signora' ('the Old Lady'), but the club has other nicknames including 'La Madama' ('the Madam'). In English, the word 'madam' has many meanings, one of which is a female procurer of prostitutes. In the opera Violetta suffers ill health and eventually dies. When in Rome six years earlier, we saw an opera called *Pagliacci* (*Clowns*) which could have described Manchester United's defending in that final. The question now was would Violetta's demise be a bad omen for the old Italian madam the following evening?

On the day of the game, Saturday, 6 June 2015, we visited the Champions Festival which UEFA had located in the centre of the city by the Brandenburg Gate. Constructed towards the end of the 18th century in a grand neoclassical style, the gate is an iconic symbol not only of Berlin but of Germany as a whole, featuring in key moments during the country's history. After Hitler came to power in 1933 Nazi stormtroopers paraded through the gate, while after the end of the Second World War long columns of defeated German soldiers marched through it on the way to captivity. In the post-war period when Berlin was divided into zones, the gate was a few yards inside communist East Germany with the infamous Berlin Wall erected immediately in front of it. In 1989 protestors chose the section of the wall right by the Brandenburg Gate as the place to start dismantling it and cross over. When I first visited Berlin in 2002 the gate was completely covered by scaffolding while it underwent restoration, but by 2015 this process had been completed, so representing the reunification and renewal of the country.

For the Champions League Final the Brandenburg Gate featured prominently in the official logo, which included a picture of the trophy standing on the Olympic Stadium with the gate in front. Some parts of the Champions Festival, such as the trophy, were located on the western side of the Brandenburg Gate, but most, including the mini pitch, were on the eastern side, down the famous avenue Unter den Linden (Under the Lime Trees).

After leaving the festival it was time to head down to Bahnhof Zoo (Zoo Station) near where the Barça Fan Zone was located (the Juventus Fan Zone was on the eastern side of the city by Alexanderplatz). Bahnhof

Zoo was named after the railway station that served the nearby zoo, and when Berlin was divided into western and eastern zones it became the main station for West Berlin. However, following reunification that role was eventually taken over by the new Berlin Hauptbahnhof. For music fans, Zoo Station is best known for the 1981 film *Christiane F. – Wir Kinder vom Bahnhof Zoo* (*Christiane F. – We the children from Zoo Station*). Set in the area around Zoo Station at the time it was made, the film told the harrowing story of some teenagers in West Berlin who got involved in drugs and prostitution. David Bowie starred, playing the part of himself as a rock star and also providing the soundtrack. One of the first scenes in the film is when the main characters, a German girl and her boyfriend, carry out a robbery in Zoo Station, then run away with the song 'Heroes' booming in the background.

On matchday, the area outside Zoo Station temporarily became a mini enclave of Catalonia, with thousands of fans in Barça replica shirts gathered by one of Berlin's most famous sights, the Kaiser-Wilhelm-Gedächtniskirch (Kaiser Wilhelm Memorial Church). Built in the 1890s, the church was bombed in 1943 and deliberately left with its badly damaged tower standing as a memorial to the horrors of war. When we were there it was a lovely summer's day, with hundreds of fans from Spain joined by others from different countries, all enjoying a drink and looking forward to the game that evening. It was hard to think that 70 years earlier much of Europe was, like the church in the centre of the frivolity, a bombed-out ruin, and the young men of Europe were fighting instead of enjoying a beer.

We managed to meet up with a few of the PBL members who made the trip, including Eduard, Cesar, Nicky and Jason. The atmosphere was pleasant except for one incident when a young male, aged about 20, decided to walk right through the middle of the crowd of Barça fans wearing a Real Madrid shirt. A few words of abuse were hurled at him, followed by beer bottles, before he managed to get away. Although violence like this cannot be justified, his action was certainly unwise. I didn't discover whether he was a provocateur, a naive tourist, a student doing it for a bet, or just an idiot.

After sampling the Fan Zone, it was time to head down to the Olympiastadion (Olympic Stadium), the venue for the final. Built for the 1936 Olympics, which will always be remembered for taking place during the Third Reich, the stadium and the surrounding complex (originally called the Reichssportfeld) are located in the west of Berlin and full of history. Adolf Hitler is said to have had a direct input into the stadium's design, insisting on the use of natural stone in its construction, over-ruling the architect (Werner March) who wanted concrete. The complex is remarkably preserved, including the adjacent Maifeld (May Field) once used for Nazi parades and two towers which still have the five Olympic rings mounted on them[62]. The main Olympic Stadium hosted athletics events during the 1936 Games

---

62 Rodiger, U. A., *The Olympic Stadium in Berlin: From the German Stadium to the Reichssportfeld* (Berlin: Rodiger Verlag 1999).

and is famous for being the scene of the success of the black American athlete, Jesse Owens, who won four gold medals, smashing Nazi theories of racial superiority. Owens won the 100m final in 10.3 seconds, prompting Hitler to leave the stadium nearly as quickly to avoid having to shake his hand[63].

Only slightly damaged by Second World War bombs, the Olympic Stadium found itself located in the British sector of West Berlin during the Cold War. The complex also included smaller venues constructed for other Olympic sports, such as an impressive swimming pool. Most of these survived, although some underwent changes of use – the British military turned the exercise academy into its headquarters and the tennis courts into a children's playground. One part that did survive untouched was the hockey stadium, which my wife was particularly interested to see having played in it during the mid-1970s. Being the daughter of a liaison officer of the British Army of the Rhine, she had attended an army school in Hohne and travelled 275km eastwards to play another BAOR school team based in Berlin. During the journey she remembered being ordered to pull the blinds down on the train while passing through the communist DDR, then peeping through them to see East German soldiers at the border followed by Soviet tanks on arrival in Berlin.

The main stadium was originally constructed as an open bowl, made up of two tiers. Two roofs were

---

63 'Ten seconds that defied Hitler': bbc.co.uk.

added along the sides for the 1974 World Cup, when the tournament was held in Germany and the stadium hosted three games. Prior to the World Cup returning to Germany in 2006 the stadium underwent further changes, including extending the lower tiers downwards by sinking the pitch to increase capacity and building a roof going all the way round the stadium, except for a narrow gap at the west end. That gap is important, because it enables the stadium to keep much of its original shape and maintain the view of the Maifeld. Originally an athletics stadium, it retained its running track surrounding the pitch, which meant that those sitting behind the goals were some distance from the action. The stadium now had a capacity of 74,500, and with each finalist only getting 20,000 tickets our only way of getting to see the game had been by ordering two of UEFA's hospitality packages.

We left early to get to the Olympic Stadium, which was just as well because the entry to the stadium was chaotic. We followed UEFA's instructions accompanying our tickets and went to the south entrance. The tickets also said that our part of the stadium would open at 5.45pm, but at nearly 6.30pm we were still standing in the boiling hot weather, waiting for the turnstiles to open. When they did finally open a steward told us that we were in the wrong section and suggested that we push through all the Juventus fans massing behind us to go along to another entrance. At that point my wife exploded and started shouting at the steward, 'Unsere Karte sagen, wir sollten durch den Südeingang kommen. Also sind wir hier. Wir können nicht an all diesen Leuten vorbeikommen. Sie müssen uns durch dieses Tor hereinlassen!'

Translated, this meant, 'Our tickets said we should come through the south entrance. So here we are. We can't push past all these people. You have to let us in through this gate!'

The steward had heard us talking in English and was surprised to find someone yelling in German amid this sea of black and white Juve shirts, so they let us through. I later joked that the last person to scream so aggressively in German at this stadium ended up in a bunker at the other end of town.

Luckily the game didn't kick off until quarter to nine, so there was still time to enjoy the refreshments in the hospitality area, tucked underneath the grandstand, although there was no German equivalent of John Inverdale to entertain us this time. We eventually took our seats in block M1, on the northern side of the stadium, in row 39 towards the back of the lower tier of the Gegentribune. We were near the corner with the Juve fans massed in the Westkurve, while the Barça fans were in the Ostkurve, the home end of Hertha Berlin, the Bundesliga club that uses the stadium.

The opening ceremony was the usual bizarre pageant, for which the pitch was covered in blue with the Champions League logo in the middle. Dozens of people began running round it in circles before stopping to make meaningless shapes and patterns. Dancers in weird costumes performed against a soundtrack of prerecorded music, a lot of which was moronic noise unrelated to Germany, football, or indeed anything in particular.

Immediately after the opening ceremony the two teams entered the arena, emerging from the tunnel on the opposite side to where we were sitting. The Juve fans held up black and white cards to create a mosaic image just before kick-off. At the time I couldn't see what the mosaic looked like, but watching a film later it appeared to be two huge outstretched hands. I don't know whether this symbol referred to the *Calciopoli* match-fixing scandal, which resulted in Juventus being demoted to the lower divisions a decade before. Some of the cards then fell down on top of us from the tier above, a case of careless hands. At the other end of the stadium the Barça fans held up blue, red and yellow cards to create a mosaic containing the club motto of 'Més que un club' ('More than a club'). At the time, this message appeared to be more wholesome than the Juventus one, but after Barça joined the Turin club and Real Madrid in being the last three remaining members of the European Super League in 2021 things looked less clear.

Soon after the mosaics went up the two teams came out to play the 60th European Cup Final. Both Barça and Juve came to Berlin in search of a treble, having already secured their domestic league and cup titles. The Barça line-up was a 4-3-3 with almost the same team as at the Parc des Princes, the exception being Alves returning in place of Montoya. Only six of the starting 11 had survived from Wembley 2011: Alves, Piqué, Mascherano, Busquets, Iniesta and Messi.

The Juve formation was a 4-1-2-1-2, with Gianluigi Buffon in goal; Patrice Evra (who had played for Manchester United against Barça in the 2009 and 2011 finals), Leonardo Bonucci, Andrea Barzagli and Stephan Lichtsteiner in defence; Andrea Pirlo at the base of a diamond in midfield; Paul Pogba and Claudio Marchisio further forward; Arturo Vidal at the head of the diamond; then Morata and Tevez up front. This was the usual Juve line-up, with the exception of Barzagli replacing Georgio Chiellini who had suffered a late injury, meaning he wouldn't have to face Suárez, the player who had been suspended for biting him at the previous year's World Cup in Brazil, when Uruguay played Italy.

As was becoming customary, Barça began a final sloppily, giving the ball away in the opening seconds, but then managed to control possession and went ahead in the team's first attack in the fourth minute. A move involving 15 passes and nine players ended with Iniesta feeding the ball through to Rakitić who shot home with his left foot from ten yards. We had an excellent view of the goal, scored at our end.

After 13 minutes Suárez crossed from the right to Alves who hit a shot from just inside the penalty area, forcing a great save by Buffon. Then, just before half-time, Messi went on one of his trademark slaloming runs, beating several defenders before eventually being crowded out. The first half ended with Barça on top but you had the feeling that the team would need a second goal with Juventus likely to score at some point.

Three minutes after the restart, Barça launched a rapid counter-attack with five players against three. Rakitić passed to Suárez on his right, but Buffon pulled off another save. The miss looked like it would prove costly because five minutes later Juve did score. Lichtsteiner crossed the ball from the right, Tevez hit an excellent shot on the turn which ter Stegen saved, but instead of catching or pushing the ball wide he merely knocked it back into the path of Morata, who had an easy finish from close range. It was another case of careless hands. Morata, a former Real Madrid player, then came over to our corner to celebrate in front of the Juve fans.

In my account of the 2011 final I referred to an elderly man and his friend who left the game early as evidence of corporate hospitality enabling people who don't deserve to be at such big games getting tickets. In Berlin there was a much worse example, because sitting in front of us were a group of about eight Brazilians, a mixture of male and female, all wearing that year's Barça replica shirt and clearly very wealthy (flaunting expensive watches, the latest smartphones, jewellery and designer clothing). On a couple of occasions they blocked our view by standing up during the game to take selfies with their back to the pitch. They cheered when Rakitić scored, but after Morata's goal one of their group asked, in all seriousness, 'Shall we support Juventus now?' For these people the Champions League Final is just another date on their calendar, something to be seen at and post pictures on social media. I thought about some of the PBL members who had travelled to Berlin for the final, but failed to get tickets, and felt angry on their behalf. Allocating 34,500 tickets to sponsors, football federations and hospitality, when each finalist only gets 20,000, surely isn't right.

The equaliser came during a good spell for Juventus, and the Italian club could have been awarded a penalty after Alves tangled with Pogba in the area. Pogba went down, but it was debatable as to whether there was enough contact to judge it a foul. From my vantage point it looked like a foul, although when I watched a recording later it wasn't so clear. Most important, of course, was the referee's opinion, and he waved away the penalty appeals. A minute later Barça restored its lead. Messi ran with the ball then shot from the edge of the penalty area. Buffon blocked the effort, but then spilled the ball into the path of Suárez, who smashed in the rebound. It was the final's third case of careless hands.

After 70 minutes Neymar headed a cross into the goal, but it was disallowed for handball. Although Barça was ahead, the game remained very tense because Juventus only needed one goal to take us into extra time. Barça then had another breakaway counter-attack with about five against three but once again failed to press home the advantage.

In the last ten minutes both sides made substitutions; Juve brought on midfielder Roberto Pereyra for future Barça player Vidal, followed by Fernando Llorente for fellow striker Morata, and then another forward, Kingsley Coman, was introduced for Evra. Barça introduced Xavi in place of Iniesta, who was carrying a slight injury, then replaced both scorers, Mathieu for Rakitić and Pedro for Suárez.

In the sixth minute of stoppage time, following a Juve free kick, Barça regained possession and broke rapidly. Neymar played a one-two with new arrival Pedro, before shooting the ball underneath Buffon from an angle with his left foot to make it 3-1. It was the final act in our footballing opera, finally killing off la Vecchia Signora.

This late strike made it an incredible 122 goals for Barça's attacking MSN trident that season. It also meant Barça had won the treble of national league, domestic cup and Champions League. This repeated the treble of 2008/09 and Barça therefore became the first club in history to get a second treble. The club had also had to do it the hard way, by beating the champions of all the major European football countries on the way: Holland (Ajax) in the group stage, England (Manchester City) in the first knockout round, France (PSG) in the quarter-final, Germany (Bayern) in the semi-final, and lastly Italy (Juventus).

The final in Berlin was also notable for being the last appearance for Barcelona of Xavi, a player described by Messi as the best player in the history of Spanish football. At the time of the final Xavi was 35 years old and had already announced that he would be leaving Barcelona at the end of the season to wind down his career in the Middle East. Altogether Xavi won 25 major trophies with the club and set a new record for the number of appearances in its colours. His last act was to mount the small number of steps above the tunnel opposite us and lift the trophy as club captain to the tune of the Champions League anthem followed by 'Cant del Barça'.

The Juve end emptied quickly as the Italian fans headed for the nearby train station to travel into the city centre or to the coach park for the road journey back to Turin. Meanwhile, we returned to the hospitality area and saw the Brazilians who'd sat in front of us. The rich South American tourists were still wearing their Barcelona replica shirts, so I guess they must have decided against changing their allegiance.

The following day I travelled south to Leipzig to see a lower league game and picked up a copy of the local paper, *Leipziger Volkszeitung*, which called Barcelona 'Die beste Mannschaft der Welt' ('The best team in the world')[64]. Back home, *The Guardian* said, 'This Barça perhaps now stand comparison with the Real Madrid team that won the first five European Cups.'[65] Talking of European Cups won, the trophy count was now Real Madrid ten, Milan seven, then Barça on equal third place with five wins alongside Liverpool and Bayern Munich. On a personal level, the Berlin trip meant achieving an ambition of seeing all of Barça's first five European Cup wins live: 1992, 2006, 2009, 2011 and 2015, finally witnessing ten big ears.

---

64 *Leipziger Volkszeitung*, 7 June 2015.
65 *The Guardian*, 8 June 2015.

13

More than a Club

IN NOVEMBER 2015, a few months after Berlin, I attended the 30th anniversary celebrations of the formation of PBL in Barcelona and was photographed holding the Champions League trophy at the dinner. Even though no club had successfully defended it in the Champions League era I expected, like many people, to see that record broken over the next few years. It was, and the victors went on to win the tournament three times in a row, in 2016, 2017 and 2018. Congratulations, Real Madrid.

Before holding the cup with big ears at the dinner, I joined 45 other PBL members at the unveiling of a new *penya* plaque by gate number 96 of Camp Nou. There are loads of plaques around the stadium, many of them with the name and badge of a supporters' club. London's *penya* already had a plaque at Camp Nou, but it needed to be replaced by one with a redesigned badge. The reason for the change was because the new *penya* badge had two stars, one for the win at the old Wembley in 1992 and the other for the victory in the rebuilt stadium in 2011. London is the only city to have hosted two of Barça's five European Cup Final triumphs; Paris, Rome and Berlin having just one each. After the first of these in 1992 the club's vice-president, Joan Gaspart, famously celebrated by jumping into the River Thames. Paris's Seine, the Tiber in Rome and Berlin's Spree cannot make such a claim.

The English capital has many other links to the Barça story, starting with the club's claim that its first win in a continental-wide tournament was the 1958 Inter-Cities Fairs Cup Final, a game played at Chelsea's Stamford Bridge stadium against a London XI. Since then, London has hosted more Barcelona away matches in UEFA competitions than any other European city. Discounting friendlies as well as the Inter-Cities Fairs Cup, which was not an official UEFA competition, but including the European Cup/Champions League, Cup Winners' Cup, UEFA Cup/Europa League and the Super Cup, Barça has visited London on 15 occasions. Only Milan comes close. Another connection is Vic Buckingham, coach of Barcelona from 1969 until 1971, who was born in Greenwich in the south-east of the city. Arguably Buckingham's most important contribution to the history of Barça came earlier in his career, when he gave a first-team debut to a young Johan Cruyff as coach of Ajax Amsterdam in 1964. Another coach with London origins was Terry Venables, who came from Dagenham on the eastern edge of the city, and won Barcelona its first La Liga title for 11 years in 1985. That same year saw the formation of Penya Blaugrana London, Barça's oldest surviving *penya* outside Spain.

On 9 November 2015, three weeks before the *penya* dinner, the Catalan Parliament in Barcelona voted in favour of a 'Declaration of the Initiation of the Process of Independence of Catalonia' from Spain, a decision with important implications for the football club.

Located in the north-east of what is now Spain, Catalonia has a long history. For example, the Senyera is one of the oldest flags in Europe, while for centuries it had its own parliament and legal system. The region was a prosperous one until the discovery of the Americas by Christopher Columbus in 1492 meant that ports on the Atlantic became more important than those on the Mediterranean. After the end of the War of the Spanish Succession, Catalonia was brought under direct rule from Madrid in 1716. Spanish rule also ended the use of the Catalan language in local administration. During the 19th century Catalonia experienced a revival, with the industrial revolution and renewed interest in the region's culture, language and national aspirations, and it was against this background that FC Barcelona was formed in 1899.

The 20th century would prove to be a seesaw, with liberties being granted then withdrawn. This started in 1913 when some political powers were devolved to Catalonia, only to be abolished during the rule of Spanish dictator Primo de Rivera in 1925, who also suppressed the Catalan language and the Senyera. After many Barça fans whistled during the Spanish national anthem at a football match the club's stadium was temporarily closed and Joan Gamper given a lifelong ban from being club president. FC Barcelona's association with *Catalanismo* took off from around that time, and support for Barça became a legal way of expressing support for Catalonia.

The seesaw continued half a dozen years later when Spain became a Republic in 1931 and Catalonia was made an autonomous region with its own Generalitat de Catalunya (Government of Catalonia) led by left-wing politicians. In 1936 the Spanish Civil War started, following a revolt by right-wing nationalist troops led by Franco. Most of Catalonia rallied in support of the Republic, but within a month of the fighting breaking out FC Barcelona's president, Josep Sunyol, a local left-wing politician, was executed by Franco's soldiers and three years later the conflict ended in a victory for the nationalists. As well as introducing a dictatorship, outlawing all opposition and executing or imprisoning many thousands of opponents across Spain, Franco also suppressed Catalonia's regional autonomy and culture. For the dictatorship, the Castilian language was a centralising force, so Catalan was suppressed and banned from official use on things like street signs, publications and names.

Originally called 'Foot-ball Club Barcelona', after the English invention of the sport and the involvement of some Englishmen in the club's formation in 1899, Barça had been given the Catalan name 'Futbol Club Barcelona' in 1906, but soon after coming to power the Francoists ordered this to be changed to the Castilian title, 'Club de Fútbol Barcelona'. A few years later in the 1950s Real Madrid's success in the European Cup led to the club from the capital being viewed by the regime as an effective ambassador of Castilian Spain, contrasting with its view of FC Barcelona which was associated with *Catalanismo*. It was this that turned the rivalry between the two clubs into one of the biggest in world football, prompting Barça's president Narcis de Carreras to coin the phrase 'Més que un club' ('More than a club') in 1968 as an expression of its identity and association with the Catalan nation under Franco.

Some limited use of the Catalan language at the club began in the last years of Franco's rule, but the restoration of the name 'Futbol Club Barcelona' had to wait until 1973, despite efforts to reintroduce it earlier. Further change only happened after Franco's death in 1975 when democracy gradually returned to Spain. The Generalitat was restored and by 1979 Catalonia had received recognition as an autonomous nation within Spain and its Catalan language made a joint official one alongside Castilian.

Incredibly, despite the restoration of the Catalan language, Castilian was still used in live television coverage of FC Barcelona matches until eight years after the dictator's death. According to the official club publication, *Barça: Centenario de Emociones*, 'The first game to be shown live on television with a commentary in Catalan was a match between Barça and Real Madrid broadcast in Catalonia only by TVE, the state-run broadcasting company, in 1983.'[66] This *clásico* was later

---

66 Vilagut, M. (ed.), *Barça: Centenario de Emociones* (Barcelona: FC Barcelona, 1999), p294.

in the year than the European Super Cup, meaning that if the first game in this book against Aston Villa was broadcast live on television the commentary would still have been in Castilian.

The international economic crisis following the 2008 credit crunch boosted nationalist feeling in Catalonia. The region had long been one of the most prosperous parts of Spain, and there was increasing concern about the amount of money it contributed to the rest of the country. The Catalan parliament's vote in November 2015 followed a regional election two months earlier which had been won by pro-separatist parties. In December the Spanish constitutional court ruled that Catalonia's moves towards independence were invalid. The Catalan parliament responded a month later by selecting a supporter of separatism, Carles Puigdemont, as head of its government. In October 2017 Catalan separatists decided to hold a referendum on independence from Spain, which was ruled illegal by Madrid.

Being so closely connected to the region and Catalan identity, FC Barcelona inevitably became involved in the controversy. The Spanish football authorities ordered Barça to play a La Liga fixture against Las Palmas on the same day as the 2017 referendum, leading to the club deciding to play the game behind closed doors, partly for safety reasons and partly as a political gesture. FC Barcelona also issued a statement which, while maintaining neutrality on the issue of whether people should support independence or remain part of Spain, upheld the right of the Catalan people to self-determination and to be free to vote on their future.

Most of those who participated in the referendum supported independence, so the Spanish central government responded by imposing direct rule over Catalonia. Two months later parties supporting independence won a majority in fresh regional elections, and in May 2018 they changed the law so that the separatist leader Puigdemont could be voted Catalan president, even though he had fled Spain to live in exile and avoid arrest. In October 2019 thousands of people demonstrated following a decision of the Spanish Supreme Court to sentence nine separatist leaders to lengthy terms of imprisonment following the failed independence attempt. Although the Spanish government released the nine from prison in June 2021, the wider political conflict was still unresolved at the time of writing.

Although FC Barcelona is associated with *Catalanismo*, in modern times its football teams often have had few players actually from the region. For example, at the first game in this book, the 1983 Super Cup, Barça's starting 11 included only one Catalan (alongside a German and nine from the rest of Spain). By the time of the famous Dream Team in the 1992 European Cup Final this had only grown to two Catalans (with a Dane, a Bulgarian, a Dutchman and six from other parts of Spain). Louis van Gaal was widely criticised for introducing too many Dutch players and undermining the identity of the club, yet his teams sometimes included more Catalans than other coaches' sides had. With Pep Guardiola, a prominent supporter of Catalan independence, as coach, more local players were given opportunities. The famous 'La Masia XI', entirely made up of graduates from the youth academy, that appeared against Levante in 2012 consisted of eight Catalans plus two from other parts of Spain and one from Argentina. However, by the time of the final game in this book at Anfield in 2019 the number of Catalans had dropped to four, with the club preferring to sign expensive outsiders rather than promoting through the youth system.

As well as taking place during an important month in the political history of Catalonia, the visit to Barcelona for the 30th anniversary celebrations of the *penya* provides a good opportunity to talk about the famous Camp Nou stadium and how it, and the club, has changed in recent times.

During Barça's first decade the club played at several locations, then in 1909 opened its own stadium on Carrer Indústria, staying there until 1922 before moving to another at Les Corts. The club's success in the 1950s meant an increasing number of spectators wanted to see its star players, so in 1955 building work started on a new stadium, which was completed two years later. The stadium consisted of a bowl, with two main tiers, three sides uncovered with a roof over just the main stand. The initial capacity was 99,000, then between 1980 and 1982 the stadium was enlarged with the addition of an extra tier accommodating 20,000 more. The refurbishment was done to prepare the stadium for the 1982 World Cup, where it hosted the opening ceremony as well as some other matches.

These days, visitors to the home of FC Barcelona can enjoy the full 'Camp Nou Experience', joining tours which take them into the dressing room, press conference room, tunnel and other parts of the stadium's interior, but when I first went there 30 years ago nothing like that was available; the whole place was practically deserted with no guide to show me around. All I was allowed to do was go among the seats in the main stand, look down at the pitch, gaze up at the other grandstands, visit the museum and pop into the shop. At that time the stadium wasn't even officially called Camp Nou, instead being referred to as 'Estadi FC Barcelona' on the picture postcard of the stadium that I bought. Although 'Camp Nou' (literally 'new field') had been used informally for years, it was only adopted as the title of the stadium as recently as 2000, following a vote by club members.

In the 1990s the stadium still had standing terraced areas, at the very top of both ends and in the section immediately behind the goalmouth in the lower tiers. I stood in the upper tier of the Gol Nord for the big match against Real Madrid in 1998, and it was a scary experience being so high up watching the game through wire fencing standing amid crumbling concrete in a crowd of 120,000. Shortly afterwards the stadium became all-seater, with a capacity of 'only' 99,000.

The growth of FC Barcelona as a global sporting institution is most clearly demonstrated by the museum and the shop. What was originally called 'Museu FC

Barcelona' was established in 1984. Seven years later, on my first trip to Camp Nou, I visited the museum, which I remember as modestly proportioned with only a handful of visitors viewing its artefacts. A year later, in 1992, the museum was enlarged and in 2010 I returned to what had been rebranded as 'El Museo del Barça'. In contrast to the earlier visit, the museum was now very crowded and by then attracted more than a million visitors per year, making it even more popular than the city's Picasso museum.

The only official club shop open at Camp Nou in 1991 was a tiny kiosk, staffed by a solitary woman. Its range of merchandise was limited to a few replicas of the current home shirt, a couple of scarves and caps, plus the odd pennant, but little else. Even the unofficial stalls which lined the road outside offered a better selection. Later in the 1990s the club opened a megastore at Camp Nou, which in 2003 became 'FCBotiga' ('FCShop'). I visited the new store in 2015, during the weekend of the *penya* dinner, to find 2,000 square metres of retail space, spread over several levels. It was packed with hundreds of customers, served by what I estimated to have been about 25 staff. The store sold around 3,000 different official FCB products which ranged from bags and blankets, hats and hoodies, shirts and scarves, to watches and wallets. The megastore serves about 5,500 customers per day.

Commercial interests caused Barça to adapt its motto, 'Més que un club', to promote the megastore in the form of the slogan 'FCBotiga: más que una tiend' ('FCBotiga:

more than a shop')[67]. The transformation of FC Barcelona into a massive global business brand over the four decades covered by this book is summed up by this slogan.

---

67 fcbarcelona.com.

14

Date with Destiny

ON THE Sunday morning after the *penya* dinner I joined a handful of other PBL members at a Barça B fixture in the Mini Estadi. It was much colder than for the first team match the previous day, so overcoats were required. Whereas 74,000 had watched Saturday's La Liga game against Real Sociedad in the adjacent main Camp Nou stadium, only a few hundred attended the second-tier fixture, which Barça B lost 2-1 to Mallorcan side Atlético Baleares. After the game I headed toward the seaside neighbourhood of Barceloneta for a late lunch, walking by the old La Masia building on the way.

Literally meaning 'the farmhouse', La Masia had provided accommodation for youth academy players from 1979 until it moved to modern premises in the west of the city a month after one of the club's finest hours, the 2011 Champions League triumph. Shortly after the move, the Barça first team fielded an entire team of youth academy graduates, dubbed 'La Masia XI'. When I walked past, the old building still looked well-maintained with neatly cut grass, but was deserted and the famous training pitches empty. Sadly, La Masia XI proved to be the high-water mark of the youth academy, and none of the Barça B side I had just seen lose in a cold and empty stadium were to establish themselves in the first team. As the great Guardiola side gradually aged, the club resorted to bringing in expensive signings to replace its stars, rather than promoting from within. It was the start of the road to ruin.

A few months after the *penya* dinner, Barça drew Arsenal in the first knockout round of the 2015/16 Champions League after topping a group consisting of Roma, Bayer Leverkusen and BATE Borisov. The opening leg away was at the Emirates on Tuesday, 23 February 2016. This time I didn't have to go down the tout route as PBL received a decent allocation for the game, providing me with a ticket in the Clock End, the same end as for the 2010 game but this time in the lower tier by the corner, in the area reserved for visiting supporters. Once again everybody stood up because sitting down in the lower tier provided such a poor view.

Barça arrived at the Emirates top of La Liga, while Arsenal was third in the Premier League, just two points behind surprise leader and eventual winner Leicester City. Barça's team and formation was exactly the same as in Berlin, but this time the players wore a light blue away kit. Barça attacked the other end in the first half and had the usual majority of possession but failed to make it count, so at half-time it was goalless. In the second half Arsenal started to get into the match more, but Barça then struck with a rapid counter-attack, a trademark of Luis Enrique's team, after 71 minutes. The move began deep in the Barça half after an Arsenal move broke down and the ball then came to Neymar, who played a brilliant one-two with Suárez down the left. When Neymar received the ball back he ran with devastating pace, before delivering a perfect pass to Messi who finished expertly past Petr Čech, silencing the majority of the 59,889 crowd. Eight minutes from time, Mathieu Flamini came on as a substitute for Arsenal and managed to give away a penalty after fouling Messi in the box within seconds of coming on. Messi converted his penalty after sending Čech the wrong way. Suárez later hit the post, but a 2-0 score and a couple of away goals was a great result.

A 3-1 victory at Camp Nou in the second leg sent Barça through 5-1 on aggregate to face Atlético Madrid in the quarter-final. Although Barça won 2-1 at home, a 2-0 defeat away at the Estadio Vicente Calderón sent Barça crashing out on aggregate.

The following campaign, 2016/17, saw Barça top a Champions League group containing Manchester City, Borussia Mönchengladbach and Celtic. Unfortunately, work commitments meant I wasn't able to travel up north to see the game against Manchester City (now coached by Pep Guardiola). In the first knockout round Barça was thrashed 4-0 away at PSG, but pulled off one of the greatest comebacks in the history of the tournament, winning the second leg 6-1. The final that year was in Cardiff and easily reached from London, so after the miraculous recovery against PSG I began to think that

Barça's name was on the cup. Think again. In the quarter-final Juventus defeated Barça 3-0 in Turin, only this time there was no coming back and a scoreless draw at Camp Nou eliminated Barça and gave la Vecchia Signora revenge for Berlin.

At the end of the season Luis Enrique departed after three campaigns in charge, to be replaced by another Spanish coach, Ernesto Valverde. Another one to go was Neymar who left for Paris Saint-Germain in a €220m deal, which more than doubled the world transfer record and still remains the highest fee ever paid. The money offered by the French club's Middle Eastern owners proved too tempting.

In the 2017/18 Champions League Barça recorded four wins and two draws to finish first in a group containing Sporting Lisbon, Olympiakos and the previous season's opponent, Juventus. This time the draw for the first knockout round selected Chelsea, with the first leg at Stamford Bridge on Tuesday, 20 February 2018. I managed to get a face-value ticket in the top tier of the East Stand, the place where I had watched the two clubs back in 2000. Going into the game Barça was top of La Liga, while Chelsea, despite being reigning Premier League champion, was merely fourth, a massive 19 points behind runaway leader Manchester City.

That night Barça appeared in a very dark maroon, almost brown, kit with orange trimmings. Notable additions to the team at the Emirates were Sergi Roberto at right-back, Frenchman Samuel Umtiti in central defence, and Brazilian midfielder Paulinho. Antonio

Conte's Chelsea team included three players with Barça connections. The first two of these were Cesc Fàbregas and Pedro, who had joined Chelsea from Barça in 2014 and 2015 respectively. The third was wing-back Marcos Alonso, whose father had played for Barça and been sent off in that Super Cup game against Aston Villa in 1983.

The home side was on top in the opening period with Willian, the game's outstanding performer, hitting the woodwork twice. Conte's team made special efforts to crowd out Messi whenever he got on the ball, doing this so successfully that he only escaped once in the first half when he went on one of his trademark dazzling runs. Barça's only chance of note resulted from a Messi cross on the left which Paulinho headed wide. I wasn't impressed with Paulinho during my only viewing of him, and wasn't surprised to see him replaced by Arturo Vidal, who played in Berlin for Juventus, after 63 minutes.

The substitution came immediately after Chelsea went ahead. Willian got lucky at the third attempt and hit a low shot from just outside the penalty area which curled round the players in front of him and crept past ter Stegen and inside his left post. The Brazilian forward had been allowed far too much space by the visitors' defence. Chelsea looked odds-on to repeat their performance of 2012 and take a 1-0 lead back to Camp Nou, but with quarter of an hour remaining Barça was gifted an equaliser after Andreas Christensen hit a risky sideways pass which was intercepted by Iniesta who quickly passed across to Messi, and he fired a left-footed shot past Thibaut Courtois.

The Barça players celebrated in front of the travelling supporters, congregated in a corner behind that goal. Surprisingly, it was Messi's first goal against Chelsea, having failed to score against the Blues in his previous eight encounters with the London side. A minute from time, Portuguese midfielder André Gomes replaced Iniesta. It was to be my last sight of Iniesta as he left the club at the end of the season to wind down his career in Japan, to be remembered as one of Barcelona's greatest players. Despite having 73 per cent of the possession, a very high amount for an away team, Barça only managed seven shots to Chelsea's 11 and had been lucky to escape with a draw. However, in the second leg Barcelona won 3-0, progressing to the next round courtesy of two goals and an assist from Messi helped by defensive errors from Chelsea.

Roma provided the opposition in the quarter-final with the first leg at Camp Nou ending in a 4-1 victory for Barça. One of those who travelled to watch the second leg in the Italian capital expecting to see a place in the semi-final confirmed was Naheed, a member of the London *penya*.

Naheed flew out from Luton airport with his two sons, Imran and Haroon, all three of them Barça *socis*. They arrived the day before the game in order to have time for sightseeing in the Eternal City on matchday morning, before collecting their match tickets then heading down to the Barça Fan Zone. For Naheed, the Fan Zone is always a highlight of his many trips to see Barça away in European competition, later telling me, 'This is my favourite event before each game, as all the Barça fans meet up together in one place.' Instantly recognisable in his garish orange FCB cap, Naheed is well known to all the regulars at the Fan Zones and has acquired legendary status among the club's travelling support as a result. About this particular Fan Zone, Naheed said, 'We sang the Barça songs, and like all the other *cules* [fans], we were in a happy and joyous mood. Never did any of us *cules* think Roma would come back from being 4-1 down from the first leg.'

After travelling with his sons to the Stadio Olimpico, Naheed then witnessed a new interpretation of the proverb 'See Rome and die'. Barça needed to start well but didn't, conceding a goal scored by Edin Džeko after only six minutes. Both sides had chances, but on this occasion only one took them. In the second half Roma was awarded a penalty which Daniele De Rossi converted to massively increase the pressure on Barça. Throughout the game Roma hit high balls into the box which Barça struggled to deal with. One of these, a corner eight minutes from the end, proved decisive when Kostas Manolas headed in from the near post without any defenders getting tight enough on him. The game ended 3-0 to Roma, 4-4 on aggregate, with Barça eliminated on the away goals rule.

After the game, Naheed said, 'The performance was terrible, Roma deserved the 3-0 win. I was very emotional after the game. Sergi from Barcelona who is a good friend of mine, came over to me, hugged me and said, "This is the life of being a Barça fan." We have to share good and bad times together. As you can imagine the trip back home was very quiet!'

The month ended with Barcelona winning both the Copa del Rey and La Liga to clinch the domestic double in Ernesto Valverde's first season as coach, but the increasing importance of the Champions League meant the collapse in Rome, coupled with Real Madrid's triumph in the Kyiv final, provided a feeling of disappointment.

The 2018/19 Champions League campaign started with Barça drawn in a group comprising Tottenham Hotspur, Inter Milan and PSV Eindhoven, meaning another game in London but at a different stadium. Incredibly, despite nine Champions League matches against Arsenal and 14 against Chelsea in the last 20 years, Barça had never played Spurs in the competition. The only encounters between the two clubs in England were a pre-season friendly in 2009, preceded by a very unfriendly Cup Winners' Cup semi-final in 1982. Like the 2009 fixture, the Champions League group match took place at Wembley, this time because the new Tottenham Hotspur Stadium was still being built.

By now I had moved out of London, so travelled up from the south coast the day before the game to join PBL members and other Barcelona supporters collecting their match tickets from FCB officials at the Cumberland Hotel near Marble Arch. The Cumberland Hotel is famous among music fans for being the residence of Jimi Hendrix shortly before his death in 1970, with pictures of the rock star displayed in the bedroom where he stayed. Talking of stars, after a few years of *Messimania* the demand to see the world's greatest player was massive, tempting a minority of supporters to sell their tickets for more than face value. To deal with this, everyone allocated a ticket also had a band fitted around their wrist, which could only be removed by being destroyed. The band had to be shown still intact on your wrist together with the match ticket before entering the stadium. The club officials at the Cumberland fitted the bands on people's left arm, but I don't know whether this had anything to do with Hendrix being a left-handed guitarist.

Luckily the wristband didn't fall off during my sleep, and on matchday, Wednesday, 3 October 2018, I joined several hundred Barça fans for a pre-match rally at Piccadilly Circus followed by drinks at the nearby Riley's Sports Bar on Haymarket. It was soon time to take the Tube up to the stadium for what was my first big game there since meeting Ronald Koeman and being filmed for his documentary *Bestemming Wembley* the previous year. Talking of Koeman, the Barça fans were allocated an area of seating in the south-east corner, the end they had occupied for the 1992 European Cup Final at the old Wembley, and where the Dutchman had scored his famous goal. This meant that the tunnel was halfway along the side to the right. When I found my seat inside the stadium it was too low down for my liking, so I swapped with another PBL member who preferred to be closer to the action and whose seat was further back, but higher up. It was unusually warm for early October, so many of the 82,000 fans in the stadium wore replica shirts all evening. The conditions and the setting were perfect and the match turned out to be a classic.

There was no colour clash, so Barça wore its traditional blue and red against the all-white of Mauricio Pochettino's Tottenham. Changes to the side at Chelsea included the Portuguese Nélson Semedo at right-back, Clément Lenglet at centre-back, plus two Brazilians, Arthur and Philippe Coutinho, the latter bought at huge expense earlier that year from Liverpool. Pochettino's team was a weakened one, missing Jan Vertonghen, Dele Alli, Mousa Dembélé and Christian Eriksen.

Messi was now Barça's captain following the departure of Iniesta, and didn't take long to make an impact. In the second minute he played a long diagonal pass from a deep position which found Alba down the left. Tottenham's goalkeeper Hugo Lloris rashly raced off his line, so Alba slipped the ball inside to Coutinho, who hit a right-footed shot into the corner of an empty net. Cue pandemonium in the Barça end.

Messi proceeded to run Spurs ragged in the opening period, one moment in midfield, the next up front, then appearing on the left before popping up on the right, passing to team-mates, while also pressing and tackling opponents. It took Spurs nearly ten minutes to settle down and it was after the midway point of the first half before the London club managed an attempt on goal. Barça extended its lead just before the half hour with Messi once again the instigator. This time he picked up the ball on the left and curled it into the path of Suárez, who chested it to Coutinho. The Brazilian shot, but although Lloris saved he only succeeded in punching it back to Coutinho who then crossed towards Rakitić. The ball bounced once before the Croatian midfielder demonstrated incredible technique to jump up, and while still off the ground, smash a half-volley in off the post. A feature of the game was Spurs repeatedly conceding possession and providing Messi with far too much space, enabling him to have two more attempts on goal before half-time.

At the break it was 2-0 and Rakitić's goal provided the main talking point over the half-time beers. Barça, now attacking our end, nearly make it three at the start of the second half, with Messi twice hitting the same goalpost. These near misses looked like they might prove costly when Harry Kane snatched a goal back 30 seconds later. However, Barça restored its two-goal cushion within four minutes. Messi passed to Alba on the left, and a one-two ended with Messi side-footing the ball past Lloris and inside his right post. Messi then ran to the Barça fans at our end and blew them a kiss, a picture that appeared in newspapers and websites around the world the following day. By this stage Spurs looked dead and buried, only for Barça's defensive frailties to hand the London side a lifeline after 66 minutes. A bad back-pass from Alba eventually led to Erik Lamela scoring from a left-footed shot, a gift which energised both Spurs and the home crowd.

Both sides made late changes, Barça bringing on Rafinha, Vidal and Thomas Vermaelen, before victory was secured in the final minute. The Spurs defenders were trying to play the ball out from the back when Alba dispossessed them before passing towards Suárez. The Uruguayan dummied the ball, letting it roll through to Messi, who took one touch with his right foot before calmly slotting it with his left past Lloris.

After the final whistle, PBL members posed for a group photo on the walkway outside the east end of Wembley to celebrate the 4-2 triumph. After being turned away from a few pubs that refused to serve away fans, one was eventually found that happily served people wearing Barcelona colours. There was plenty to talk about: four goals, 61 per cent possession, eight shots on target to Tottenham's five, but most of all Lionel Messi.

The Argentinian had a hand in the first two goals and scored the third and fourth himself, meaning he had scored a total of four goals in his last three competitive games in London. People rightly rave about Messi in the 2009 and 2011 Champions League Finals, but for me that match against Tottenham was his finest display that I saw live. Whereas in those finals Messi played alongside Xavi and Iniesta, by 2018/19 he had to perform without them. For years observers had admired Messi's dribbling and goalscoring, but now they started to appreciate his passing and playmaking too. The following day British newspapers used words such as 'glorious' and 'masterclass' to describe Messi's performance, while in Spain *Mundo Deportivo* headlined with 'WEMBLEO'.[68]

After Messi's goals against Spurs, the Barcelona fans at Wembley worshipped him by bowing down in a 'we

---

68 *Mundo Deportivo*, 4 October 2018.

are not worthy' gesture, while similar performances had encouraged some Barça fans to call their star player 'D 10 S', incorporating his shirt number into 'dios', the Spanish word for 'god'. A few months after the Tottenham game, Messi's compatriot and football fan, Pope Francis, felt compelled to comment on such actions. During an interview with the Spanish television channel La Sexta, the Pope said, 'He's great to watch, but he's not God,' and added, 'Only God can be worshipped.'[69] This is quite possibly the only papal ruling against a footballer's divinity, but far from being the sole connection between religion and Barça.

FC Barcelona's associations with religion started during the political turmoil of the 1930s, when the Catholic Church in Spain was associated with the political right and some left-wing extremists carried out assassinations of clergymen in various parts of the country. In Barcelona the football club provided a safe haven for clerics at its Les Corts stadium before they were able to escape the city. Camp Nou opened in 1957 and the following year it became the first major football ground to have its own place of worship, with a chapel installed near the tunnel. Pope John Paul II blessed the chapel during his visit to Barcelona in November 1982, before performing mass at the stadium in front of 120,000 worshippers. After the ceremony he was given a lifelong Barça membership card (*soci* number 108,000).

---

69 timesnownews.com.

The two patron saints of Catalonia both have links to FC Barcelona. The first, of course, is Sant Jordi (St George), patron saint of both England and Catalonia. The saint's red cross on a white background appears on the Barça badge, but it is the city's second patron saint, Our Lady of Montserrat, that I shall focus on. Popularly known as 'La Moreneta' ('The Little Dark One'), Our Lady of Montserrat is a black Madonna image of Mary the mother of Jesus. Carved from wood during the 12th century and about a metre tall, the statue is located by an ancient monastery at Montserrat. Literally meaning 'serrated mountain', Montserrat rises steeply above the surrounding land with spectacular craggy outcrops on its summit. According to legend, local people saw a religious vision on Montserrat in the ninth century, and a place of worship was consequently built on the site. Our Lady of Montserrat was proclaimed a patron saint of Catalonia by Pope Leo XIII in 1881, and because of the statue's cultural importance Camp Nou's aforementioned chapel contains a replica of it. In 2020 it was reported that Barça's black and gold away kit was inspired by the colours of the chapel's Moreneta[70].

In 1985 Barça's players celebrated their La Liga title by cycling the 50km journey from Barcelona to Montserrat. Six years later, I took the less strenuous route, travelling on the hour-long train ride from Barcelona's Plaça d'Espanya station followed by a hair-raising cable car ascent up to the monastery at an altitude of over 700m. On seeing

---

70 footyheadlines.com.

the black Madonna in the basilica next to the monastery, I felt it gave off a rather eerie vibe, although that could have been caused by the autumn mist that mingled with Montserrat's dark peaks on the day of my visit.

Some have speculated that Montserrat was the inspiration for Monsalvat, a castle containing the Holy Grail in *Parsifal*, Richard Wagner's 19th-century opera. According to legend, the Holy Grail was a treasured relic from biblical times possessed with special powers. In October 1940 Hitler visited Spain to try and persuade Franco to enter the Second World War on Germany's side. During the Nazi visit, SS leader Heinrich Himmler popped up to Montserrat to investigate whether it was indeed the home of the Holy Grail. However, Himmler's mission, like Hitler's, proved unsuccessful.

Although La Moreneta is one of the most famous black Madonnas in the world, it is not unique. My sightseeing has taken in others at cathedrals in Toledo and Zaragoza in Spain, and there are about 300 across the globe. Although some are paintings, most take the form of statues. A common explanation for the colour of black Madonnas is that it's the accidental result of natural ageing and the effect of candle smoke. However, this cannot explain why other icons, sometimes housed in the same church or shrine, have not also darkened. Others argue that the shade is deliberate and based on *Song of Songs* in the Old Testament which reads, 'I am black but comely, O ye daughters of Jerusalem,' and point out that some, though not all, black Madonnas appear to have features like sub-Saharan African women. Another explanation is that black Madonnas show the influence of older pagan goddesses. Many black Madonnas date from the late Middle Ages, and although some appeared miraculously (according to legend), others may have been brought back to Europe by returning crusaders.

During their trip to London for the 1992 European Cup Final, some visitors from Barcelona went on a pilgrimage looking for black Madonnas, inspired by their own ones at Montserrat and Camp Nou. The nearest and most important destination for such pilgrims is Willesden, within sight of Wembley Stadium. Willesden's first St Mary's Church was founded in the tenth century and within a few hundred years it established a black Madonna shrine called Our Lady of Willesden, also known as 'The Black Virgin of Willesden'. The shrine was destroyed during the English Reformation in 1538 and its statue is believed to have been burnt by the bank of the River Thames.

In the early 20th century St Mary's Church, by then High Anglican, installed a gold Madonna followed by a black one in 1972. However, of more interest is another place of worship, the nearby Roman Catholic Our Lady of Willesden Church. Originally a mission serving the area's large Irish Catholic community, it created its own black Madonna in 1892 before developing into a full church and moving to the present site in 1931. When visiting the church I found this black Madonna, located in a chapel to one side of the nave. Made in a traditional style, it was carved out of wood from an oak tree growing on the site of the original shrine that had been destroyed centuries before. Although there are a small number of other black Madonnas in Britain, the priest explained to me that his church contained the only one recognised by Roman Catholics.

Unlike the black Madonna at Montserrat, this one didn't give me any unsettling vibes, although I did discover some weird coincidences. For the first, we go back to 1954, which Pope Pius XII chose as the first ever Marion Year, commemorating the centenary of a papal ruling about the Immaculate Conception. Part of the celebrations included Willesden's black Madonna being carried 5km from the church to Wembley Stadium, where it was crowned by Cardinal Bernard Griffin in front of 94,000 worshippers[71]. The crowning of the black Madonna of Willesden at the old Wembley Stadium took place on 3 October 1954, exactly 64 years to the very day before another massive crowd filled the new Wembley on 3 October 2018 to witness a different kind of glory.

Investigating whether 64 years held any significance in Marion terms, I came across accounts of an early-19th-century German Roman Catholic nun called Catherine Emmerich. Born into a poor peasant family, Emmerich claimed to have experienced visions about scriptural events and became known as the 'Mystic of the Land of Münster'. In 1822, two years before her death, Emmerich had a vision about the death of the Virgin Mary. When asked how old Mary was when she died, Emmerich is

---

71 Schofield, N., *Our Lady of Willesden: A brief history of the Shrine and Parish*, pp52-59.

reported to have replied, 'I have just seen the figure X six times, then I, then V; is that not 64?'[72]

In 2004 the Papacy decided to beatify Emmerich, a step towards sainthood. Her beatification and its timing provoked some debate because Emmerich's visions had inspired Mel Gibson when making his controversial film, *The Passion of the Christ*, released just a few months earlier. Emmerich's beatification was performed by the Pope in St Peter's Square at the front of the Vatican before a crowd of 20,000. Which Pope beatified Emmerich? John Paul II, the very same pontiff who was Barça *soci* number 108,000 and in 1982 had blessed Camp Nou's chapel containing its black Madonna. The date of Emmerich's beatification ceremony: 3 October 2004[73].

---

72 'The Life of the Blessed Virgin Mary by Blessed Anne Catherine Emmerich': ecatholic2000.com.

73 'Beatification of Five Servants of God': vatican.va.

15

From the Sublime
to the Ridiculous

FOLLOWING MESSI'S sublime display at Wembley, Barça was highly fancied to win the Champions League Final at the end of the season. In the first knockout round, Barça was drawn against Lyon, progressing after a goalless draw in France followed by a thumping 5-1 win at Camp Nou. In the quarter-final Barça faced Manchester United, now coached by Ole Gunnar Solskjær following José Mourinho's sacking just before Christmas. The first leg was away at Old Trafford on Wednesday, 10 April 2019, and fortunately work commitments didn't get in the way this time.

After arriving in Manchester around midday the first task was collecting my match ticket complete with wristband from FCB officials at the National Football Museum. Founded in 2001, the museum was originally at Preston North End's Deepdale stadium, a historic location as the oldest ground in terms of continuous use by an English league club, and home of the first winners of the Football League title in 1889. In 2006 I went to Deepdale to see Leeds in the play-off semi-final and visited the museum. However, after funding difficulties the museum closed in 2010 before reopening at its present location in Manchester city centre two years later. The second museum is bigger than the first, and the Barcelona game provided the perfect opportunity to view its thousands of exhibits, including footballs, shirts, boots, match programmes, pictures and other memorabilia from the history of the sport.

Next up was a lunch organised for Barça supporters at the Manchester Smokehouse and Cellar. This was a great event, which typified what's best about Barcelona supporters. Many English fans would probably just meet in crowded pubs and stand up drinking alcohol on an empty, or near empty, stomach, but with Barça fans, venues are chosen where it's possible to sit down and enjoy food and conversation, so there's less drunkenness, you can enjoy the football and even remember it next day. There is no *penya* in the north of England, so the FC Barcelona Supporters' Clubs World Confederation organised the event. The lunch was well attended, with members of *penyes* from Spain, Poland, Romania, Brazil and Ireland as well as England represented. Many of us later appeared in a photograph of the event that appeared in *Blaugranes*, the official magazine of the *penya* world confederation as well as on the club website. About 100 people went to the lunch, with a total of 600 *penyistas* going to the game itself, which was a good proportion of the total away attendance[74].

Suitably fuelled with sticky pork ribs, chips, cheesecake and Estrella beer, I made my way to Old Trafford, in the west of the city. Since my trip there with Barça for the 1994 Champions League fixture it had changed dramatically. Old Trafford was now nearly twice the size with 74,093 at the game, but the additional stands gave it a haphazard, piecemeal look. The Barça fans were allocated seats in the south-east corner, practically opposite where I had been 25 years earlier.

As in 1994 there was a colour clash, so Barça wore a change kit, this time of fluorescent yellow. The team lined up with exactly the same formation as the Tottenham game. The decisive moment came after 12 minutes. Messi received the ball inside the penalty area on the left, then without even looking up hit a perfect lob across to Suárez who headed the ball down, off Luke Shaw, and into the goal. Everyone in the Barça section went crazy, but it soon became apparent that the players were not lining up for kick-off and that the linesman over on the far side had raised his flag. This is when VAR makes its first appearance in this book.

Video Assistant Referee was introduced into the Champions League in the 2018/19 round of 16 to inform the referee when there may have been an incorrect decision relating to four situations: goals; incidents in the penalty area; red cards; and mistaken identity. The Barça goal

---

74 *Blaugranes*, official magazine of the FC Barcelona Supporters' Clubs World Confederation, July 2019, pp8-9.

clearly came into the first two categories. Although television viewers at home were told immediately that the goal had been disallowed for offside and was being subjected to a VAR review, fans inside the stadium were not informed of this. Instead, some of us who were positioned towards the back of the Barça section were able to look at television screens in the executive boxes immediately behind and see that the replays suggested offside was the issue and that VAR was being used. After an agonising delay, the referee pointed to the centre circle signalling a goal, with VAR deciding that Suárez was not offside when Messi crossed the ball. Although enabling a correct decision to be made on this occasion, VAR had interrupted the fans' celebrations and would lead in future to supporters hesitating before knowing whether or not to cheer a goal, so further diluting the crowd atmosphere already dealt a severe blow by allocated places in all-seater stadiums.

Barça was fortunate to go ahead as Suárez's header was probably going wide until it hit Shaw, and after taking the lead the visitors seemed to try and settle for going home with an away goal. Barça was sloppy in possession, with little of the usual slick passing, not helped by poor movement of the players and effective pressing by the home side. Sergio Busquets, for example, gave away the ball more than I had seen before, although playing the right pass could be more difficult without Xavi or Iniesta to find. The players, perhaps remembering recent failures in the Champions League knockout stages, looked uncertain. Apart from one moment of brilliance with his assist for the goal, Messi had a quiet day, not helped by an elbow in the face from Chris Smalling after half an hour, which caused a lot of bleeding. Messi's team-mates proved unable to supply him with the ball, meaning that he was forced to drop deep to get it and was therefore too far from goal to do damage. On the rare occasions when Messi gained possession he was frequently surrounded by several opponents. Fortunately for Barça, Diogo Dalot missed the home side's best opportunity with a header which went miles wide.

Apart from his goal, Suárez was wasteful, missing a good chance from a Semedo pass by shooting into the side netting after an hour. Barça then made a couple of changes, bringing on Vidal for Coutinho and Sergi Roberto for Arthur, then just before the end replaced Busquets with Carles Aleñá. Vidal, who had been charging like a madman, jumped into Smalling in the penalty area, a needless challenge that could have conceded a last-minute penalty.

The match ended 1-0 to Barça, who had enjoyed 66 per cent of the possession and managed three shots on target, while all of Manchester United's ten efforts missed. Those statistics, and the all-important away goal, meant the *penya* members I spoke to as they posed for a group photograph with their banners outside Old Trafford after the game were upbeat. However, looking back on the match, Barça played nothing like the team that had defeated Tottenham and the problem of *Messidependencia* seemed to have returned.

Despite a bright start in the second leg at Camp Nou, hitting the bar early on, Manchester United was ruthlessly punished for giving Messi too much space. The Argentinian scored twice, while Coutinho added a third to clinch a 4-0 aggregate victory, a semi-final against Liverpool and raise hopes of a place in the final.

Barça won the first leg of the semi-final 3-0 at Camp Nou, through a goal scored by former Anfield favourite Suárez followed by a couple towards the end from Messi. However, the home side was lucky to come away without conceding an away goal with Jürgen Klopp's team having more possession and chances on goal. Liverpool would be expected to win at Anfield, possibly by a couple of goals, but most expected Barça to convert at least one chance, meaning Liverpool would have to score five. Even in this age of amazing comebacks, surely that would be too much. The only nagging doubt was that Ousmane Dembélé, who came on at the end, had a great chance to score a fourth in stoppage time, but hit his effort straight at the Liverpool keeper from close range. The question was, would it matter?

I hoped that it wouldn't, particularly because before Christmas I had booked my flights, accommodation and match tickets (via UEFA) to see the final. Booking the trip early meant that although I didn't know who would be contesting the final, it did ensure that travel and accommodation would be considerably cheaper and easier to obtain than if I waited until after the semi-final, when thousands would be trying to make arrangements. The location was especially important because that year the final was in Madrid (at the new

Atlético stadium) so providing an opportunity to get over the disappointment of 2010.

I entered PBL's raffle for match tickets for the away leg of the semi-final, but was initially unsuccessful. This was frustrating because I had already purchased train tickets for my second 550-mile return journey from the south coast to the north of England as well as hotel accommodation. At the time I booked my train travel the game could potentially have been either on the Tuesday or the Wednesday, so I decided to travel up on the Tuesday and stay two nights to be covered either way. This increased my accommodation costs, so I opted for a budget hotel. After Barcelona scandalously charged visiting Liverpool fans over £100 for a match ticket to see the first leg, Liverpool retaliated by charging Barça fans the same amount for their tickets at Anfield. This high price reduced demand for the tickets, and when more became available I was lucky enough to get one.

On the morning of the second leg, Tuesday, 7 May 2019, I got up just after dawn to take an early train from Sussex to London, before once again boarding another train at Euston to head towards the north-west. Barça had a three-goal lead to take to Anfield and had won five of its past seven away games against English teams in the Champions League. What could possibly go wrong?

From early that morning I started to have a funny feeling, until by the time I arrived in Liverpool around midday I feared Barça would get knocked out. After reporting to a posh city centre hotel to collect my expensive match ticket from FCB officials and have a wristband fitted, it was time to check in at my own hotel, which turned out to be above a Chinese restaurant. The room key had to be collected from the staff in between them serving egg fried rice or crispy chow mein, and by then I feared the match would leave a sour rather than a sweet taste in my mouth.

After walking through the city centre I reached Church Street and bumped into Tony (Liverpool fan, PBL member and survivor of the Barcelona Blackout Tray four years before). Optimistically wearing shorts even though it wasn't that warm, Tony thought there was no way Liverpool could go through. Like many others, he believed Liverpool could conceivably score two or even three goals, but Barça was bound to get one, meaning that the Reds would need five, which was practically impossible. I told Tony of my fears of a collapse worse than Roma, but he wasn't to be persuaded and continued to view the tie as over, although he would still be taking his usual place on the Kop that evening.

Unlike Manchester, there was no official pre-match lunch for the travelling Barça fans. Instead, there was an informal gathering at the Around the World Bar, near the riverfront and opposite the Hilton Hotel where the Barça team was staying (and no, the squad didn't have a Chinese restaurant below their rooms). I discovered that I wasn't the only person feeling apprehensive about the evening's match after bumping into Naheed, who had attended the previous season's collapse in the Stadio Olimpico. Another of the fans I met in the pub was Jason. Formerly a West Ham fan from Essex who decided The Only Way Is Catalan (TOWIC), he had become a regular contributor to the official FC Barcelona website and two years later would publish his book *Messi: The King of Camp Nou*[75]. Jason shared my fears for the game, and when he told me he was going to Anfield early to meet some Liverpool-supporting friends, I decided to leave the pub with him and take a bus up to the stadium.

Anfield, the home of Liverpool FC, is in the north of the city. Our bus arrived there around five o'clock, three hours before kick-off. One of the friends Jason was meeting sang and played guitar in a band providing pre-match entertainment outside the turnstiles at the famous Kop end. One of the songs they performed was a cover version of the James track 'Sit Down', only with the words changed to 'Mo Salah, Mo Salah, Sit down next to me.' Hearing this rendition momentarily raised my spirits because the Egyptian forward would be missing that night due to injury, as would his strike partner Firmino. Between them they had scored 42 goals already that season, although this still left Sadio Mané who had got 24. If the home fans were paying homage to a player who wasn't even going to play, perhaps they didn't have much faith in his replacement, or perhaps 'Origi, Origi, Sit down next to me' didn't sound right?

After a few drinks in a pub outside the stadium, I took my place in the lower tier of the Anfield Road

---

75 Pettigrove, J., *Messi: The King of Camp Nou* (Cardiff: St David's Press, 2021).

stand about an hour and a half before kick-off. My seat was right behind the goal, opposite the famous Kop. I had only been to Anfield on one previous occasion, to see Leeds United secure a vital point just before the conclusion of its successful title-winning campaign in 1992. That afternoon Anfield was subdued and the Kop a disappointment. I remember the Leeds fans singing, 'Where's your famous atmosphere?' Over a quarter of a century later, I was about to find out.

The song 'You'll Never Walk Alone' is widely credited to Rodgers and Hammerstein, first appearing in their 1945 musical *Carousel*, but possibly has earlier origins. Widely covered by various artists, by far and away the best-known version is the one by Gerry and the Pacemakers. In the early 1960s the city of Liverpool was famously the centre of pop music, with groups such as The Beatles leading the Merseybeat phenomenon. In the days before all-seater stadiums and ordering your ticket in advance, fans would pay at the gate to watch football. Lock-outs, turning away later arrivals, sometimes happened, so to be sure of gaining entry fans would arrive early. As they stood waiting on the terraces for an hour or more supporters needed entertainment, and at Anfield it became the custom to play the Top Ten in the music charts, with fans sometimes singing along. When local group Gerry and the Pacemakers released their version of 'You'll Never Walk Alone' in 1963 it was particularly popular with the crowd on the Kop, and fans continued to sing it long after the single dropped out of the charts.

Over the years, I had seen Liverpool play English opposition on many occasions, and although the club's fans usually sang 'You'll Never Walk Alone' at some point in the proceedings, the intensity varied. For example, I was fortunate enough to attend the first all-Merseyside FA Cup Final at Wembley in 1986. Gary Lineker opened the scoring for Everton (joining Barcelona later that summer) before Liverpool came back to win 3-1 and secure the club's first league and cup double. In those days Liverpool versus Everton was referred to as the 'friendly derby' – it is only in recent decades that hostility between the two sets of supporters in the city has developed. Consequently, when the Reds sang 'You'll Never Walk Alone' that afternoon, swaying from side to side with their scarves, some of the Blues joined in. However, on my only previous trip to Anfield in April 1992 the crowd was quiet, and when 'You'll Never Walk Alone' was played before kick-off most of the home fans ignored it. These examples suggest that 'You'll Never Walk Alone' is only really sung enthusiastically by fans on special occasions; however, a Champions League semi-final is definitely one of those. Anfield's big European nights under floodlights are legendary, so I anticipated a better rendition of the song than in 1992, but I didn't expect what I was about to witness.

Just before the teams marched out of the tunnel to my right the vast majority of the 53,300 crowd sang 'You'll Never Walk Alone' with a volume and intensity I had not experienced before. The crowd scenes were the most passionate I had ever seen in England. It wasn't just the noise of the singing, but the sight of the red and white colours on thousands of scarves and dozens of large flags and banners, many boasting about the club's European pedigree. I have been fortunate enough to attend some big clashes – Ajax versus Feyenoord, Dortmund against Bayern, Milan facing Juve, Barça playing Real Madrid, and various major finals – but in terms of atmosphere and choreography only the Belgrade derby surpassed what I experienced that night at Anfield. The Barça fans concentrated on taking photos and recording films on their smartphones of the scenes on the Kop at the other end rather than attempting to sing back, and sadly for them their team also seemed mesmerised.

Just as in Manchester, the home side wore red so Barça played in yellow, lining up in a 4-3-3 with two changes to the starting 11 at Wembley and Old Trafford, Sergi Roberto replacing Semedo in defence with Vidal instead of Arthur in midfield. Liverpool kicked off, attacking my end. All the talk before the game mentioned the importance of not conceding an early goal. So, what do Barça do? Concede an early goal.

With only seven minutes gone, Xherdan Shaqiri played the ball to Joël Matip deep in the Liverpool half. Matip then hit a long diagonal pass forward which Alba tried clearing, only to head the ball to Mané, who fed it to Jordan Henderson. The Liverpool captain did well to drive through several Barça defenders and get in a shot. Ter Stegen dived down low to save Henderson's effort, but parried the ball to Divock Origi, who finished from close range in front of me. The goal was rapturously received by the other three sides of Anfield. My immediate thought was, 'Oh no, surely not,' and in our section a feeling of déjà vu began to fester. However, Barça rallied and actually had three chances of its own in the first half, from Messi, Coutinho and Alba, all of which were saved by Alisson.

The first half ended with mixed feelings in the Barça end. On one hand, the team hadn't conceded any more goals after the bad start, while edging it in terms of possession and managing to create a few chances, although the failure to convert any could prove costly. Some of the Barça fans I spoke to at the break were more optimistic than me, one London-based Catalan saying his team usually played better in the second half of games. However, the omens were not good, with worrying signs of a repeat of Roma the previous season. Firstly, on Barcelona's last encounter with Liverpool in England (a pre-season game at Wembley in 2016) Origi scored and the final result was 4-0. Secondly, Liverpool's kit in 2018/19 was a darker shade of red than normal, looking more like the colours Roma had worn in the Stadio Olimpico. Thirdly, Alisson had kept goal for the Italian side that night and threatened to frustrate Barça again one year later. Finally, Roma had scored after six minutes and went in 1-0 ahead at half-time, while at Anfield Liverpool scored after six minutes and also went in with a single-goal lead. Would the English club repeat Roma's achievement by overturning a three-goal deficit?

In the first half Suárez, who was constantly booed by his former supporters, had injured Andy Robertson, causing the Scottish full-back to be replaced at the break by Georginio Wijnaldum, as James Milner filled in at the back. Suárez's action backfired soon after the second half kicked off. With Barça attacking my end, I hoped to have a close view of the goal which would kill the tie, leaving Liverpool needing at least four more. Both sides had a chance soon after the restart, Virgil van Dijk for Liverpool and Suárez for Barcelona, but the two efforts were saved by the goalkeepers. When another goal came early on, it was not at my end and not for Barça.

Nine minutes after the restart Rakitić tried to pass the ball to Alba inside the Barcelona half, but Trent Alexander-Arnold robbed him down Liverpool's right flank and hit in a cross which was fired home from near the penalty spot by Wijnaldum. By now Anfield was truly rocking while confidence appeared to drain away from the Barça players and their supporters. The restart was held up for a VAR check on a potential red card, although exactly what incident it involved was never explained. Within 31 seconds of the restart it was 3-0. This time Milner fed Shaqiri down the left, and the Swiss player launched in a cross to Wijnaldum who out-jumped the Barça defenders and headed the ball past ter Stegen and just inside his left post.

The tie was now level on aggregate, meaning if there were no more goals it would go to extra time then penalties. However, if Barça could snatch that crucial away goal, then Liverpool would need at least two more. Barça did have a chance after 65 minutes, but Messi's effort was once again saved by Alisson.

Ernesto Valverde rarely gave off a positive impression, hardly ever smiling, but at Anfield his dark grey suit, white shirt and black tie made him look like an undertaker. It was certainly a deathly mood in the away end. Standing in his technical area, the funeral director decided to make a couple of substitutions. Semedo replaced Coutinho, and with quarter of an hour remaining Arthur came on for Vidal, but there was little time for that change to work before the visitors conceded a fourth.

After Liverpool was awarded a corner on the right, Alexander-Arnold stood over the ball as if he was going to take it, then walked away suggesting he'd changed his mind and decided to leave it for someone else. As there wasn't another Liverpool player nearby the Barça players assumed there'd be a delay, but Alexander-Arnold quickly turned back to the ball and whipped in a cross. Some of the Barça players switched off and had their backs to the ball when it reached Origi, who finished from close range. Being at the other end of the stadium meant that there was an important part of the goal which I missed, namely the contribution of an alert ballboy in front of the Kop who threw a spare ball to Alexander-Arnold, enabling him to take the corner quickly. There were briefly two balls on the pitch which may have added to the confusion, although one was removed before the corner was taken. The ballboy concerned was Oakley Cannonier, who two years later signed a professional footballer contract with

Liverpool, aged 17, having previously been a youth player at his home club, my very own Leeds United[76].

It was now 4-0 and Barça, for the first time, was behind on aggregate, with 11 minutes remaining. Both sides made late changes, Barça's being the replacement of Rakitić with Malcom. The travelling fans made no effort to rouse their beaten team. Even now an away goal would change everything, but few expected it, and it didn't happen. Five minutes of stoppage time provided false hope before the final whistle blew, meaning Barça was out. It was the first time since 1986 (when Barcelona beat Gothenburg) that a side recovered from a three-goal deficit in the first leg of a European Cup semi-final. One piece of television commentary said, 'It's the greatest ever semi-final comeback in the history of the competition.'[77] Back in Barcelona, the local paper *Sport* headlined its report 'El Mayor Ridículo de la Historia' ('The Most Ridiculous in History')[78].

As soon as the game was over the Barça section of the Anfield Road stand emptied. The way back to the city centre involved going round the stadium and past the Liverpool fans leaving through their exits. I wasn't wearing colours, but my face must have told a story as I was taunted by a Liverpool fan while passing the Kop end. It had been dark for some time as I strolled back towards the city centre, and on the way my mind drifted back to 2010, the last time the final was in Madrid, when

76 dailymail.co.uk.

77 Liverpool vs Barcelona, BT Sport commentary, 7 May 2019.

78 *Sport*, 8 May 2019.

Barça had also fallen at the semi-final stage. Seeing Barça win the Champions League in the Spanish capital would have been a tremendous experience. After an hour's walk I was back at my hotel. I tried to think of better times, such as the trip to Berlin to see the trident of Messi, Suárez and Neymar win the 2015 final, but with my room now smelling of Chinese food things were more MSG than MSN.

I wasn't due to return home until Thursday, so had all of Wednesday for sightseeing in Liverpool and decided to book a place on one of the city's many Beatles tours. Having made my way down to the docks I boarded a bright yellow bus, a modern version of the vehicle used in *Magical Mystery Tour*, a surreal comedy film that The Beatles released in 1967, parodying working-class day trips and popular culture of the time. As I boarded the bus the guide welcomed everyone aboard saying in his Scouse accent, 'Hello everybody. You've chosen a great time to be in Liverpool, wasn't last night's game fantastic?' The bus then drove off, taking us to the south of the city to see the childhood homes of John Lennon, Paul McCartney, George Harrison and Ringo Starr, before visiting places like Penny Lane and Strawberry Fields.

Still suffering from *Beatlemania* after the tour, I popped into the famous Cavern Club, the iconic venue where the Fab Four performed in their early days. The door of the Cavern displayed a sign with an FC Barcelona badge saying 'Benvinguts a Liverpool!' ('Welcome to Liverpool!') and during the days leading up to the game hundreds of travelling Barça supporters had accepted the invitation. According to *Mundo Deportivo* their impeccable conduct was praised by the Cavern's owners, who sadly may have been more accustomed to misbehaviour from visiting football fans[79]. At the time of my visit, the Barça fans still in the city were licking their wounds from the previous night's drubbing, so hardly any of them were in the Cavern which made it easier to find a seat. I settled down with a beer while a musician played an acoustic guitar on the small stage.

I later learned that the sign on the door wasn't the famous basement venue's only connection with Barça. After the original Cavern Club closed in 1973 it was then recreated in the 1980s. After reopening, the landlords leased the club to Tommy Smith, the former Liverpool footballer[80]. A few years earlier in March 1976, Smith had played for Liverpool in both legs of a UEFA Cup semi-final against Barcelona. The first leg at Camp Nou ended with a 1-0 win for Liverpool and Barça fans throwing cushions on the pitch in protest at their team's poor display, although, by contrast, they sportingly applauded Smith and his victorious team-mates after the full-time whistle[81].

The second leg took place at Anfield a couple of weeks later. Among the crowd of over 55,000 was a 20-year-old student called Alan. During a break from his studies at Reading University, Alan had returned to Liverpool, the

---

79 'The Cavern Club congratulates the Barça fans': 10 May 2019, mundodeportivo.com.

80 cavernclub.com.

81 liverpoolfc.com.

city of his birth, and met up with some of his old school friends. Two of them, both Liverpool fans, had decided to go to Anfield to watch the Barcelona game. Although Alan was a Toffee, a dyed-in-the-wool Evertonian, he decided to tag along. Alan later told me, 'I don't recall the chance to see Johan Cruyff being a big factor, and even though it was a huge game it was more that I just liked getting out, going to the pub, games, gigs, whatever. It might have been simply a matter of my mates having a spare ticket.'

One of those friends had a car and kindly gave Alan a lift from his home to the stadium. It wasn't Alan's first trip to Anfield – his Liverpool-supporting father had taken him to the wrong side of Stanley Park on several previous occasions, but always to sit along the sides, whereas that night he stood on the famous Kop terrace behind the goal. Alan added, 'I remember the stadium was really busy and I couldn't get a programme despite trying at several kiosks, but they had all sold out. It was murder getting in as loads of fans had no tickets. I always loved night games played under floodlights, especially the first view of the pitch, so green in the dark.'

Once again, Tommy Smith was one of the Liverpool defenders tasked with stopping a Barcelona team wearing yellow away shirts with a *blaugrana* diagonal sash. Alan says, 'I can remember Cruyff, although he wasn't in the game that much, and also his Dutch team-mate Neeskens. I think Liverpool dominated the game then Barca got a lucky equaliser, but nonetheless Liverpool went through.'

Alan worked with me in a north London library 15 years later, and because of his attendance at that UEFA Cup semi-final in 1976 he is the only person I know to have seen Johan Cruyff play live in the flesh for Barcelona. If that wasn't enough, three years after the Anfield game Alan's employer posted him to Glasgow. During his brief stay, Argentina played Scotland at Hampden Park, so Alan decided to pop along and consequently saw future Barça star Diego Maradona's first goal for his country.

Highly skilled at Subbuteo table football, Alan was my very first opponent when I played with the team of orange plastic figures, hand-painted in the colours of the 1992 Dream Team.

Number four in that team was the miniature model of Ronald Koeman, pictured in this book and shown to the free kick specialist when we met at Wembley Stadium, much to the Dutchman's disdain. In 2017, at the time of that encounter, Koeman was the coach of Alan's Everton.

By coincidence, in the same year as the 1976 UEFA Cup semi-final two Catalan Beatles fans, Joan and Ricky, opened a bar in Barcelona as a tribute to the Fab Four. Named La Garrafa dels Beatles (literally 'The Bottle of The Beatles'), the bar is located on Carrer de Joan Guell, less than half a kilometre from Camp Nou. Inside it is packed with Beatles memorabilia and every night the staff perform cover versions of Beatles songs from a small stage reminiscent of the one at the Cavern. The temporary closure of the Liverpool venue in the 1970s means that

La Garrafa dels Beatles is actually the longer-running of the two establishments[82].

Talking of garrafa, it looked like the city's football team had lost its bottle in the 2019 Champions League semi-final. I talked about this after bumping into Jason, just before embarking on my long train journey back to the south coast. We chatted about the disaster that had recently unfolded before our eyes, so starting my post-mortem. Here are its conclusions.

Although the Barça players had played in *clásicos* and major finals, it looked like the atmosphere generated by the Kop intimidated and overwhelmed them. Conceding an early goal was disastrous. It came from mistakes at the back, specifically from Alba and ter Stegen. After the first goal, fears of a repeat of Roma the previous year began to prey on the players' minds. Despite being in this situation before, it looked like Valverde and his team still didn't know whether to concentrate on defending their aggregate lead or go for the killer away goal, and in the end did neither.

On the train home, I read a report of the game in *The Independent* newspaper, headlined 'Reds summon Istanbul spirit but Barcelona switch off at vital moment'[83]. This presumably referred to the loss of concentration before Alexander-Arnold's corner kick, but for me the second goal was the pivotal moment. Barça had rallied after conceding the first goal, while the match was already

82 'The bar every Beatles fan has to go to – but there's a catch': liverpoolecho.co.uk.

83 *The Independent*, 8 May 2019.

lost by the time of the fourth. At 2-0 any remaining confidence drained away from the Barça players and the team fell apart, conceding the third goal seconds later. For quite some time the players have lacked a Puyol-type leader to encourage them or kick them up the backside when needed.

Thinking about the goals, three of them had come from wide areas. As well as exploiting Barça's weakness on the flanks, the victors had also hit long balls forward which the visitors struggled to deal with, partly because of a lack of height in the team. Age had been a factor too; Liverpool only had one player over 30, while Barça had seven. Helped partly by their relative youth, the Liverpool players had an intensity and pace that Barça could not cope with.

Despite most of the possession and a better pass completion rate than Liverpool, Barça still lost because too much of its possession and passing lacked an end product. The problem of *Messidependencia* had been solved with the arrivals of Neymar and Suárez, but returned with the departure of the former and loss of form of the latter. Barça only brought two top-class forwards to Anfield: Messi and Suárez. Dembélé, who had missed a sitter in the first leg, was injured for the second, so when Barça desperately needed to bring on more firepower at Anfield there was no one available.

Barça had already retained its La Liga title before the trip to Liverpool, but its hold on the domestic double was lost with a defeat to Valencia in the Cope del Rey Final a few weeks after Anfield. Chapter five of this book describes the 4-0 defeat to Milan in 1994 and how it was the beginning of the end for Cruyff's Dream Team. That process started immediately with the first recriminations allegedly taking place on the bus back to Athens airport. By contrast, the consequences of the 4-0 at Anfield were delayed by just over half a year, but when they came were far more profound.

16

Super Bronca: Political Bust-ups

BARÇA'S 2019/20 Champions League campaign began well enough, with four wins and a couple of draws to finish first in a group containing Borussia Dortmund, Inter and Slavia Prague. However, 13 January 2020 proved to be unlucky for Ernesto Valverde, who was sacked that day. Reasons included unconvincing displays, poor away results in La Liga and memories of second-leg collapses against Roma and, especially, Liverpool. The timing seemed strange, with Valverde's side not only unbeaten in Europe but also top of the Spanish league. After several candidates turned down the job, the club finally appointed the former Real Betis coach Quique Setién as Valverde's replacement.

Valverde's sacking started a series of events that rapidly escalated into a massive crisis, summarised at the end of this chapter. Barça's Champions League round of 16 first leg in Naples in February 2020 ended in a 1-1 draw, but the return leg was postponed after UEFA suspended all its matches because of the coronavirus pandemic. Following the resumption of the season in the summer, Barça lost its hold on La Liga, with Real Madrid becoming champions. The second leg against Napoli was eventually held nearly six months after the first. Despite having to play in an empty Camp Nou, Barça secured a 3-1 victory and a 4-2 aggregate win. However, there would be no home advantage in the quarter-final the following Friday when the opposition was Bayern Munich, after UEFA introduced major changes to the remaining part of the competition because of the pandemic. The quarter- and semi-finals would now be single-leg ties, rather than the usual home and away format, held in a mini-tournament in August in Lisbon. Istanbul had been scheduled to host the final, but UEFA decided that the Portuguese capital was more suitable.

With it being impossible to attend matches, the next best thing was to watch a television screening at Bar & Co, a boat on the River Thames and the home of PBL. Built around 1920, it was originally a barge used for travel up and down the Thames called *Wilfred*. Today the boat is moored at Temple Pier on the north bank of the river, with great views of the London Eye. About 25m long with two decks, it was thoroughly renovated by its present owner Jorge to comply with Westminster Council's licensing requirements. Renamed Bar & Co as a play on the Spanish word 'barco', meaning 'ship', it has been PBL's base since 2008.

Usually the boat can hold 125 people, but for the Bayern game it had a reduced capacity to comply with coronavirus regulations, and all customers had to sit at tables and maintain social distancing. PBL members are generally optimistic and predict victory for their team, but not on this occasion. Although some thought the revised format might help as it was arguably better to play Bayern once rather than over two legs. However, not even the most pessimistic could anticipate what was about to happen, or at least not its scale. As this book is an eyewitness account, I won't talk in detail about the Bayern game because it was impossible to attend it. Instead, my focus will be on the one thing I did see, namely the fans at Bar & Co and how they reacted.

Shortly before kick-off I ordered a meal of barbecued sausages and chose the bigger screen at the end of the lower level to watch, rather than one of the relatively smaller televisions. I'd hardly started to cut my chorizo when Thomas Müller exchanged passes with Robert Lewandowski to similarly dissect Barça's defence and put the German side ahead, although, to be honest, the sausage offered more resistance. Soon after Müller's goal, Bayern's David Alaba wildly sliced the ball into his own net for the equaliser. Cue the ritual playing of 'Cant del Barça' over the boat's loudspeaker in celebration of an unexpected gift. Momentarily energised, Barça nearly went ahead with Messi hitting the post soon after. Unfortunately for those on the boat, Bayern then proceeded to score seven more times with only a single Suárez goal in response. Adding insult to injury, the final two goals were scored by Philippe Coutinho, still a Barcelona player but on loan to Bayern and bizarrely allowed to play against his own club.

The final score of 8-2 was the first time a team had conceded so many goals in a Champions League knockout tie, and the first time Barça had let in eight in any competition since 1946. After the game the fans at Bar & Co were naturally shocked, with one of them pointing out that the starting 11 for Bayern had cost less in combined transfer fees than Dembélé. Here are some of the reactions.

Raimon, a supporter originally from the city of Barcelona but now living in the UK, simply said, 'It is a disaster.' Chris, a member of PBL from London, was shocked not by the defeat, but by its scale. After the game he told me, 'Ten years ago we had a team that was a perfect blend of experience, headline signings and a consistent flow of graduates from La Masia. We were at the top of world football, commanding respect and admiration for our football ethos that other clubs tried, without success, to replicate. Since the 2011 Champions League win and the departure of Pep Guardiola, the board has failed to move the club forward, relying instead on Messi and the "Barcelona Brand" and at the same time selling some of our most talented young players without replacing them with proven quality. Until the board is changed and we return to our core Barcelona values we will stagnate.'

Sitting next to me, socially distanced of course, was Florin, a Romanian Barça fan, now living in London. Fierce-looking at the best of times (think of a character from *Pirates of the Caribbean*), after the game he was furious and echoed the view that the club had betrayed its philosophy and neglected youth, saying, 'This wasn't a surprise for those who knew how sick this team was and still is. I said three years ago, when Luis Enrique left we needed to rebuild and get back to our ideology and focus on teenagers from La Masia. We had and still have plenty of talent that this board ignored for years, and instead went and paid hundreds of millions on panic buys. [Club president Josep Maria] Bartomeu and the board are a disgrace to this club, they have transformed us into a circus, an absolute joke.'

Florin also mentioned Alphonso Davies, Bayern's 19-year-old left-sided player, saying, 'Davies destroyed Semedo and everyone who dared to come near him. But he joined Bayern from Vancouver Whitecaps in Canada for only €10m, and this proves we need to be open-minded and extend our scouting programme in order to find the best talent out there.' More controversially, Florin also argued that Barça's captain was partly responsible, 'I do appreciate Messi for everything he's done for us, but why did it take this long to realise he's not a leader and never will be, and that he and his entourage are a big problem for the club?'

Sitting at the far end of Bar & Co was Mubarik, also a PBL member. Not one to normally criticise the club, he thought that an emphasis on money-making rather than training had been a factor, telling me, 'I believe there's a major flaw in the team's fitness level. The players often look slow, unfit, tired and dejected and have been like that for the past two seasons. Questions should be asked about whether the training standards were met and if not the board should be held accountable. From what

I see the players are too busy focusing on commercials, documentaries and endless promotional videos. The players have been too busy acting as celebrities for commercial gain rather than focusing on the real game of football. It's definitely taken a heavy toll on team performance.'

Wisely watching the horror show on one of the smaller screens was Anna, another PBL member living in London. She also criticised the club's transfer policies, saying, 'Barça's fall from grace was a long time coming. By never replacing the Xavis, Iniestas and as was evidently clear against Bayern the right-back position after Alves left with the same calibre of player, we have left ourselves in a state of free-fall which has got to be sorted out.'

Angelo, a Canadian living in London and a PBL member, agreed with Anna's comment about the failure to replace the likes of Xavi, Iniesta and Alves, but added that it was a mistake to attempt to continue with a style of play that depended on players of that quality. He said, 'We suffered this calamitous result because for several years the club was crying out for a solution to fill holes in the squad, mainly in defence, but also in midfield. We no longer have the players to play tiki-taka football, but in this match we tried to carry out a version of tiki-taka (if you can call it that), which completely got blown back in our face. This is the result of not fixing a team that lost 3-0 to Juventus, 3-0 to Roma and 4-0 to Liverpool.'

The crisis at the club immediately intensified, with Barcelona magazine *Sport* headlining its match report

'Humillación Histórica' ('Historical Humiliation')[84]. Three days later, Setién was sacked to be replaced by Ronald Koeman. In October 2020 Bartomeu resigned to avoid a vote of no confidence from club members. Presidential elections delayed from January because of the pandemic were finally held on 7 March 2021, resulting in victory for former incumbent Joan Laporta.

Within weeks of being elected, Laporta was faced with a fresh crisis when news broke that Barça was one of 12 clubs forming a new 'European Super League', alongside the two Madrid clubs, the so-called 'top six' from England, plus Juventus, Milan and Inter from Italy, with three as yet unnamed clubs expected to join later. This breakaway competition would be a closed league on the American model, without promotion or relegation, and on an invitation-only basis.

News of the ESL rocked the world of football, prompting a furious response from other clubs. Within days most of the 12 clubs withdrew from the ESL, but three remained: Real Madrid, Juventus and Barcelona. When Bartomeu announced Barça's involvement in the ESL during his resignation speech he explained that it was subject to approval by club members, consequently the club had to wait until the project was officially dead or the members' vote had been held before leaving. Although English fans demonstrated outside stadiums against the ESL, there were no such actions in Spain. Fans had gathered outside Camp Nou to protest against Bartomeu,

---

84 *Sport*, 15 August 2020.

but none took to the streets against the ESL. In fact, the response of the Barça fans I spoke to was rather more mixed, with some believing that if the ESL was going to be formed anyway Barcelona couldn't afford not to be in it, particularly because of the club's financial situation. However, others were appalled at the idea, believing that clubs should earn the right to participate and concerned about the consequences for the rest of football. Joan, an architect from southern Catalonia settled in the UK and a member of the London *penya*, told me at Bar & Co, 'I think it's mostly for the rich clubs, and it will convert football into a money-making machine and we will probably lose the spirit of the game.'

Barça then agreed a joint statement with Real Madrid and Juventus protesting against what it called 'threats' if the clubs didn't abandon the ESL, referring to possible fines by UEFA and suspension from its competitions. During his election campaign Laporta, returning for a second spell as president, paid for a giant banner to be displayed down the side of a tall building near Real Madrid's Bernabéu stadium, with the slogan 'Ganas de volver a veros' ('Looking forward to seeing you again'), although it said nothing about agreeing statements together.

When the Barça members' assembly met on 20 June 2021, Laporta told delegates that the ESL remained 'alive, but not mature enough to leave it in your hands'; consequently it was deemed 'not possible' to put the issue to a vote and as the club's website reported, the president was 'given clearance to continue discussing a European

Super League' because 'the proposed new tournament will benefit the club'. Such political manoeuvrings may have been because of the ongoing legal action and the financial penalties of opting out of the ESL. Laporta also told the delegates, 'The memory of our historic error of not accepting an invitation to play in the European Cup when it was created because we decided to continue playing in the Fairs Cup. Another club accepted the invitation in our place and went on to win the first five editions.'[85] This statement is puzzling because Real Madrid finished the 1954/55 La Liga season as champions, five points ahead of second-placed Barcelona, so the club from the capital qualified on merit and did not accept an invitation to participate in the first European Cup (1955/56) in Barça's place.

At the end of July the courts ordered UEFA to halt its action against the three remaining members of the ESL, while the wider issue of UEFA's monopolistic position in European football was referred to the European Court of Justice[86]. With political and financial turmoil off the pitch, Barça finished second in its Champions League group followed by knockout-round elimination at the hands of Paris Saint-Germain. Koeman did well in difficult circumstances, winning the Copa del Rey and hauling back Atlético Madrid's lead at the top of La Liga, only for a poor end to the season to squander chances of an unlikely domestic double.

---

85 'Laporta given clearance to continue discussing a European Super League,' fcbarcelona.com, 20 June 2021.

86 fcbarcelona.com/en/club/news/2202247/statement-on-the-european-super-league.

The club's financial crisis continued into the following pre-season when it was required to cut the wage bill by €200m to meet the Spanish football authority's salary cap, but found it difficult to find takers for some of its now unwanted players because of their high earnings. Although a mixture of selling players and wage cuts found half the money, more savings were needed before Barça could register all its new signings and, more importantly, retain Lionel Messi. The Barça star's old contract expired at the end of June 2021, and although Messi agreed to a halving of his salary a new deal could not be registered, prompting the club to announce his departure to Paris Saint-Germain in early August.

So how did the turmoil at Barça in 2020/21 compare with previous crises at the club? After Barcelona's shock exit from the European Cup back in November 1992 at the hands of CSKA Moscow, I picked up a copy of the newspaper *Marca* from a Madrid street kiosk which gleefully reported on the recriminations at Camp Nou, headlining its article 'Super Bronca' as a play on the slogan 'Super Barça'.[87] The word 'bronca' usually translates as 'row', so 'Super Bronca' meant 'Super Row'. FC Barcelona's centenary publication referred to the 'anarchic' spirit of Catalans finding an outlet in football, adding that arguments had been 'a constant feature in the life of the club' and suggested they performed a positive role by helping keep Barça together[88]. Johan Cruyff took

---

87 *Marca*, 6 November 1992.

88 Vilagut, M. (ed.), *Barça: Centenario de Emociones* (Barcelona: FC Barcelona, 1999), p280.

a less positive view, claiming in his autobiography that politics was the most serious problem at Barça[89].

In the four decades covered by this book there have been many rows at Camp Nou. As a former councillor, I like a good political bust-up, so here is my selection in historical order, with marks out of ten.

Men Behaving Badly: 1982/83

In the 1982/83 season, president Josep Lluís Núñez and coach Udo Lattek faced two main challenges. The first was keeping their new world record signing Diego Maradona, plus Allan Simonsen and Bernd Schuster, happy under the two foreign players only rule. The second task was controlling their players following a UEFA fine the previous season. How did they do? Not very well. After being dropped, Simonsen stormed off to England, so was unavailable when Maradona fell ill with hepatitis. Lacking their star player, Barça resorted to persistent fouling in defeat to Aston Villa at the 1983 Super Cup, with two players sent off and four suspended, prompting another fine from UEFA. A few weeks later Lattek was sacked, blamed for losing control of his squad (Schuster had publicly called him a 'drunk'). Towards the end of the season, Maradona deliberately smashed a valuable cup in the Camp Nou trophy room during a row with Núñez[90].

Super Bronca rating: 6/10

---

89 Cruyff, J., *My Turn: The Autobiography* (London: MacMillan, 2016), p149.
90 Maradona, D., *El Diego* (London: Yellow Jersey Press, 2000), pp68 & 72.

Gobby Lot: 1986/87

In October 1986 the Grup d'Opinió Barcelonista (Barcelona Opinion Group) published a manifesto demanding Núñez's resignation as president and fresh elections, arguing that he had damaged the image of the club and been disrespectful of its history. Sadly for the GOB, nostalgia was never likely to bother a president whose business, Núñez y Navarro, specialised in demolishing old buildings and redeveloping the sites.
Super Bronca rating: 1/10

El motín del Hesperia: 1988

After it was exposed that FC Barcelona had failed to disclose the entire earnings of its footballers to the Spanish taxman, the players were ordered to pay fines and unpaid taxes. Club captain Alesanco read out a statement on behalf of the squad which argued that the club should pay the bill as it was responsible. Described in full in chapter three, the incident became known as *'El motín del Hesperia'* ('The Hesperia Mutiny') after the hotel where it took place. The mutineers also called for Núñez to resign, but most fans sided with their president, judging the players to be greedy, while coach Luis Aragonés, who had backed the squad, was replaced by Cruyff.
Super Bronca rating: 9/10

Russian Roulette: 1992

Already in a dispute with Núñez over players' bonuses, the shock defeat by CSKA Moscow prompted rumours that Cruyff would leave. In the end, the coach stayed

to deliver two further La Liga titles for Barcelona. So despite what *Marca* printed, this was just handbags really.
Super Bronca rating: 1/10

Hanky-panky: 1996

Having dismantled his Dream Team, Cruyff tried to assemble another one. On 6 April 1996 I was in Camp Nou to see Barça beat Real Sociedad and move within three points of La Liga leaders Atlético Madrid. However, a run of only one win in the next five games meant that for the second successive year there were no trophies, so the following month Núñez got his vice-president, Joan Gaspart, to tell Cruyff he was sacked. The Dutchman replied by calling Gaspart 'Judas'. White hankies waved around Camp Nou in protest at the sacking, while Cruyff felt betrayed by his friend and assistant, Carles Rexach, who replaced him as caretaker.
Super Bronca rating: 4/10

Elefant Blau: 1998–2000

In March 1998, while in Barcelona to attend *El clásico*, I noticed posters all over the city advertising a campaign by the Elefant Blau (Blue Elephant) group. On the day of the game a vote of no confidence in Núñez took place, which he survived. However, in the long run he lost, finally resigning in 2000, tired of constant criticism by the media, to be joined by coach Louis van Gaal, who quit in solidarity.
Super Bronca rating: 6/10

Barçagate Plus: 2020–21

Starting 2020 top of La Liga and unbeaten in Europe, Barça then imploded with two coaches sacked and sporting director Eric Abidal publicly critical of the squad. President Bartomeu was accused of hiring a media company to campaign against some of the players, creating a scandal dubbed 'Barçagate'. The club's already precarious finances worsened dramatically after the outbreak of the coronavirus pandemic. Possessing the largest stadium meant Barça lost more income than its rivals when Camp Nou had to be closed to spectators. FCB imposed cutbacks and accused its players of refusing to accept wage cuts. The players denied this, and eventually offered to accept an even bigger cut in their wages to provide funds to pay other employees at the club.

After a humiliating 8-2 defeat by Bayern in the Champions League, Messi attempted to leave on a free transfer. Determined not to lose its prime asset without a fee, the club claimed that Messi's escape clause expired in June, and insisted he should stay. Although Messi eventually decided against taking Barça to court and reluctantly stayed at Camp Nou, fear of losing their favourite player caused fans to take to the streets in protest. After more than 20,000 club members signed a motion against Bartomeu, he resigned in October 2020 to avoid a vote of no confidence.

In 2021 Barça became one of three remaining clubs in the abortive European Super League, a venture which damaged the club's reputation and put its participation in UEFA competition at risk, until the threat of suspension was successfully challenged in the courts. New president Joan Laporta then entered into conflict with the previously highly regarded *penya* confederation. Arguably the worst news came in August 2021 when Lionel Messi left the club following failure to agree a new contract that complied with La Liga financial fair play regulations.

Super Bronca rating: 10/10

17

La gent blaugrana: Barça Fans

WRITTEN IN 1974 to celebrate FC Barcelona's 75th anniversary, 'Cant del Barça' is regularly sung by the club's supporters at games. The lyrics include 'Som la gent blaugrana' ('We're the blue and red people'), but who exactly are these blue and red people? Here are my own experiences and impressions of Barcelona supporters.

Barça supporters are often called *culés* (sometimes written as *culers*), a nickname dating from the time when the club played at its old ground on Carrer de la Industria in the early 20th century. The stadium wasn't big enough for all the fans who wanted to watch, so some would sit on top of a perimeter wall displaying their rears to passers-by. The word *culés* refers to people showing their backsides.

It is widely reported that FC Barcelona is run by its fans. It would be more accurate to say that Barça is a privately owned club run by some of its fans. These people are the *socis* (literally 'partners'). The joining process has changed over the years, but has recently required prospective members to take out a 'Commitment Card' which costs about £120 per year, and has to be renewed annually in person at the club's offices in Barcelona. After three years of this probationary membership, Commitment Card holders can then apply to become a *soci*. Successful applicants then pay about £160 per year to be a *soci*, giving them the right to vote in presidential elections (usually every four years) and, if selected, participate in the assembly of delegates which acts like a members' executive. In between elections, real power at the club lies with the president, the board and their financial backers.

Interestingly, all *socis* have only had voting powers within FC Barcelona since 1978, when the club's first elections took place, replicating the introduction of democracy in Spain as a whole in the years after Franco's death. Before that, only male members voted[91]. Progress to full democracy remains slow, with the club granting postal votes only in Spain and refusing to offer them to *socis* residing outside the country during the coronavirus pandemic. Consequently, *socis* living in the UK, who were not allowed by British government rules to travel abroad, were unable to vote in the 2021 presidential elections. With elections approximately every four years, this meant these *socis* each paid over £600 since the last election, only to be refused a ballot paper when the vote came around.

In 1899, when FC Barcelona was founded, there were 32 *socis*; by the time of the first game in this book in 1983

---

91 *FC Barcelona: The Complete History of the Club* (Barcelona: Dos De Arte FC Barcelona, 2018), pp44 & 63.

the number had risen to 108,000, and by 2020 it stood at 144,000. Other top European clubs generally charge much less than £160 for club membership, but such schemes only provide things like priority access to match tickets and discounts on merchandise, not a say in how the club is run. However, Barcelona membership enables participation in the running of the club (principally through voting in elections and approving the club's budget and accounts), so the high cost inevitably means that it attracts higher earners or, if you like, more 'middle-class' people.

The second organised part of Barcelona's fanbase is made up of *penyistas*, members of the supporters' clubs such as Penya Blaugrana London, which I joined in 2011. Some *penyistas* are *socis* but others are not. Similarly, not all *socis* decide to join a *penya*, although many do.

The first *penya*, called Penya Solera, was formed in 1944, in the years just after the Spanish Civil War. By 1979 the number of *penyes* had grown to 96, and in that year Barça reached the Cup Winners' Cup Final in Basel. The club claims that the 35,000 Barça fans who travelled to Switzerland for the game was the largest movement of people since the end of the Second World War. It was Barça's first major game abroad after the death of Franco and the restoration of democracy, and from that time the number of *penyes* grew rapidly[92].

The primary function of the *penyes* is to organise support for the football team at matches, or if that is

92 Vilagut, M. (ed.), *Barça: Centenario de Emociones* (Barcelona: FC Barcelona, 1999), pp284-285.

not possible screenings of the games. However, it is not just a question of watching football, let alone acting as a ticket agency; instead, being welcoming, organising social activities and, above all, acting as ambassadors for the club is central to the *penya* ethos.

According to the magazine *Blaugranes*, half of the fans who travelled within Spain to attend away matches in La Liga in 2018/19 were *penya* members. However, for European competition, the focus of this book, the proportion of those who travelled abroad to Champions League matches that same season who were *penyista*s rose to nearly three-quarters[93].

When Barça plays abroad in European competition it is traditional for the local *penya* to host a dinner on the eve of the game. This is not just a ritual or an opportunity to eat and drink. Instead, it provides club officials with a chance to keep in touch with the *penyes* and promote the club. If there is no local *penya* in the vicinity of the match the FC Barcelona Supporters' Clubs World Confederation has recently started to organise such events. The first of these was in Eindhoven for the trip to play PSV in November 2018, followed by the lunch on the day of the game at Manchester United in April 2019, already described in this book.

It is also customary for the local *penya* to arrange a rally in a public place on the afternoon of the match, which in London has included gatherings in Trafalgar Square, Covent Garden and Piccadilly Circus. Leaflets

---

93 *Blaugranes*, official magazine of the FC Barcelona Supporters' Clubs World Confederation, July 2019, p8.

and other forms of publicity are used to encourage Barça fans from other *penyes* to meet, sing and wave the colours. Noticeably different to gatherings of many English fans abroad, these events pass off peacefully, without drunkenness or aggressive behaviour. Local media are often invited to attend these informal Fan Zones which serve as effective ways of promoting the club.

Penyes were initially set up just in Spain. One of the first created outside of Spain was Penya Blaugrana London in 1985. The first *penyes* abroad were generally established by Catalan émigrés, but later branches started to be organised by local people, and in recent years this has been the main way they have started. The FC Barcelona Supporters' Clubs World Confederation was established in 2015 to give the movement an international focus. The confederation now has 1,273 *penyes* affiliated to it, of which 1,122 are in Spain and 151 in the rest of the world. The *penyes* have a total of 171,100 members across the globe, meaning there are more *penyistas* than *socis*[94].

Internationally, about a third of *penyistas* are under the age of 35, while over a quarter are female. If we take Penya Blaugrana London as an example, it has a similar age and gender profile, while in terms of nationality, about a third of members are Catalan, another third originate from other parts of Spain, with the remainder from the rest of the world. This last portion includes around 30 different nationalities with a significant number of UK citizens. In terms of occupations, PBL members tend to reflect the

---

94 confederaciopenyes.fcbarcelona.com.

London workforce, with many involved in finance and other services. *Penyistas* tend to reflect the 'progressive' and humanitarian values of the club. For example, the international *penya* movement has participated in projects such as charity work for children affected by poverty or rare diseases, and in 2020 the FC Barcelona Supporters' Clubs World Confederation joined the Catalan Red Cross to back the Welcome Project in support of refugees. Sympathy for Catalan independence is also strong among *penyistas*, although not universal.

Like many other *penyes*, PBL grew rapidly in size during the time of *Messimania*, from about 2009 onwards. The football on offer, headed by the world's greatest player, attracted a younger and wider audience. It will be interesting to see whether that changes if Barça enters a less successful period of transition following the end of the Messi era.

The huge number of Barça fans who went to the 1979 Cup Winners' Cup Final in Basel was made possible because the relative prosperity and freedom in post-Franco Spain provided increased opportunities for travel. Unfortunately, it also allowed hooliganism to develop in the 1980s, and although the problem was never as serious as in England, it did exist on a smaller scale at Barcelona. In 1981 the Boixos Nois (a misspelling of 'Crazy Boys') was set up as the main hooligan group. The Boixos Nois originally tended towards the political left, but later evolved in a right-wing direction. When Barça played Juventus in the European Cup in 1986 a banner was displayed at Camp Nou containing swastikas and a slogan mocking the Juve fans who died at Heysel the year before. It is not known which group was responsible, but suspicion fell on fans with far-right sympathies.

While I didn't see crowd trouble at any of the games featured in this book, I did see a Boixos Nois banner in the Barça end by the tunnel at Wembley in 1992 and many of the fans at the game waved scarves with 'Boixos Nois' printed on them. The Boixos Nois also had banners at the European Cup Final in Athens a couple of years later and at Rotterdam in 1997 for the Cup Winners' Cup Final. The first Barcelona president to take action against hooliganism was Laporta, who from 2003 ended the club's indulgence of groups such as the Boixos Nois, although their banners could still be seen three years later in the Stade de France and for the club's other Champions League finals in Rome in 2009, Wembley 2011 and Berlin 2015.

In recent times, crowd trouble involving Barça fans has been rare. The only trouble I have witnessed with Barcelona involves Real Madrid: racist chanting by some home fans at Camp Nou directed at Madrid's three black players in 1998; a minor altercation between a couple of fans of the two clubs outside the Bernabéu in 2011; and bottle-throwing in the Barça Fan Zone in Berlin before the 2015 Champions League Final.

The rivalry with Real Madrid is so huge that other Barcelona fixtures tend to lack the same meaning and consequently have less atmosphere and intensity. These days Camp Nou is probably one of the safest places in the world to watch a major football match. In fact, things have gone to the other extreme, with increasing numbers of 'tourist fans' from abroad attending matches. In October 2020 Carles Tusquets, representing the Barça board, said, 'The club depends on tourism.'[95] Although these 'tourist fans' provide an income for Barcelona, they tend to sit quietly, wait for their superstars to score a goal, then politely clap and take a selfie. Together with the conversion of Camp Nou to an all-seater stadium, these 'tourist fans' have diluted the atmosphere. One noticeable thing is that when Barça struggles in a match the fans don't get behind their team. As with most clubs, Barça fans attending away games tend to be more supportive than the home crowd, but even they tend to become silent when their team goes behind, unlike those of many English clubs who continue to vocally back their team when losing.

Taking *socis*, *penyistas* and other Barça fans together, my impression is that they seem to be even more demanding and impatient than English ones. The fans expect their team to thrash lesser clubs, with tighter victories only acceptable against Real Madrid. Barely a year after nearly winning the European Cup, most Barça fans stayed away from Camp Nou during the final games of Terry Venables' time as coach in 1987. Ten years later, Bobby Robson complained after Barça fans jeered his team following a 6-0 win against Rayo Vallecano, something inconceivable in England[96].

Wider television broadcasting of matches has impacted on the support of many clubs, including Barcelona. In

---

95 thesun.co.uk.
96 Robson, B., *My Autobiography* (London: MacMillan, 1998), p183.

chapter one, we heard that La Liga fixtures weren't shown in China until 2003, while they were still a rarity in the UK until the mid-1990s. Today, with cable TV and internet streaming, viewers can watch games throughout the world. This has greatly boosted Barça's profile and attracted a new type of fan who watches games on screen, rather than attending stadiums. The rise of social media in recent years has provided another forum for football fans, including those of Barcelona, and is especially popular with foreign-based supporters. A glance at chat forums for any of Europe's big clubs shows that many of these fans expect uninterrupted success, with coaches and players only as good as their last game. However, this feeling seems stronger at Barcelona than most other top clubs, bordering on entitlement. Social media and wider international broadcasting of games has also encouraged the phenomenon of people simultaneously following several teams and in the case of 'Messi fans' supporting an individual player. When some of the latter announced on Facebook that they would start following PSG after Messi left Camp Nou the postings attracted a hostile response from most readers, although I suspect that others defected without advertising it. Such phenomena undoubtedly bring more money into the game, through TV subscriptions and merchandising, but at the cost of diluting the intensity of support.

The *socis* and *penyes* provide an organised form of support and connection between fans and their football club, encouraging many to want to act as ambassadors for both Barça and Catalonia. However, the relationship between FCB and its organised fan groups has not always developed smoothly. The number of *socis* and *penyes* expanded under the presidency of Josep Lluís Núñez in the 1980s and 1990s. After becoming president in 2003 Joan Laporta then banned the Boixos Nois, which in hindsight could be interpreted not only as a wise move against hooligans but also a reflection of his uneasy relationship with supporters' groups. In 2019 under Josep Maria Bartomeu, the FC Barcelona Supporters' Clubs World Confederation moved into plush premises in the east of the city. However, when Laporta returned in 2021 he quickly conflicted with the confederation. Some could argue that Laporta saw the confederation as costly to sustain, so it became an unfortunate, but financially necessary, victim of the need to make economies. Others believe that Laporta preferred to deal with *penyes* individually rather than as part of a united, international organisation, and so the new president embarked on a policy of divide and rule.

To sum up, in my experience *la gent blaugrana* are generally different to many English supporters in the following ways. Their age profile is slightly younger, more of them are female, they don't drink as much alcohol and behaviour is usually less boisterous or aggressive. Barça fans frequently combine higher expectations of their team with a failure to back it in times of difficulty.

Having looked at Barcelona's fanbase and how it is organised into *socis* and *penyistas*, I shall now consider an example of how and why individuals decide to follow the club.

Originally from Poland, Kuba was born in 1980 in the city of Bielsko-Biała, in between Kraków and the border of what was then Czechoslovakia. The month after he was born the Polish communist government recognised *Solidarność* (Solidarity), the first independent trade union in the Eastern Bloc. Communist rule continued for the first nine years of Kuba's life, and during that time he became a supporter of the local football team BKS Stal Bielsko-Biala. After the collapse of communism in 1989, Kuba developed an interest in football in the west and at the age of 12 watched Barcelona's triumph in the 1992 European Cup Final on television. Kuba was also impressed by Olympique Marseille's success in the same competition the following year, but he turned away from the French club after it was involved in a match-fixing scandal, and from then on became committed solely to Barça.

FC Barcelona has supporters throughout the world, but is especially popular in Poland. When asked to explain this, Kuba replied, 'I think it's because of politics. For many years Poland was not free, we were controlled by the Soviets. After the end of communism many Polish football supporters looked to the west and developed an identity with Barça because Catalonia was also not free. At the time Johan Cruyff coached the team, and the football was great to watch.'

The first Barça game Kuba attended personally was on 28 August 2002, the second leg of a Champions League qualifying round against Legia Warsaw, during Louis van Gaal's second spell in charge. At the time Kuba was 22 years old and he travelled to the Polish capital to see the match at Legia's stadium. Since totally rebuilt, the stadium was more basic in those days, with a crowd of only 11,500 in attendance. Defending a 3-0 lead from the first leg, Barça won 1-0 in Warsaw through a penalty converted by Gaizka Mendieta, after Patrick Kluivert had been brought down in the box. The team included one of Kuba's all-time favourite players, Luis Enrique, as well as future stars Víctor Valdés, Carles Puyol and Xavi. On the bench for Barça that day was German goalkeeper Robert Enke, who made very few appearances for the club, and would tragically commit suicide seven years later. Although pleased to see Barça for the first time, Kuba was not impressed with the performance, saying, 'I remember Mendieta's penalty, but otherwise Barça didn't play well. The team wasn't so good at that time.'

Although Legia's ground was often referred to as the Polish Army Stadium, Kuba decided that being a soldier was not for him, and a few months after the game he emigrated to avoid service in the Polish military, which was compulsory in those days. He moved to England and settled in London, gaining employment as a chef as part of the city's large Polish community, before in later years studying psychology.

Kuba estimates that he has attended about 35 Barça games in total, with about ten of these in the UK and the other 25 abroad. These include six *clásicos*, of which one was away at the Bernabéu. Kuba's claim to fame is having attended both Guardiola's first match as Barça coach, a 6-0 away win in Edinburgh against Hibernian in a pre-season friendly in July 2008, as well as his final match, a 3-0 win in the final of the Copa del Rey against Athletic Bilbao played in Madrid in May 2012. This is a very rare, possibly unique, achievement.

A father of two children, Kuba's wife is Italian and her family supports Juventus, making the 2015 Champions League Final a special event for them. Kuba graduated from a *penyista* to a *soci* in 2018, and according to him the best thing about following Barca is 'seeing beautiful attacking play'.

18

Conclusion: Mortgage to Catalonia

I FEEL extremely fortunate to have seen, during four decades, some of the finest football in history, including all five of Barça's European Cup/Champions League Final victories. However, *Ten Big Ears* starts and finishes with the club in disgrace and in conflict with UEFA. FC Barcelona ended in this predicament partly as a victim of its own success and ambitions.

After winning its fifth pair of big ears in Berlin, the Barcelona team slowly but surely lost some of its greatest players. In successive seasons, Xavi, Dani Alves, Neymar and Andres Iniesta left the club, eventually followed by Lionel Messi. Although Barça won three La Liga titles after Berlin, in 2016, 2018 and 2019, these achievements were overshadowed by failure in Europe, with the Champions League replacing La Liga as the benchmark for success. Former club employees Terry Venables and José Mourinho claimed that Barcelona was obsessed with Real Madrid. Years later, when the team from the Spanish capital won a hat-trick of Champions Leagues between 2016 and 2018, Barça over-reached itself by spending approximately €1bn attempting to catch up.

Unfortunately, most of the new signings failed to live up to their price tag or adequately replace the lost legends, while Barça secured the services of those that remained by putting too many on costly long-term contracts. As the players aged and their wages rose, it became difficult to prune the squad when needed, because other clubs couldn't afford their salaries. The result was the biggest wage bill in world football. In January 2021 it was reported that although the club topped the Deloitte Football Money League, making it the world's richest club for the second year running with revenue of €715m, its debt was also huge at €1.4bn, which made the club the richest in the world in terms of income, but in danger of bankruptcy because of its debt[97]. In May 2021 new club president Joan Laporta was reported to have borrowed up to €500m from an American investment bank, with a fifth of this sum used to pay players' wages[98]. It looked like the club was mortgaging its future, and a couple of months later we heard that FC Barcelona had the biggest short-term debt in Europe, needing to pay back €731m within the next 12 months[99].

---

97 'The Barcelona Riddle: Deloitte Calls Club Soccer's Richest Even As Report Claims It's Nearly Bankrupt': forbes.com.

98 espn.co.uk.

99 football-espana.net.

Another factor was the success of the club encouraging a feeling of entitlement, with many around it (not least the fans) unprepared to accept periods of consolidation or team-building, demanding instead an immediate and uninterrupted supply of European trophies. Ernesto Valverde had been dismissed despite winning La Liga in his first two seasons, partly as a consequence of his unpopularity, because the style of football wasn't considered as good as Pep Guardiola's, and his failure to win the Champions League while seeing Real Madrid win it during his reign. This was not new. Twenty years earlier, Louis van Gaal had quit despite winning La Liga in his first two seasons, partly as a consequence of his unpopularity, because the style of football wasn't considered as good as Johan Cruyff's, and his failure to win the Champions League while seeing Real Madrid win it during his reign. In both cases, Valverde's and van Gaal's immediate successors took the team to a lower level.

Desperation to emulate Real Madrid's success in Europe proved to be the club's undoing, encouraging it to lose faith in La Masia, preferring quick fixes by buying expensive and often unsuitable players to try and replace departing stars. It was sadly fitting that Josep Maria Bartomeu's disastrous reign ended with a resignation speech announcing that the club would be joining Real Madrid in a new European Super League, to ensure participation in the proposed senior continental competition and guarantee the club's financial future, ignoring that it was the very search for European glory which had overstretched the club financially in the first place.

In the period covered by this book, football has changed almost beyond recognition. My story started in 1983, queuing up outside the Holte End, paying £2.50 at the turnstile and pushing through crowds before finding a place to stand on the terraces, then ended in 2019 paying £103 in advance for a ticket, collecting it from men in suits at a posh hotel, before taking my reserved place in an all-seater stadium. At Villa Park in 1983 the hosts, then reigning European champions, begged volunteers to work unpaid and supply their own equipment to film the club's matches. By the end of this story in 2019 we had dozens of cameras and professional operators at Anfield, including VAR, while television had not only increased the popularity of football among a global audience, but pumped vast sums of money into the game.

In the starting 11 at Villa Park for the 1983 Super Cup, Barça's most expensive player, Bernd Schuster, had been signed for a transfer fee of £800,000 and earned about £1.1m per year[100]. Different players have distinct qualities and therefore value, but as an extremely rough guide if the costs had risen by the rate of inflation since 1983 then we might have expected the player with the biggest transfer fee in 2019 to cost something like £2.7m. In fact, the most expensive signing at the Anfield semi-final was Philippe Coutinho, signed for a whopping £142m. Similarly, the highest earner at Anfield was Messi, and

100 Rossi, G., Semens, A., Brocard, J. F., *Sports Agents and Labour Markets: Evidence from World Football* (Routledge, 2016).

again at the rate of inflation since 1983, his income could have been anticipated to be something like £3.7m per year (or if you think he was ten times better than Schuster, £37m). However, when details of Messi's contract were leaked to the press in early 2021 his gross annual salary (so subject to deductions for tax and additions such as bonuses) was reported to be an incredible £122m[101]. To be fair to Messi, it can be argued that he generated more for the club through ticket sales, merchandising, advertising, television revenue and prize money than he cost. Messi was also reported to have agreed a cut in his salary to try and stay at Barça in 2021. However, the problem is the inflationary effect of a star player's wage, with other squad members of lesser ability demanding wages they don't deserve.

In 1978 Cruyff left Barça and the next campaign saw the club win its first UEFA trophy, the Cup Winners' Cup. The season following Diego Maradona's departure, Barça won La Liga after an 11-year wait before coming within a penalty shoot-out of winning its first European Cup 12 months later. After another superstar, Ronaldinho, was sold in 2008 the club had its greatest trophy haul, which included a third European Cup. At the time of writing, we don't know how Barça will fare post-Messi. European success like the three examples above would be an incredible achievement, but also highly unlikely given the club's financial difficulties, although given Barça's history nothing can be ruled out.

---

101 Dailymail.co.uk.

Talking of money, the travelling, accommodation and above all match tickets for the 24 games covered in this book proved to be extremely expensive, wiping out most of my savings. Like FC Barcelona, the hunt for European glory came at a high price for me. However, as I write this, amid a global pandemic, international travel restrictions, reduced access to stadiums, artificial crowd noise and a game being overrun by television and financial greed, I feel very glad to have done it when there was the opportunity.

Visca el Barça!

Bibliography

Books:

Balagué, G., *Barça: The Illustrated History of FC Barcelona* (London: Carlton, 2014)

Ball, P., *Morbo: The Story of Spanish Football* (London: WSC, 2003)

Burns, J., *Barça: A People's Passion* (London: Bloomsbury, 1999)

Cruyff, J., *My Turn: The Autobiography* (London: MacMillan, 2016)

FC Barcelona: The Complete History of the Club (Barcelona: Dos De Arte FC Barcelona, 2018)

Finestres, J., *Universal Barça* (Barcelona: Angle Editorial, 2009)

Gray, E., *Marching on Together: My Life with Leeds United* (London: Hodder & Stoughton, 2001)

Hunter, G., *Barça: The Making of the Greatest Team in the World* (BackPage Press, 2012)

Ibrahimović, Z., *I am Zlatan Ibrahimović*
(Penguin, 2013)

Inglis, S., *The Football Grounds of Europe* (London:
Collins Willow, 1990)

Maradona, D., *El Diego* (London: Yellow Jersey
Press, 2000)

Robson, B., *My Autobiography* (London:
MacMillan, 1998)

Rodiger, U. A., *The Olympic Stadium in Berlin: From
the German Stadium to the Reichssportfeld* (Berlin:
Rodiger Verlag, 1999)

Rossi, G., Semens, A., Brocard, J.F., *Sports Agents
and Labour Markets: Evidence from World Football*
(Routledge, 2016)

Schofield, N., *Our Lady of Willesden: A brief history of
the Shrine and Parish*

Venables, T., *Born to Manage: The Autobiography*
(London: Simon & Schuster, 2015)

Vilagut, M. (ed.), *Barça: Centenario de Emociones*
(Barcelona: FC Barcelona, 1999)

Newspapers and magazines:

Blaugranes

Daily Telegraph

The Guardian

Independent

Leipziger Volkszeitung

Marca

Mundo Deportivo

Official programme, Aston Villa vs Barcelona, 26 January 1983

Official programme, Charlton Athletic vs Crystal Palace, 4 April 1983

Official programme, UEFA Champions League Final 2017

Official programme, UEFA Cup Winners' Cup Final 1997

Sport

The Times

Tottenham and Wood Green Journal

World Soccer

Websites and social media:

abc.es

athensguide.com

adevarul.ro

bbc.co.uk

best-quotations.com

billedbladet.dk

cavernclub.com

dailymail.co.uk

ecatholic2000.com

espn.co.uk

fcbarcelona.com

football-espana.net

footyheadlines.com

forbes.com

ft.com

goal.com

informer.rs

italymagazine.com

liverpoolecho.co.uk

liverpoolfc.com

meyba.com

mundodeportivo.com

psychologytoday.com

quemedices.es

theguardian.com

thesun.co.uk

timesnownews.com

uefa.com

vatican.va

youtube.com

Radio, television and films:

Bestemming Wembley, Wasserman and Captains Studio, broadcast on Ziggo Sport (Dutch TV), 3 June 2017

The European Cup Final, BBC, 20 May 1992

Liverpool vs Barcelona, BT Sport commentary, 7 May 2019

Manchester United vs Barcelona, BT Sport commentary, 10 April 2019

Michael Laudrup: En Fodboldspiller, video, directed by Jørgen Leth (Zentropa Entertainments, 1993)

Take the Ball, Pass the Ball, DVD (Zoom Sport International, 2018)